ASTROPOLITIK

Cass Series: Strategy and History
Series Editors: Colin Gray and Williamson Murray
ISSN: 1473-6403

This new series will focus on the theory and practice of strategy. Following Clausewitz, strategy has been understood to mean the use made of force, and the threat of the use of force, for the ends of policy. This series is as interested in ideas as in historical cases of grand strategy and military strategy in action. All historical periods, near and past, and even future, are of interest. In addition to original monographs, the series will from time to time publish edited reprints of neglected classics as well as collections of essays.

1. *Military Logistics and Strategic Performance*, Thomas M. Kane

2. *Strategy for Chaos: RMA Theory and the Evidence of History*, Colin Gray

3. *The Myth of Inevitable US Defeat in Vietnam*, C. Dale Walton

4. *Astropolitik: Classical Geopolitics in the Space Age*, Everett C. Dolman

ASTROPOLITIK

Classical Geopolitics in the Space Age

Everett C. Dolman

School of Advanced Airpower Studies, Maxwell Air Force Base, AL

FRANK CASS

LONDON • PORTLAND, OR

First published in 2002 in Great Britain by
FRANK CASS PUBLISHERS
2 Park Square, Milton Park,
Abingdon, Oxon, OX14 4RN

and in the United States of America by
FRANK CASS PUBLISHERS
270 Madison Ave,
New York NY 10016

Transferred to Digital Printing 2006

Website www.frankcass.com

British Library Cataloguing in Publication Data

Dolman, Everett C.
Astropolitik: classical geopolitics in the space age. –
(Cass series. Strategy and history; no. 4)
1. Outer space – Political aspects 2. Outer space –
International cooperation 3. Geopolitics 4. Astronautics,
Military 5. National security
I. Title
333.9'4

ISBN 0-7146-5200-8 (cloth)
ISBN 0-7146-8197-0 (paper)
ISSN 1473-6403

Library Congress Cataloging-in-Publication Data

Dolman, Everett C., 1958–
Astropolitik: classical geopolitics in the Space Age/Everett C.
Dolman.
p. cm. – (Cass series – strategy and history)
Includes bibliographical references and index.
ISBN 0-7146-5200-8 (cloth) – ISBN 0-7146-8197-0 (paper)
1. Outer space – Exploration – Political aspects. 2. Geopolitics. 3.
Astronautics – Government policy. 4. Astronautics – International
cooperation. 5. Space industrialization – Political aspects. 6. Space
industrialization – Law and legislation. 7. Astronautics,
Military – Government policy. I. Title. II. Series.
TL788.4 .D685 2001
327' .0919–dc21

2001047183

Typeset in 10½/12 Minion by Cambridge Photosetting Services

Publisher's Note
The publisher has gone to great lengths to ensure the quality of this reprint but points out that some imperfections in the original may be apparent

Printed and bound by CPI Antony Rowe, Eastbourne

For Denise and Mary

Love and Hope

Contents

List of Plates

List of Figures

Series Editor's Preface

One of our objectives as Series Editors for the Cass Series on Strategy and History is to challenge readers with frontier studies. Everett Dolman's *Astropolitik* all but defines such a one. In this extraordinary book, Dolman takes strategy into outer space in a way that has not even been attempted before, let alone effected successfully, as here. Many people may have difficulty crediting the claim, but it happens to be the case that until now, nearly 60 years into the space age (from the testing of the first V-2 rocket in 1942), there has been next to nothing worth reading on space as a strategic environment.

The world is becoming ever more dependent on the convenience of space systems. Those technologies quintessentially are signature features of 'globalization'. So routine has become the use of Earth orbit, that we no longer marvel when CNN, *inter alia*, shows us footage from halfway around the world via a live satellite feed. But how should we think about outer space? Is it the new 'great commons' for mankind, somehow uniquely and benignly devoid of the kind of strategic hazards so familiar to us from the land, sea and air environments? Or, is it simply a matter of time before strategic history climbs the new high ground? Anyone seeking answers to Big Questions such as these will have a research problem. The literature on space is vast, but – beyond the explicitly fictional – comprises technical manuals, works of political advocacy, and – in the military realm – a library of 'studies' pro and con the proposal of the day for ballistic missile defence (BMD).

Regardless of where one stands on BMD, a subject on which few people are short of a firm opinion, the public debate on the matter has a Gresham-like effect on the strategic consideration of the space environment. Whatever one says about the military utility of orbit is placed swiftly into the quasi-ideological context of contending theories of (Cold War-derivative) strategic stability. Thus far, there has been virtually no public discussion of the space realm as such. Of course, space is different in scale from the other geographies. But the fact of that near-infinite vastness is of only limited significance for humans who are likely to be confined for many decades to come to function within the Earth–Moon system. So how should we function in space? Should we eschew military behaviour? Well, it is too late for that by more than 40 years. How about prohibiting weaponization? Thus far only weapons of mass destruction are banned from orbit (by the Outer Space Treaty of 1967). Should we seek to protect satellites by international arms-control agreement? Since an anti-satellite (ASAT) weapon could be anything that impairs the performance of a space system, it is apparent that, as usual, formal measures of arms control could not work. ASATs could menace ground-control stations, electronic up and down links, as well as vehicles in orbit. More to the point, perhaps, should we be thinking about war in space at all?

Everett Dolman performs a great public and scholarly service by treating the space environment as just another geography. True, it is extra-terran geography, but no matter. Naturally, it is Earth's gravity well that dominates movement in the Earth–Moon system. Dolman's *Astropolitik* is a complex, but more than satisfactory, blend of international history, strategic theory and orbital mechanics. This book provides not only a prescient guide to the meaning of space for the human future, but also offers the reader an excellent explanation of movement into, in and out of particular orbits. Much as there are basic features to the land, sea, air and now cyber environments which limit what can and cannot be done on, in and through them, so also there are for space. For example, some grasp of the laws of orbital motion is necessary in order for one to appreciate why the People's Republic of China will not be able to monitor/target from space (low-Earth orbit) a US carrier task force moving on the high seas – except at economically prohibitive cost.

Astropolitik, together with Jim Oberg's *Space Power Theory* (1999), may be said to open a new phase in the strategic understanding of space. The Royal Navy practised sea power long before Alfred Thayer Mahan wrote in 1890 telling the world what they had been doing. So it is with space power, at least up to a point. A great navy seizes and exercises sea control (including sea denial) in order to enable friendly maritime mobility and to project power against the shore. Space power implies a function parallel to sea control in space control. But in order to seize and exercise space control, first a polity needs to understand space as an environment for war, in essence no different from the land, the sea, the air or cyberspace. Everett Dolman brings to bear upon the distinctive space geography our accumulated learning in strategic theory, and the historical experience of international terrestrial conflict. The result is a book that we are proud to publish as a true milestone on the road to holistic strategic understanding of the space environment.

Colin S. Gray
Series Co-Editor

Abbreviations

AABNCP	Advanced Airborne National Command Post
ABM	anti-ballistic missile
AEC	Atomic Energy Commission
AHCOPUOS	Ad Hoc Committee on the Peaceful Uses of Outer Space
ASAT	anti-satellite
BMD	Ballistic Missile Defense
C3I	Command, Control, Communications, and Intelligence
CNES	French National Space Agency
COPUOS	Committee on the Peaceful Uses of Outer Space
DEW	Defense Early Warning
DoD	(US) Department of Defense
ELINT	electronic intelligence
EMP	electromagnetic pulse
ESA	European Space Agency
FSA	First Strike Advantage
GPS	Global Positioning Satellite
GSLV	Geostationary Space Launch Vehicle
HOPE-X H-II	Orbiting Plane – Experimental
HUMINT	human agent
IC	Intelligence Community
ICBM	intercontinental ballistic missile
IGY	International Geophysical Year
INPE	Brazilian National Space Agency
ISRO	Indian Space and Research Organization
LDC	Less Developed Country
LEO	Low Earth Orbit
LoW	launch on warning (of attack)
MAD	Mutual Assured Destruction
MRBM	Medium Range Ballistic Missile
NASA	National Aeronautics and Space Administration
NASDA	Japanese National Space Agency
NAVSTAR/GPS	Global Positioning Satellite
NPT	Non-Proliferation Treaty

NSC	National Security Council
OST	Outer Space Treaty
PSLV	Polar Space Launch Vehicle
SAC	Strategic Air Command
SBIRS	space-based infrared system
SDI	Strategic Defense Initiative
SLV	space launch vehicle
SMEC	Strategic Missiles Evaluation Committee
SRBM	Short Range Ballistic Missile
TMD	Theater Missile Defense
TREE	Transient Radiation Effects on Electronics
UNCLOS	United Nations Convention on Law of the Sea
WTO	World Trade Organization

1

Introduction: Realism and Geopolitics

Astropolitik is grand strategy. Indeed, it is the grandest strategy of them all. The entirety of the Earth is reduced to a single component of the total approach, critically important to be sure, but in many cases no more than a peripheral component. Within this brief text, an attempt is made to outline the framework of a consistent strategic approach to the current and near future realms of state rivalry in outer space. This is not an operational or tactical account. Technologies of war and the intricacies of force application are considered only to the extent that they illuminate and rationalize strategic policy.

In its narrowest construct, *Astropolitik* is the extension of primarily nineteenth- and twentieth-century theories of global geopolitics into the vast context of the human conquest of outer space. In a more general and encompassing interpretation, it is the application of the prominent and refined realist vision of state competition into outer space policy, particularly the development and evolution of a legal and political regime for humanity's entry into the cosmos. This work considers the former view, begun with a few keen insights from Dandridge Cole and Marc Vaucher but never adequately synthesized into a coherent theory, to be more academically provocative.[1] The basic format of this more precise and rigorous model is fully delineated here for the first time. The latter view, which encompasses a sizable and growing body of pertinent literature, nowhere expressed better than in the magnificent study of superpower confrontation in the space age by Walter McDougall, is addressed to reinforce and help explain the former view.[2]

This is not meant to denigrate or minimize the importance of the realist, even harsh *Realpolitik*, view of humanity's tendency toward confrontational diplomatic exchange in the history of space exploration. Political realism is a central theme of this work. Without the jurist's and historian's painstaking chronicle of the Space Age, astropolitics as elaborated upon here might not be comprehensible. It is simply to acknowledge that others have served the genre much better, and that if this work is judged to have any merit it will not be for adding significantly to that splendid astrohistorical collection. The effort herein is primarily an attempt to place a more stringent conceptual framework around and among the many vectors of space policies and chronicles, to establish a separate domain of realist academic and theoretical study in the space arena, and to reinforce what is astropolitical and what is not. Just as the term geopolitics is over-used, diminishing its explanatory power and reducing its utility, astropolitics has been likewise abused. If everything that happens in space is astropolitical, then the term loses its meaning.

Thus I propose corralling the elements of space and politics recognized as realist into their proper places in grand strategy. Colin Gray, in his penetrating analysis of the meaning and place of modern strategy, makes an almost unassailable case that the elements of strategy are unchanging, and applicable across all levels of analysis – that is, across system, across level, and across time.[3] His argument is wholly compatible with the tenets of astropolitics and *Astropolitik*: 'there is an essential unity to all strategic experience in all periods of history because nothing vital to the nature and function of war and strategy changes'.[4] In his rigorous definition, Gray asserts that strategy is 'the use that is made of force and the threats of force for the ends of policy'.[5] Threats may be implicit or explicit, but the connection between violence and policy is vital to an understanding of grand strategy. While it may seem barbaric in this modern era to continue to assert the primacy of war and violence – 'high politics' in the realist vernacular – in formulations of state strategy, it would be disingenuous and even reckless to try to deny the continued preeminence of the terrestrial state and the place of military action in the short history and near future of space operations. Even as states publicly denounce the use of violence and force in space operations, all spacefaring states today have military missions, goals, and contingency space-operations plans. A case will be made here that the reality of confrontation in space politics pervades the reality of the ideal of true cooperation and political unity in space which has never been genuine, and in the near term seems unlikely.

At this juncture it is probably necessary to set down a defense of the selection of an admittedly contentious term for the title. Astropolitics is innocuous enough. It conjures a sense of commingled realms of politics and space-age technology. It is narrower and more powerful than that, as will be shown, but as an appellation it should not rankle. *Astropolitik*, as the saying goes, is another kettle of fish. Yet it is chosen carefully and with much thoughtful deliberation. The text nowhere concludes that a harsh realist outlook is the only one for the future of space exploration and exploitation. It simply avers that this has been the pattern, and that policymakers should be prepared to deal with a competitive, state-dominated future in space. Nor is there any intimation that such an environment is inevitable or even probable. In the author's view, in the long term, such a sustained policy is counterproductive and detrimental. The colossal effort to conquer space will be done much more efficiently by a united world, if for no other reason than that the enormous expense of a truly large-scale conquest and colonization effort may require the enthusiasm and support of all Earth's people. Simply put, in a world of modern territorial nation-states (whose demise has been prematurely announced[6]), collective action dilemmas will prevent those political entities from cooperatively exploiting the realm, and efforts to enjoin states to do so will have negative if not countervailing results. These views are discussed in greater detail in Chapters 4–6. In the short term, despite our best intentions, we may be relegated to a harsh, discordant, entirely realist paradigm in space.

Therefore the term *Astropolitik* is chosen as a constant reminder to those who would read this book, and carefully weigh many of its claims, of the horrible depths to which other geopolitical-based *Realpolitik* strategies of dominance ultimately degenerated. The German school of *Geopolitik*, despite the equivocal intentions of its founders, became a racist and utterly unscientific invective about the superiority of the 'Aryan' race and its inevitable domination of the world. *Geopolitik*, too, was a grand strategy, an action plan for conquest. The good intentions of the author of the current work aside, the potential for misuse and abuse of *Astropolitik* is plain. The theory describes the geopolitical bases for power in outer space, and offers suggestions for dominance of space through military means. Policymakers ignore such a strategy at their state's peril. When the time has come for a theoretical perspective to emerge, and that perspective cuts across the grain of extant ideology, wishing it were not so cannot make it go away. Some state will likely employ the principles of *Astropolitik* and may come to dominate space as a consequence. It is to be hoped that this state will be a relatively benign one. It is with some trepidation and angst, then, that this argument is put forward. The author understands and accepts the opinion that practitioners who believe the world is evil and dangerous will in their actions continually tend to recreate it. Before this degenerates into a self-absorbed *mea culpa*, it is essential to note that astropolitics and *Astropolitik* make no distinction among the many motives of those who might apply them. The following chapters do make a few specific calls for action. A new regime for outer space that could reignite the fervor for space exploration that culminated during the 1960s, and a military policy based on territorial control are pre-eminent among them. Neither of these moves by themselves, nor the realist foundations upon which they are based, necessarily engenders evil or malicious outcomes. The tenets within, however, cannot and should not escape the past from which they were drawn, and so the title is chosen as a constant reminder of that past, and as a grim warning for the future.

The simple fact that Gray's definition of strategy is accepted, and is itself a modification of Clausewitz's renowned if widely misinterpreted dictum that war is a continuation of political discourse by other (extreme) means, indicates the hard-realist paradigm of ever-present violence and fear cannot be separated from *Astropolitik*; and nor should it be. *Astropolitik*, like *Realpolitik*, is hardnosed and pragmatic, it is not pretty or uplifting or a joyous sermon for the masses. But neither is it evil. Its benevolence or malevolence will become apparent only as it is applied, and by whom. For instance, it is anticipated, that a critical understanding of the propositions cautiously proffered here could lead the reader to anticipate a future where violent competition is transferred to an economic realm. In that case, states will employ competition productively, harnessing natural incentives for self-interested gain to a mutually beneficial future, a competition based on the fair and legal commercial exploitation of space. The axioms of astropolitics and *Astropolitik* fit just as well in an economically competitive environment as in a continuously warring one.

There is some hope for this view. Mounting empirical evidence points to the proliferation of modern liberal democracy as a pacifying force in international relations. Liberal-democratic states have not gone to war with each other, and, although they have had considerable conflicts of interest, appear content to resolve common disputes with rare resort even to the threat of military violence. Such is the enormous drain on national economies that advanced liberal-democratic states are the most likely to undertake and *sustain* a dominating space program. As more states democratize, these observations lead to the promise of an ever-widening democratic zone of peace, ultimately encompassing the globe then spreading out to the cosmos and ushering in an era of true cooperation and stability.

Although David Singer and Melvin Small first empirically described the phenomenon, it was Michael Doyle who provoked a storm of activity with his attempt to tie the observation to Kant's claim that liberal-democratic states would be naturally less prone to war.[7] Tests of the hypothesis showed that democratic states appear just as likely to engage in war as any alternative politically organized state. What remained intriguing, and promising, was the empirical evidence and rationale that democratic states do not go to war *with each other*.[8] Causal explanations tend to cluster around structural and normative factors of government capacities and leadership qualities, and represent some of the most sophisticated international analyses in ongoing political science debates.[9] If mutual liberal democracy is in fact a sufficient precondition for inter-state peace, then democratic peace theory provides both the means and end for a stable and pacific world (and presumably space) order. Any policy that efficiently enhances the process of democratization in authoritarian and developing states will have positive inter-state results, and should be thoughtfully considered. When all states are democratic, war will be a social relic. Astropolitics and *Astropolitik* encompass the social and cultural effects of new technologies, in this case space technologies, on the subsequent evolution of political institutions (Chapters 2 and 5). The direction of influence on democratization of astropolitical variables is introduced here, though it is not definitively announced. If, however, primarily democratic states enter and exploit space, and these states are best equipped to sustain robust space programs, then the tenets of *Astropolitik* are structurally less malicious – since these states are unlikely to pursue violent confrontation with each other – and so can be used for commercial and system stability (policing) and productive economic advantages.

Needless to say, a contradictory thesis is prevalent. For many traditional peace theorists, who concentrate on eliminating war by reducing and eliminating the military capacity to engage in combat, democratic peace theory appears fully complementary to their views. Since war is the problem democracy is held to correct, they presume that the tools of war are, by association, 'anti-democratic'.[10] The widely held belief that disarmament promotes peace has long been acknowledged, and then quickly dismissed, by such eminent theorists as Friedrich Schumann and Hedley Bull.[11] Still, the notion hangs on and is the prescriptive cornerstone of the World Peace Movement.[12] Reducing or eliminating arms promotes peace and decreases external threats, so the argument goes, which in turn fosters domestic development of individual liberty. William Thompson makes precisely this point as he argues that peace causes democracy, not the reverse.[13] Moreover, say the peace theorists, when all states are democratic there will be no need to maintain the military forces necessary to prosecute war, and all states will be able, if not compelled by socio-economic necessity, to complete any remaining process of disarmament. For these advocates, astropolitics and *Astropolitik* will be considered politically and socially reprehensible, if not dangerous. The preferred prescription is that humanity begins its entry into the cosmos without weapons, warriors, or Clauswitzian theorists. If the non-weaponized model is pursued, peaceful coexistence is inevitable. Unfortunately for their utopian position, the short history of space exploration already belies that hope. The militarization and weaponization of space is not only an historical fact, it is an ongoing process.

Most international realists choose to discount the democratic peace (this work is a distinct exception). They aver that the correlation is a coincidental facade, that democratic states have not gone to war simply because traditional power politics inducements have not yet presented themselves.[14] Democratic states have too short a history, and in that brief time they have always been allied against ideological positions that sought the end of liberalism – first monarchy, then fascism, then communism. It is only recently that liberal-democratic states have shared borders, the realists will point out, as their numbers have risen to important minority status in the community of states only since 1945. They argue it is not weapons or armed force that destabilizes, it is the attitudes and perceptions of the potential wielders of weapons that matter. States must anticipate increasing resource and market competition in the future, and should expect democratic states to act as any other power-optimizing state, regardless of domestic governing arrangements. Stable peace, wholly desirable but fragile, can be obtained only via balancing strategies based on mutual positions of strength.[15] Democratic states may be especially vulnerable in a less militarized world, since their societies tend to be more open, mobilization is public and difficult, and they are thus susceptible to first strike attacks.[16] Under these conditions, all states should avoid eliminating or unduly weakening their armed forces. To do so would be an invitation to war.

The concerns of the realists are well argued, and cast a wary doubt on the abundance of empirical evidence cited by the democratic peace proponents. If one accepts for the moment, as an *analytical assumption* only, the proposition that liberal-democratic states do not go to war with each other, then an alternate and exceptionally cooperative future can be projected. Indeed, if such states do not go to war with each other, then the level of armaments they possess or the military attitudes they project should not be a serious threat. Calls for disarmament may be economically efficient, but they should not be necessary. Liberal-democratic states have nothing to fear from other such states, and the size and strength of their armed forces need not be of concern. If one further accepts that a stable inter-state peace is the goal of both liberal and realist theory – a reasonable one in that a stable peace has been the holy grail of international theorists since the possibility of global destruction via nuclear devastation has been hypothesized – then a compatible path is opened. The means of one school (realist military preparedness) are reconciled with the means (liberal democratization) and ends (global then interstellar peace derived from the condition of full democracy) of the other. The point of harmonization is democracy itself.

The bulk of democratization theory correctly emphasizes socioeconomic factors as the foundation of democracy, and my analysis is not intended to contradict this significant body of established theory. If anything, the relationship between rising wealth and rising democracy is an 'iron law' of political science. Should the vast wealth of space be tapped and brought to constructive use on Earth, the wealth of all people should dramatically rise (at least in terms of per capita income, but undoubtedly in more meaningful ways as well). Significant infusions of capital, such as that observed in the sixteenth century after the discovery of the New World by the Spanish, serve to ignite systemic economic booms. The principles of astropolitics and *Astropolitik* promote such economic endeavors, and rising wealth should have a complementary effect enhancing democratization, in this way limiting the negative effects of space-based militarization. To be sure, the state that too aggressively pursues military power will lose ground in commercial productivity. If war never occurs, then all attempts to prepare for it are (in the liberal view) wasted. On the other hand, if the democratic peace is not so robust, and in the future democratic states may indeed go to war, then the realists have not sacrificed their defensive postures. Vigilance and force of arms will be ready to assure the peace in a breakdown of theory. Astropolitics and *Astropolitik* constitute but one view of the future, which cannot accurately foretell real world events. It can only provide predictions of what the model will output if certain expressed assumptions are accepted. Readers will find evidence both for and against a prognosis of peace, but by itself it is neither a threat to that peace nor a guarantee of hostile military action.

The paradox that maintaining effective means for war is the best guarantor of peace has been staunchly defended by balance-of-power realists and relentlessly attacked by pacificists. Based solely on calculations of capacities for war, there appears to be no compromise solution. John Owen points out that realists and liberals 'have been loathe to cede any ground' when discussing the democratic peace. Nonetheless, Owen cites John Elster's argument that opposite tendencies can cancel each other out in practice and promote a working synthesis, and he joins Stephen Walt's balance of threat and Alexander Wendt's ideational framework as a possible realist–liberal synthesis along Elster's model.[17] In a side argument, *Astropolitik* proposes shifting the dispute to the role of military forces in shaping social and political institutions. Under a precise (and historically rare) set of organizing conditions, military forces can both promote democracy and enhance deterrent policies, an argument to be taken up in Chapter 2. Despite a requirement for specific military preparation, however, war is neither necessary nor beneficial to the process of democratization, and so *Astropolitik* does not project a certain future of applied violence in space. In this manner, the means of both liberals and realists are supported *en route* to a common goal. This is to be the ultimate contribution of astropolitics and *Astropolitik*: a full and heuristic understanding of the geopolitical determinants of space, an application of the assumptions of realism to the astropolitical model, and, in the end, an economically robust and peaceful exploration of the cosmos by humanity.

Chapters 2 and 3 identify and evaluate the relationship between outer space geography and geographic position (*astrography*) and the evolution of current and future military space strategy. Throughout, five primary propositions are explored. First, many classical geopolitical theories of national military development are fully compatible with, and will prove readily adaptable to, the realm of outer space. Second, the most applicable of these theories will be military power assessments of geographical position in light of new technologies. Such assessments have been made for sea, rail, and air power, and can be viewed with analytic perspicacity as segments of an evolutionary process. Space power is their logical and apparent heir. Third, the special terrain of solar space dictates specific tactics and strategies for efficient exploitation of space resources. These strategies impact on political development, highlighting the geo/astrodeterminist political relationship. Fourth, the concept of *space* as a power base in classical, especially German, geopolitical thought will require some modification, but will easily conform to the exploitation and use of outer space as an ultimate national power base. Finally, a thorough understanding of the astromechanical and physical demarcations of outer space can prove useful to political planners, and will prove absolutely critical to military strategists. An optimum deployment of space assets is essential for victory on the current terrestrial and future space-based battlefields. In order to animate these positions, and in accordance with the examples set by Sir Halford Mackinder and Nicholas Spykman, the formulation of a neoclassical astropolitical dictum is established: Who controls low-Earth orbit controls near-Earth space. Who controls near-Earth space dominates Terra. Who dominates Terra determines the destiny of humankind.

Critical to assessing the outcome of a possible *Astropolitik*-generated future, it is useful to have a basic grasp of the historical and political events that have shaped the current international structure, or regime, that dominates this area. Chapters 4 and 5 provide a realist interpretation of that foundation, in order to show that international accord in outer space, in every case, was shaped by competition. It will be argued that the guise of cooperation has been freely employed as a tool of astropolitical diplomacy and statecraft, and that cooperation in space as it exists today is dependent upon – and would not exist without – international competition.

To accomplish this task, several analyses will be presented. The first will describe the international setting from which the current regime emerged. It should become evident that the cooperative end result was merely the vehicle for consistent foreign policies in a decentralized, decidedly uncooperative international environment of Cold War antagonism. The United States, its dominance in space challenged by the Soviet Union, felt compelled to ensure that no other nation could carve out an empire in space. The highly touted international cooperation that produced the 1967 Outer Space Treaty was not in truth evidence of a newly emerging universalism; rather, it was a reaffirmation of Cold War realism and national rivalry, a slick diplomatic maneuver that both bought time for the United States and checked Soviet expansion. Related descriptions will include: the competitive military environment which provided the motivation and technology for space exploration; evidence that the scientific roots of the world's first satellite endeavors were grounded not in international fraternity but in epistemic conflict and Cold War manipulation; proof that, once the criteria for cooperation were accepted, the very terms of cooperation became points of contention; the air and sea law foundations for negotiation, suggesting the Outer Space Treaty is itself the jumbled consolidation of a body of conflicting precedents; and a chronology of the negotiations for the 1967 Outer Space Treaty that highlight its devolution into a perverse competition of who could out-cooperate whom.

Analyses in these chapters will further examine the notions of common heritage and collective ownership as they apply to space. This is done to support a recommendation for a new outer-space regime. The political realism pervasive among the participant states, to include the peculiar effects of a geopolitical heritage on their decision-making processes, will be described. An exploration of the negotiation history and positions of the major players will provide a structure for analysis. Included will be a brief description of the major treaties and declarations of the international outer-space regime, including two unratified but significant agreements that may signify a future shift in basic political outlooks. Suggestions of the future role this regime will play in a political world that has fundamentally changed since the regime was emplaced, to include an assessment of its validity and prospects for stability and order, will be offered. Finally, the outline for a new regime, one that harnesses the self-interested nature of the continuing territorial state, will be offered.

Chapter 6 describes the current status of national policy and strategy for outer space in astropolitical terms. The theoretical environment is quite sparse. In an era when change is the norm, few have come forward to propose a bold, new approach. Michael Doyle has urged that, in times of theoretical flux, a return to the classics of international theory is warranted. Of the base models – realism, liberalism, and Marxism/socialism – realism has suffered the most from a lack of theorists willing to promulgate its applications (much less its virtues) into the realm of outer space. Without question, military planners recognize the need for space support and are increasingly likely to raise the call for weapons in space, but only a few have successfully merged military force and political strategy in a manner reminiscent of Alfred Thayer Mahan's call for a new diplomatic paradigm based on sea power.[18] Astropolitics and *Astropolitik* take up the challenge and in this chapter provide a simple but effective blueprint for space control.

Chapter 7 reiterates the foundations of cooperation in a competitive world. As humanity stands poised at the beginning of a new millennium, a unique opportunity is presented. The state-rivalry focus of geopolitical theory has remained at significant odds with globalist recommendations for space exploitation, but a compromise may be possible. Truly efficient exploration of space, in the latter view, presupposes a unity of effort unimpeded by national rivalries. Indeed, the effort of space exploration is presumed so encompassing that only a world government shorn of the distractions of inter-state rivalry and war could focus the resources necessary to accomplish such a massive project. With the surety of their convictions and the imperatives of evolution, the globalists insist that humans have filled and dominated the biological niche that is earth, and must now spill out into the heavens to meet their collective destiny. Such future endeavors are best articulated under some framework of effective world government, they aver, but would be minimally possible given a politically stable terrestrial environment – one in which states have achieved a sturdy peace and an equitable working agreement for the division of space resources. At a time when the possibility of effective one-world government is remote, *Astropolitik* offers a plan for achieving those minimum conditions.

NOTES

1. Among Dandridge Cole's many works on the subject, see *Beyond Tomorrow: The Next 50 Years in Space* (Amherst, WI: Amherst Press, 1965); with D. Cox, *The Challenge of the Planetoids* (Philadelphia, PA: Chilton Press, 1963); and with I. M. Levitt, *Exploring the Secrets of Space: Astronautics for the Layman* (London: Prentice-Hall International, 1963). See also M. Vaucher, 'Geographic Parameters for Military Doctrine in Space and the Defense of the Space-Based Enterprise', in U. Ra'ana and R. Pfaltzgraf (eds), *International Security Dimensions of Space* (Medfors, MA: Archon, 1984), pp. 32–46. My own initial attempt to formalize the model was published as 'Geopolitics in the Space Age', *Journal of Strategic Studies*, Vol. 22 (Fall) 1999, pp. 83–106, also included as a chapter in C. Gray and G. Sloan (eds), *Geopolitics: Geography and Strategy* (London: Frank Cass, 1999), pp. 83–106.
2. W. McDougall, *... the Heavens and the Earth* (New York: Basic Books, 1987). This book, for which McDougall won the 1986 Pullitzer Prize for history, spans the history of space exploration only through 1985. For a text that does an admirable job of continuing the saga to the late 1990s, see M. Von Bencke, *The Politics of Space: A History of US–Soviet Competition and Cooperation* (Boulder, CO: Westview, 1997).
3. C. Gray, *Modern Strategy* (London: Oxford University Press, 2000), p. 1. Specifically, Gray says 'elements common to war in all periods, in all geographies, and with all technologies'.
4. Ibid.
5. Ibid., p. 17.
6. As early as 1957, John Herz was proclaiming 'The Rise and Demise of the Territorial State', *World Politics*, Vol. 9 (1957), pp. 473–93. More recently, see A. Linklater, 'Citizenship and Sovereignty in the Post-Westphalian State', *European Journal of International Relations*, Vol. 2 (1996), 77–103.
7. D. Singer and M. Small, 'The War-Proneness of Democratic Regimes', *Jerusalem Journal of International Relations*, Vol. 1, No. 4 (Summer 1976), pp. 50–69; M. Doyle, 'Kant, Liberal Legacies, and Foreign Affairs', Parts 1 and 2 in *Philosophy and Public Affairs*, Vol. 12, Nos 3 and 4 (Summer and Fall 1983), pp. 206–35 and 323–53, see also 'Liberalism and World Politics', *American Political Science Review*, Vol. 80, No. 4 (December 1986), pp. 1151–69.
8. See S. Chan, 'Mirror, Mirror on the Wall ... Are Freer Countries More Pacific?', *Journal of Conflict Resolution*, Vol. 28, No. 4 (December 1984), pp. 616–48; E. Weede, 'Democracy and War Involvement', *Journal of Conflict Resolution*, Vol. 28, No. 4 (December 1984), pp. 649–64; and Z. Maoz and N. Abdolai, 'Regime Types and International Conflict', *Journal of Conflict Resolution*, Vol. 33, No. 1 (March 1989), pp. 3–35. See also D. Bremer, 'Dangerous Dyads: Interstate War, 1816–1965', *Journal of Conflict Resolution*, Vol. 36, No. 2 (June 1992), pp. 309–41, and 'Democracy and Militarized Interstate Conflict', *International Interactions*, Vol. 18, No. 3 (Fall 1993), pp. 231–49; and W. Dixon, 'Democracy and the Peaceful Settlement of International Conflict', *American Political Science Review*, Vol. 88, No. 1 (March 1994), pp. 14–32.
9. J. Owen, 'How Liberalism Produces Democratic Peace', *International Security*, Vol. 19, No. 2 (Fall 1994), pp. 87–125; J. O'Neal, F. O'Neal, Z. Moazand B. Russett, 'The Liberal Peace, Interdependence, Democracy, and International Conflict, 1950–1985', *Journal of Peace Research*, Vol. 33, No. 1 (Winter 1996), pp. 11–28.
10. David Apter's view is typical: 'The Military Is a Particularly Important Obstacle to Democracy', in *The Politics of Modernization* (Chicago, IL: University of Chicago Press, 1965), p. 450.
11. F. Schumann, *International Politics*, 5th edn (New York: McGraw-Hill, 1953), p. 230; H. Bull, *The Control of the Arms Race* (New York: Praeger, 1961), pp. 31–3.

12. G. Blainey, *The Causes of War* (New York: Free Press, 1973), pp. 135–7, 151–2.
13. W. Thompson, 'Democracy and Peace: Putting the Cart Before the Horse', *International Organization*, Vol. 50, No. 1 (January 1996), pp. 141–74.
14. See J. Mearsheimer, 'Back to the Future: Instability in Europe After the Cold War', *International Security*, Vol. 15, No. 1 (Summer 1990), pp. 5–56; Also R. Schweller, 'Domestic Structure and Preventative War: Are Democracies More Pacific?' *World Politics*, Vol. 44, No. 2 (January 1992), pp. 235–69; D. Lake, 'Powerful Pacifists: Democratic States and War', *American Political Science Review*, Vol. 86, No. 1 (March 1992), pp. 24–37; C. Layne, 'Kant or Cant: The Myth of the Democratic Peace', *International Security*, Vol. 19, No. 2 (Fall 1994), pp. 5–49; and S. Peterson, 'How Democracies Differ: Public Opinion, State Structure, and the Lessons of the Fashoda Crisis', *Security Studies*, Vol. 5, No. 1 (Autumn 1995), pp. 3–37. Ed Mansfield and Glenn Snyder warn that instability in democracies in transition may undermine the pacifying effects of stable liberalism, see 'Democratization and War', *International Security*, Vol. 20, No. 1 (Summer 1995), pp. 5–38; Henry Farber and Joanne Gowa find 'no statistically significant relationship between democracy and war before 1914, [and] it is only after 1945 that the probability of war or serious disputes is significantly lower between democratic states than between members of other pairs of states', 'Polities and Peace', *International Organization*, Vol. 20, No. 2 (Fall 1995), p. 124.
15. Whether a balance (J. Mearsheimer, *Conventional Deterrence* (Ithaca, NY: Cornell University Press, 1983)) or a preponderance of power (A. Organski and J. Kugler, *The War Ledger* (Chicago, IL: University of Chicago Press, 1980)) is more stable is still disputed. See E. Mansfield, *Power, Trade, and War* (Princeton, NJ: Princeton University Press, 1994); R.H. Wagner, 'Peace, War, and the Balance of Power', *American Political Science Review*, Vol. 88, No. 3 (September 1994), pp. 593–607; and R. Powell, 'Stability and the Balance of Power', *World Politics*, Vol. 48, No. 1 (January 1996), pp. 239–67.
16. See B. Russet, *Grasping the Democratic Peace: Principles for a Post-Cold War World* (Princeton, NJ: Princeton University Press, 1993) for the best overview.
17. J. Owen, 'How Liberalism Produces Democratic Peace', *International Security*, Vol. 19, No. 2 (Fall 1994), pp. 122–3; J. Elster, *Political Psychology* (Cambridge: University Press, 1993); S. Walt, *The Origin of Alliances* (Ithaca, NY: Cornell University Press, 1993); and A. Wendt, 'Anarchy is What States Make of It: The Social Construction of Power Politics', *International Organization*, Vol. 46, No. 2 (Spring 1992), pp. 391–425.
18. Colin Gray asks who will be the Mahan of Space (in 'The Influence of Space Power upon History', *Comparative Strategy*, Vol. 15, No. 4 (1996), pp. 293–308)? It is presumptuous to lay claim to the mantle, and I certainly do not do so here. What I do hope to accomplish, however, is to shift the dialogue to a trajectory where the next Mahan can emerge.

2

Foundations: From Geopolitics to Astropolitics

With its long and distinguished line of adherents and proponents, geopolitics ranks among the oldest and most recognizable bodies of written political theory. Yet it has atrophied in the modern era to such an extent that while almost everyone is acquainted with the term, scarcely anyone uses it correctly and fewer can precisely define it. In the United States, for example, geopolitical events are popularly understood to be issues and actions that take place overseas.[1] The term 'geopolitical' is so broadly construed as to be meaningless. This lamentable conceptual degeneration is due almost entirely to the defeat of the Axis powers in World War II. Nazi misuse of geopolitical theory through the German school of *Geopolitik* (to be more fully described later in this chapter), as a purposeful guide and moral justification for their particular brand of racist militarism, made post-war geopolitical studies – whatever perceived merits it may have once had – an academic taboo subject.

It is not just precision in definition that eludes us. Much of the theoretical focus of geopolitics has been lost as well. To be rigorous in our definition, then, we must recognize that geopolitics embraces several research schools, including some that have been in academic hiding but many that have flourished under different terms. In a convincing argument for the resuscitation of geopolitical theory into mainstream twenty-first-century academic discourse, Daniel Deudney outlines five overlapping clusters of historically recognized geopolitical themes.[2] These include: (1) *Physiopolitics*, a type of naturalist social science that sees man's physical and political development as the product of his attempts to adapt to his environment; (2) the German school of *Geopolitik*, the most notorious of the geopolitical theories and its most regrettable; (3) *Balance of Power* politics between states, in its most recognized form the term *Realpolitik* suffices; (4) *Political Geography*, separated from geopolitics when *Geopolitik* was at its apex, dealing with the effects of man-made borders and boundaries on human activity; and (5) classical *Global Geopolitics*, which attempted to incorporate the roles of transportation, communication, and technology into a coherent view of the political world.

Ultimately, Deudney advances his own model, which he terms *Neoclassical Geopolitics*, or 'structural-functional security materialism.'[3] He uses this model to analyze the evolution of security practices in a world of changing material conditions. Though Deudney's model is not applied directly to the problem of outer space, his analysis pervades this manuscript, and the described movement of the geopolitical toward astropolitics follows the logic at Figure 2.1 (adapted from Deudney's description and Martin Glassner's more conventional 1993 model[4]).

Since the format of astropolitics is drawn from geopolitical predecessors, some precise definitions are necessary to set the terms of the argument. Making such distinctions is not simply a semantic exercise. Identification and categorization are the keys to knowledge. It is epistemologically essential to construct or, as is intended here, add on to an existing field of theory. Geoffrey Parker has defined *geopolitics* in its broadest connotation masterfully. He calls it 'the study of states as spatial phenomena, with a view toward understanding the geographical bases of their power'.[5] This definition simultaneously accounts for the object (states) and format (geocentric or global worldview) of study. Moreover, it accents the pivotal focus of interest, raw power, and suggests the hard realist paradigm with its *ultima ratio* of violence as the expression of state power. Geopolitics therefore has an implicit, and, for some modern theorists, an explicit emphasis on war.[6] Perhaps more eloquent in his definition than Parker, if not more exacting, Sir Halford Mackinder has stated that geopolitics *must* have 'a correlation between the larger geographical and the larger historical generalizations', so as to describe 'geographical causation in universal history'.[7]

Geodeterminism (or for Deudney, *physiopolitics*) is the tenet that geographic location – influenced by such factors as climate, the availability of natural resources or endowments, and topographic features including mountains, plains, rivers, and oceans – ultimately decides the character of a population and the type of government and military forces that emerge. When the military planner accounts for the largest-scale effects of geography to influence decisions on deployment of forces, *geostrategy* is invoked (in Deudney's conception, geostrategy is most nearly associated with *global geopolitics*, and to a lesser extent, *Realpolitik*). It is important to note at this juncture that geostrategy is concerned with the worldview, and is therefore quite distinct from tactical, operational, or conventional strategic military thinking (such as the 'Art of War' treatises of Sun Tzu, Machiavelli, Jomini, von Clausewitz, and innumerable military field manuals[8]). Ideally, geostrategists attempt to gain a global advantage over competing states. If they are unable to accomplish dominance for themselves, they invoke geostrategy to deny the geographically advantaged state's potential domination through their own maximization of scarce geopositional resources.

Flowing from geodeterminism are theories of the *Organic State*. In this

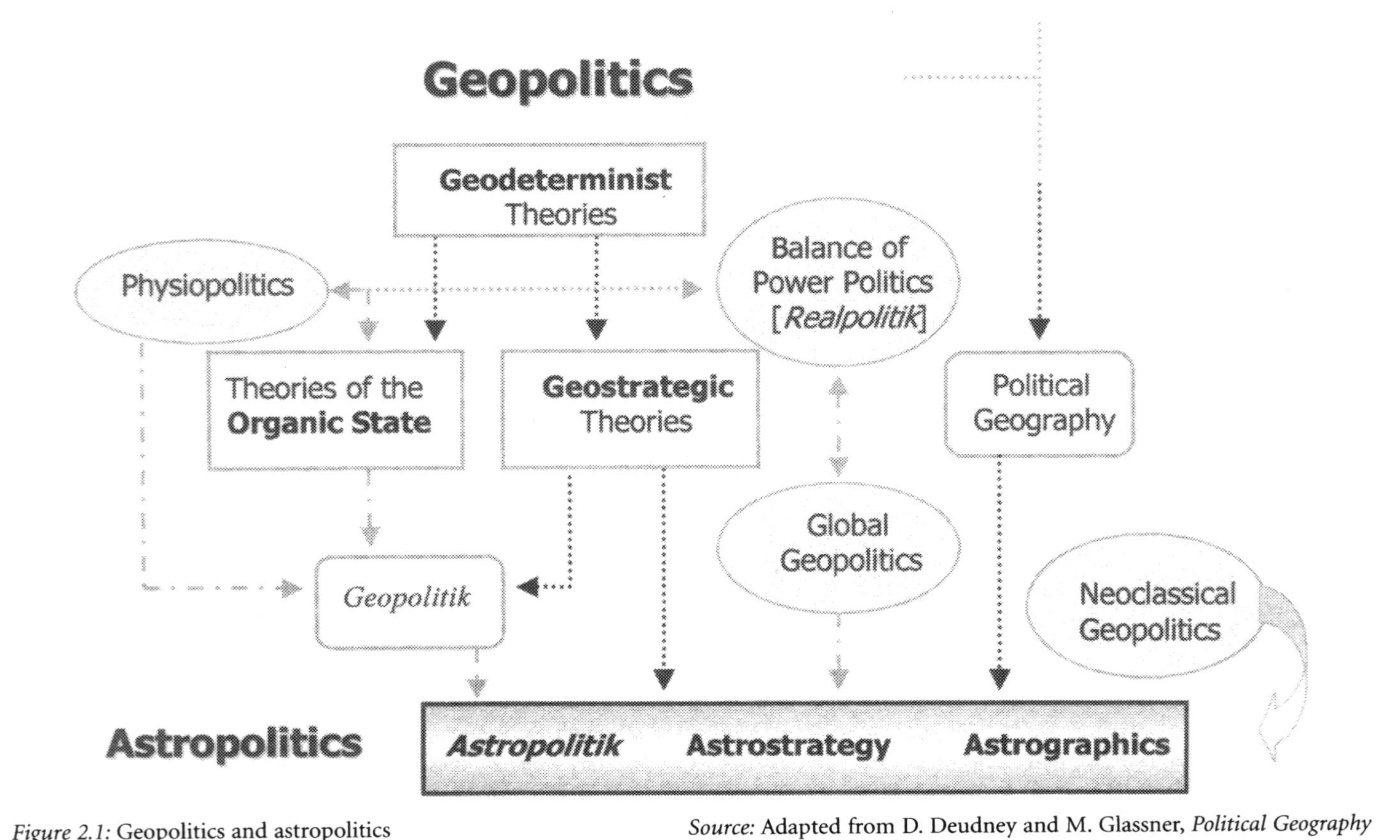

Figure 2.1: Geopolitics and astropolitics

Source: Adapted from D. Deudney and M. Glassner, *Political Geography*

view, the state is reified then brought to life so that comparisons between living organisms and the social and political construct can be made. Generally employed to justify expansionist or state-growth policies, and in the modern era inextricably bound to notions of Social and Cultural Darwinism,[9] when combined with geostrategy the outcome is a necessarily competitive world-view. The state and people that best adapt within their geographic niche, in other words that state which in the cauldron of war emerges triumphant, is fittest. The clear connotation is that the state that dominates the world *ought* to dominate it. Nature demands it. The most radical of these theoretical hybrids was the German school of *Geopolitik*, a fully and (perversely) morally justified action plan for the domination of Europe by the mythical Aryan race expounded in the 1920s and 1930s.[10]

From these historic tendrils, we can draw out the proposed distinctions of *astropolitics*, here defined as the study of the relationship between outer space terrain and technology and the development of political and military policy and strategy. *Astrostrategy*, following the pattern already established, is the identification of critical terrestrial and outer space locations, the control of which can provide military and political dominance of outer space, or at a minimum can insure against the same dominance by a potential opponent state. Astrostrategy is the dominant theme of Chapters 3 and 6 of this book. *Astropolitik*, a term specifically chosen for its negative connotations, is identified as a determinist political theory that manipulates the relationship between state power and outer-space control for the purpose of extending the dominance of a single state over the whole of the Earth. It presumes the state that dominates space is specifically chosen by the rigors of competition as the politically and morally *superior* nation, culture, and economy. Should humanity ever drop the state-dominant model (unlikely in the near term, but probably inevitable in the long), unite as a species, and strike out for the cosmos as one people, *Astropolitik* would furnish the necessary blueprint for exploration and the moral justification for success. To be sure, one of the possibilities not discussed in depth here is how the discovery of extra-terrestrial intelligence would assuredly unite the entirety of the human race. In that event, *Astropolitik* would exchange its statist connotation and underpinnings for species-based ones. Humanity could in this manner be inspired by a modern version of manifest destiny to conquer space. Please note that *Astropolitik* is but one possible outcome of an ongoing astropolitical analysis. It is neither necessary nor inevitable; it is not sought after or desirable. But it is imperative that we never forget the insidious depths which the modern study of one subset of unbridled geopolitical theory ultimately reached, and if at all possible prevent a similar descent for astropolitics.

Political Geography is formally separated from the geopolitical emphases. It focuses instead on the man-made relationships between artificial conceptions of nation, state, and territory.[11] Political geography is therefore a subdivision of *human geography*[12] that studies the relationship between political boundaries and dynamic social and political processes.[13] It differs from geopolitics in that it does not inherently seek a nature-derived topo/geographically deterministic outcome. Artificially created human boundaries (for example, by gerrymanders) are generally far more interesting (and deterministic) to the political geographer than physical ones. In the present context, *political astrography* is the outer-space counterpart to the Earth-bound disciplines of physical and political geography. It is the description of the physical characteristics of outer space overlain with politically and technologically derived boundaries and features (such as the geostationary belt, the narrow band of space that allows a satellite in orbit to appear fixed above a given point on the Earth's equator) that is interesting. Unlike political geography, however, which claims no synergistic relationship with geopolitics, astrography is a foundational element of astrostrategy.

GEODETERMINISM AND THE ENVIRONMENT OF OUTER SPACE

The investigation of geographical influences on social and political development has been evident since antiquity. Astrodeterminism is merely the last in a logically coherent evolution of such thought. Deudney finds a reference he attributes to the Greek geographer Strabo that may be the earliest on record.[14] In his *History of the Peloponnesian War*, the Greek historian and political realist Thucydides clearly argues for natural imperatives driving the divergent developments of Athens and Sparta.[15] Its advantageous position astride natural trade routes and the agriculturally poor rocky soil of Attica compelled Athens to engage in commerce to satisfy its desire for growth. This necessitated dynamic contact with numerous and diverse cultures, in turn naturally leading to the development of a more open society, enamored with arts and education, and, of course, a maritime military proficiency. Alternatively, Sparta, located inland at the center of a fertile plain, found its desire for growth in direct competition with nearby agrarian societies. It naturally developed a martial tradition, conservative politically, and proficient in land campaigns, as it sought to dominate its neighbors and pacify its territorial holdings. Trade, the conduit for learning and wealth, and thus the foundation of a life of leisure, was unacceptable as a vocation to the Spartan warrior-citizen who spent his entire life in military training. The import of new ideas, especially the political notion of radical democracy, was a direct threat to the state, and Sparta is renowned for its conservatism and stability.

Without doubt, the geographically influenced and disparate reliance of the Athenian and Spartan civilizations on commerce and conquest shaped the character of their peoples and the structures of their states, but it is not the only determining influence we can perceive. A common theme of geopolitical theorists is the manner in which new technology is adapted to geographic imperatives, thereby becoming an intervening variable in the direct relationship between geography and politics. Although technology changes are more often associated with geostrategy, in the purely geo-determined world they also have a place, and so a brief historical excursion is inserted to make the point. In the Age of Classical Greece, the technological innovations most closely associated with changing political structures are the *hoplon* and the *trireme.*

The Age of Mycenaean Warlords (1600–1100 BCE) incorporated many of the same strategies, tactics, and organizing principles of contemporary civilizations of the ancient Near East and the Egyptian New Kingdom.[16] These were the dominant states of the period, and Greek militaries copied their successful innovations carefully. The rapid introduction and widespread distribution of bronze and then iron weapons technology created successive military revolutions throughout the Mediterranean and Middle Eastern regions. Complementary tactical and strategic innovations were developed for the introduction (and quick decline) of the chariot, followed by the rapid ascendance of the cavalry. Both horse-dependent tactics provided speed and shock unmatched on the battlefield. Horses were also quite expensive, and thus limited to the individuals who could afford to purchase and maintain them, creating a privileged class of knights who used military service as a path toward political power.[17]

In this age, war was the prerogative of kings, fought by and for the ruling elite. Most disputes between the petty aristocracies were settled in skirmishes of the nobility and their retinues, supplemented where needed by roving mercenaries. In larger conflicts, campaigns for significant territorial expansion and in defense of the same, where state survival might well be at stake, mass armies could be deployed. But arming the masses was widely recognized as a dangerous gambit of last resort. While heavily armed aristocrats were individually the most formidable element on the battlefield, they could succumb to sheer weight of numbers if the mass army's morale was high. For this reason, and usually only when desperation demanded it, the poorer classes of society could be pressed into light, unarmored, pike and shield-type infantry service, in tight though undisciplined mob formations. Training for these forces was limited, usually *ad hoc*, and specific to the battle at hand. Peasants, serfs, and slaves would of necessity be armed by the state, not having the economic wherewithal to arm themselves. They would be as lightly armed as possible, naturally, the best weapons being reserved for the nobility.

Middle-class farmers, tradesmen, and artisans were also occasionally pressed into service, but they generally equipped themselves with the highest level of armaments they could afford. This was a common and practical custom for the ancient soldier, regardless of his social or economic rank. In an age of swarming every-man-for-himself combat, each individual would be highly motivated to arm himself to the best of his ability. The alternative was to accept the state's inferior basic issue and huddle with the rest of the ill-trained mass of battle fodder, an unappealing option to any who could afford better. The well armed would have a greater chance of survival on the battlefield, and each survivor could expect to share in the available and allowable booty. The decision to purchase one's own arms was in this way not only practical, but could also be cost-effective.

Mercenaries were the preferred supplement to the state's noble forces. These included skilled foot and horsed archers, seasoned warriors on horseback and as heavily armed and armored infantry, and the most elite fighters, knights, and charioteers. Although the state could supply or supplement the mercenary's armaments, these professional soldiers were combat veterans who, like other master craftsmen of their day, were expected to maintain their own specialized gear. Indeed, part of their appeal was that they brought their own weapons, often of superior quality. More important, after the battle they were expected to take their pay and go home, effectively ridding the ruler or rulers of a potential armed internal threat. For reasons of battlefield prowess and efficiency, and not least of post-war internal stability, when they could be afforded mercenaries were always preferable to armed throngs.[18]

The prime concern of early military strategists was to get this hodge-podge army to the battlefield intact, well fed and supplied. Mass armies and individual knights fought in grand melee. Once blows were exchanged, little if any battlefield organization could be discerned. The leader of each side maneuvered his force into striking distance of the enemy; all the while, ballistae and archers harried the merging forces. Battle was joined when the leader of one side or the other recognized a tactical advantage, and gave the order to charge – or when the masses of infantry and cavalry, working themselves into a seething bloodlust, could no longer be held back. Upon release of an opponent's force, the options for the receiving side were to stand fast, break, and retreat, or charge in response. In the latter event, each side attacked the other in a sudden crash, intent on overwhelming the opposing force and sending it into flight. This style of combat was undoubtedly terrifying. Discipline and morale were the sole means to overcome it and prevail.

The preceding description succinctly characterizes civilized Greek warfare in the age of the Trojan War. With the demise of the Mycenaean and Minoan civilizations, after a series of barbarian invasions by northern tribes, the Greek region entered into a profound Dark Age (1000–800 BCE). Links to the Near Eastern military tradition were severed. Greece, finding itself in a political, cultural, and military backwater, reverted to a primitive if unique style of *heroic* warfare. Impressing poorer classes into mass infantries stopped. Battles during the period were characterized by groups of aristocratic champions facing each other in single combat, and were 'fluid, free-for-all encounters in which the great aristocrats of one state dueled with those of another'.[19]

The principal change in strategy during this period was a decrease in the already poor ability to wage war offensively, or at any distance away from the politicomilitary center.[20] Defensive capacity reigned supreme as once-extensive communication and transportation nets were degraded or destroyed. Dark Age Greece, in terms of military organization and strategy, closely resembled Dark Age Europe some 1,500 years later. In this power deflation and political retrenchment, anyone with the might of arms could carve a principality from the rugged terrain of Greece. A dispersion of political authority from king to warrior-lords fragmented the ancient monarchies, and the military aristocracy grew larger as the old hereditary one declined. The lot of the Greek farmer, too poor to arm himself with the newer iron weaponry and now tied directly to the land in a feudal relationship, degenerated miserably. In this dark time the distribution of *political* power was easily discerned; it was simply held by those having their own equipment for war, and a predisposition to use it. Indeed, the very notions of Greek warrior and nobleman in this way became synonymous: 'The "nobles" of 800 BC were simply those who had weapons and horses, with experience of how to use these. With these things they were able to make lesser people obey and to ensure possession (and ultimately legal ownership) of lands and other forms of wealth in their own families.'[21] The entire Greek military structure was aligned to favor authoritarian political outcomes. 'The net result [was] that about 900 BC the individual had almost no rights, being absorbed in a totalitarian kinship group, in a system of such groups with no state and no real idea of public authority.'[22]

From this violent period of totalitarian dominance, the world's first known post-primitive democracies emerged. By 450 BCE, the poorest residents of the most powerful city-states would reach a zenith in personal rights, liberties, and responsibilities. The historical record shows that profound military structural reorganization, prompted by topographic and geopolitical realities, preceded and directly contributed to the astounding political reversal.

The heavily armored *hoplite* infantryman, operating in a closely coordinated mass formation called a *phalanx*, is the military innovation that most clearly effected this remarkable transition. Precise dating is difficult, but the phalanx formation probably developed between 750 and 650 BCE in the Greek settlements on the Aegean coast of Asia Minor.[23] The dramatic success of the new style of armaments and battle against the older methods of the mainland Persian armies ensured its spread to peninsular Greece by at least 700 BCE. The critical point to be made is that subsequent to the introduction of the hoplite phalanx, and within a remarkably short period, Greek political institutions began radical reforms. Lykurgous, founder of the Spartan Constitution, enacted his political reforms in or about 675 BCE.[24] Solon, Athenian democracy's great lawgiver, was chief magistrate beginning in 594 BCE. Although his reforms were superseded by the succession of tyrants who followed him, Solon's actions were generally reinstituted upon the return of popular government, and his reforms are generally regarded as the foundation of Athenian democracy.

By 700 BCE, the Greek world had progressed commercially and industrially so that a significant percentage of the population outside the established aristocratic kinship groups could afford to equip themselves with the best available iron weapons and bronze armor. These turned out to be the helmet, shield, leggings, and pike of the hoplite infantryman. As increasing numbers of individuals acquired not only the panoply of equipment that marked a warrior, but the retinue that carried his provisions and sustained him on marches, they began to assert themselves politically. The difference was that the hoplites asserted their claims as a group, not as individuals. Bands of well-trained and disciplined foot soldiers working in concert were able to defeat the mounted knight who so clearly represented the old aristocracies, but only if they relied upon and worked closely with each other.[25] This fusion of individuals into a coherent whole represented the kernel of the democratic ideal. 'The cohesion of the whole mass of men counted more than individual heroics. The Homeric Kings, who went out before their people to challenge their equals in single combat, had no place in the phalanx; pre-eminent strength, beauty, and swiftness of foot were no longer the first qualities demanded of a leader.'[26] A dominant leader was, in the age of the phalanx, a master tactician and organizer rather than a battlefield hero. The catalyst that ushered the downfall of the traditional nobility was a drastic change in warfare tactics, based on a very minor change in weapons technology.

As has already been described, combat since the Dark Age of Greece consisted of individualistic sparring. Warriors rode onto the battlefield, dismounted (the stirrup had not yet been invented, making horseback combat precarious and a blow from a rider considerably less forceful than one from a well-based infantryman), threw some javelins or other projectiles to harass and disrupt the enemy, moved quickly to engage an opposing warrior, and fought until one side capitulated or fled. The shield of the warrior had a strap at the center for battle, and a sling for carrying the protective instrument over his back, decidedly valuable in the event of a retreat.

The phalanx style of combat was entirely different. The heavily armed soldiers making up the phalanx were named after their particular shield, the round *hoplon*. An innovation in holding the shield allowed it to be heavier and integrated into the mass of the formation. The shield was smaller than previous ones, but instead of one handle it had two – one at the center for the hand and one on the side, where the arm was inserted up to the elbow. The soldier could now carry more weight in battle. The hoplon was smaller but heavier than its predecessors because it was covered entirely with metal. Previous shields, normally made of wood, were ringed with metal edges and usually incorporated a small metal disk mounted at the center front. The hoplon shield allowed a warrior to absorb an enemy's blow with the full strength of the arm, and to push with it, making it an auxiliary weapon. Conspicuously absent was a sling by which to throw the hoplon over one's back for protection in retreat. This was an intended advantage for unit morale. The only option the hoplite had to facilitate a panicked retreat was to drop his shield and run, unfettered but also unprotected. His chances of survival were maximized by his remaining in solidarity with the mass.

Another important change due to the hoplon was in its impact on coordinated drill and battlefield cooperation. The hoplon shield was small and protected only the left two-thirds of the body, leaving the right side somewhat vulnerable. The tactic employed was to march in formation with each soldier's right side protected by the overlap of the next soldier's shield. This led to an instinctive and powerful sense of reliance upon one's associates for protection, and must have added immeasurably to the hoplite warrior's sense of group loyalty. This artificial type of kinship, based on battlefield association instead of blood ties, was a powerful bond found in the military experience, and it fully transferred to civilian political relationships after battle.

Of course, if everyone is protecting the person to his left, the rightmost file had no protection but its own sword or pike, and so the formation had a tendency to drift to the right as it moved in battle. This helped bring about a sophisticated set of coordinated maneuvers to maintain control of tactics to overcome the problem. Military science was enhanced by the phalanx as doctrines for group weapons employment and movements had to be developed, tested, and employed. Properly and intensively trained groups of infantryman could use the force of combined mass to their advantage, countering the strength of any individual warrior no matter how strong or skilled. While battlefield tactics advanced considerably, the actual engagement still consisted of two sides moving toward a great collision of arms. The side that could put more force into its charge would generally prevail, and mathematical formulae were posited to maximize combined energy. The effectiveness of the phalanx was determined by its depth. While the front row was too occupied to lock arms and push, subsequent rows were not so constrained. They would heave and push on forward rows, shouting encouragement all the while. The resulting image is more that of rugby scrum than melee, a not inappropriate illustration. In this way, too, all members of the formation were necessary and valuable to ultimate victory. All members had equal responsibility for success, whatever their positions in the formation.

The phalanx owed its dominance in part to oddities of the Greek terrain and culture. Rugged mountains isolated the valley battlefields of Greece. Cavalry could not maximize its strategic movement, and so was rarely decisive. The common history, language, and culture of the Greeks tended to make warfare a relatively civilized (if somewhat irrational) institution. Battles were fought in open and flat terrain. Ambushes were unheard of. Rules of engagement were for the most part observed and maintained. But the reasons for developing the hoplite formation are far less important than the subsequent political development that was influenced by it. The key point in the rise and routinized employment of a coordinated infantry formation tactic was that group victory, not to mention *individual* safety, now no longer depended on individual prowess or courage or other heroic capacity. It depended entirely on tight discipline and *group* cohesion. The battle experience of the nobility was wasted against a determined formation of hoplites. [27]

The phalanx as a type of coordinated pike infantry tactic was not original to the Greeks, though they may have been completely unaware of its predecessors. Yigael Yadin observes that a phalanx-type formation, complete with shields and coordinated pikes, had its antecedents in Sumerian warfare.[28] The Stele of Vultures (*c.* 2500 BCE) shows a formation of soldiers marching in step behind locked rectangular shields and presenting a formidable array of joined spears.[29] That this type of formation was used is not surprising. It is a straightforward tactical innovation that any intelligent general should have been able to design. What is surprising, given its presumed battlefield superiority over disorganized groups of individuals, is that in Sumeria, as in every other place it may have been tried before being institutionalized by the Greeks, it was quickly abandoned.

The only rational explanation for abandoning such an effective military formation is that the ruling elite of the great despotisms of the Ancient Near East could not allow the political and social upheavals associated with a phalanx-type military. In discussing the Stele of Vultures, Robert O'Connell observes: 'They are clearly people with a stake in society, the very types necessary for a style of warfare which demands that the participants fight at close range and face danger in a cooperative fashion.'[30] In Greece, there was no central imperial authority that could perceive the danger the phalanx-type formation posed to concentrated rule and effectively halt its deployment. Moreover, emerging Greek notions of *polis* citizenship, increasing as the size of the military-based aristocracy increased, helped solidify the relationship between military service and political rights.

If terrain and geopolitical imperatives influence the development of military technology, which in turn can impact the subsequent development of political structures, then technology is properly an intervening variable in the geodetermined evolution of the state. The interesting question to be posed now is, since so many states used the phalanx, why was democracy so uniquely radical in Athens? To be sure, some level of political power dispersion existed everywhere the phalanx was in use for more than a generation, and the power was dispersed directly to those who served in the formation. But Athens' infantry was no larger relative to its population than that of most other Greek city-states. What critical component added to its maximally broad diffusion of political power?

The answer lies in Athens' extraordinary reliance on naval power. While most Greek city-states had navies, Athens alone had outgrown its ability to feed itself – owing, as Thucydides explained, to its poor and rocky soil (see above, p. 16). Without trade to bring in foodstuffs and other essentials, Athens simply could not survive. In the Mycenaean and Dark Ages of Greece, military ships and fleets were used exclusively as an adjunct of supply and reinforcement. They moved troops and victuals, and were primarily trade vessels pressed into military transport service. It was the Phoenicians who developed the first war galleys. These ships were devoted solely to naval operations, but were still primarily used for transport and occasionally for maneuvering to the side of another ship for boarding. Sometime quite shortly after the development of the phalanx the Greeks perfected the *trireme*, a long and narrow multi-oared craft designed for high speed, maneuverability, and ramming. We know very little about the trireme physically, none have survived, but ancient descriptions of the craft give us a fairly good sense of its capabilities.[31] It was fast and deadly, unmatched on the seas – the trireme quickly became the Greek's naval fighting vessel of choice.

Two techniques for naval combat then predominated: boarding, in which ships would negotiate near enough to an opponent so that boards could be slung from deck to deck and hoplite passengers would engage directly in land-style hand-to-hand combat; and ramming, in which one ship would propel itself toward another, employing its heavily armored prow to crash through the opponent's hull. Both techniques required a tremendous amount of skill, coordinated rowing, discipline, stamina, and morale. Unlike trading or transport vessels, which required quality officers but unmotivated, even disinterested labor for propulsion, the trireme required highly skilled and inspired rowers to achieve a combat advantage. Just as in land combat, rabble and slaves (in this case as oarsmen instead of foot soldiers) were not as effective in naval battle as trained and highly motivated freemen. The same psychological urgings of morale and teamwork that influenced hoplites to seek democratic political institutions acted on the trireme rower, but in an even more egalitarian fashion.

Quigley notes that in the debate over which tactics were preferable in naval engagements, democrats tended to prefer ramming while oligarchs went for boarding.[32] This is in part because oligarchs believed in the superiority of the individual combatant, and boarding agreed with their view of the navy as merely a conveyance to and from battle. Theoretically critical, despite the fact that the individual hoplite was the combatant in boarding operations, the phalanx formation could not be employed in ship-to-ship battles. Hoplites fought alone, an advantage for the style of heroic warfare in vogue in pro-authoritarian military organizations. Democrats preferred ramming because it required more sophisticated rowing and maneuver, says Quigley. It thus elevated the importance of the rowers, effectively making them integral combatants and not merely a labor source. Democracies in this period were unhindered in using their abundant supply of free citizens as rowers, while oligarchies had to coerce servants and serfs, or hire mercenaries, to do their rowing for them.

But Athens did more than tap into its free citizenry for rowers. Its extensive need for naval vessels meant it had to expand its citizen base to load its many hulls. For this reason alone, Athens became renowned as particularly adept at the art of naval battle. Athenian ships, unit for unit, were unsurpassed, and by the time of the Persian War, Athens had already developed the world's largest and most powerful combat navy. Probably some 4,000 oarsmen were needed to operate its ships. At the height of Athens' naval capacity during the Peloponnesian Wars, up to 10,000 rowers may have been trained and employed.[33] In Athens, unlike anywhere else in Hellas, the oarsmen were recognized as being as vital on water as the hoplite was on land, and were thus accorded equal privilege and political status.

The most far-reaching Athenian innovation in naval warfare stemmed from the recognition that poorer elements of society were being called on to shoulder a full share of the burden for the states' military and political autonomy, and were forced to provide a vastly disproportionate share of their personal resources in order to do so. Athens remedied the disparity by providing all citizens with a pike and hoplon, and for the first time on record paying wages for combat sailors. This was a remarkable innovation for its day, coming at a time when Athens did not and would not pay for land or sea mercenaries (still relying solely on un-reimbursed citizen volunteers to fill the ranks of its phalanxes until the ill-fated Sicilian expedition), and at a time when it had no form of compulsory military service to draft for its needs. To be sure, military participation was expected. It was a sign of vibrant political participation, but it was not mandatory. Thucydides goes so far as to have his hero Pericles say that a man who ignores politics to concentrate on personal welfare is a man who has no business in Athens. The philosophical problem was that a poor citizen living at subsistence might show the highest patriotism and desire to serve his polis, but might not have the means to arm himself and do so. All of his productive time would be spent in the pursuit of sustenance for his family. Volunteering for naval service was possible, since no armaments needed to be purchased, but to do so meant that his family might starve. With the introduction of pay for naval service (only), even the poorest citizen could now fully participate in the defense, and hence the politics, of the city-state. Indeed, pay for service became an attractive option to civilian pursuits, and many citizens were able to make more in military service than in private life. The result was that a vastly greater number of poor citizens were taking up arms and fighting for the polis than rich ones, and so gaining a proportionately greater share of political power. Not only was the fleet and its unique manning requirements a spur to democracy, it became a bulwark for it. Thucydides reports that when the Athenian Assembly panicked after the failed Sicilian expedition, and the so-called Council of Four Hundred was established to rule as an oligarchy, the Fleet refused to comply, and forced the return of democracy to Athens. After the Persian Wars, and until its subordination to the Macedonian armies of Alexander, the Athenian state was a 'sailor's republic'.[34]

Applying new technologies in familiar terrain has marked the evolution of geodeterminist and geostrategic thought, but we have just scratched the surface of variations on this theme. Before discussing the potential structural impact on political institutions of space technology and military strategy, the thread of geodeterminist theory must be followed. The Arab philosopher Ibn Khaldûn examined similar geo- and topographic features to Thucydides, and asserted that they, along with climactic variations, could be used to predict the number, size, and moral character of peoples and their governments within a given region.[35] For example, a flat open plain, like that of Mesopotamia, favored military expansion and control, thus prompting the establishment of large empires. Rugged terrain split by mountains and water made sweeping land campaigns difficult, and numerous independent states could be anticipated in this alternate environment. Contradicting Thucydides, Khaldûn argued that fertile soil and a temperate climate tended to create a population that was given over to abundance, easy living, and sumptuous architecture (Sparta was a distinct martial anomaly). Harsh climate and rugged terrain tended to instill appreciation for the soldierly arts and an independence of spirit.

Following Khaldûn's lead, Arnold Toynbee effectively represents the many geodeterminists who place climactic factors at the core of geopolitics.[36] Toynbee maintained that the existence of climactic harshness was imperative for the development of civilization, for without it people cannot be expected to toil with the purpose of overcoming their environments. A harsh winter climate forced a people to be industrious, congenial, and forward-looking, as they must work together and save for the colder months. Once ensconced in the compulsory inactivity of winter, the arts and letters would flourish as these hardy folk passed time constructively. To the contrary, he argued that an easy climate and abundant foods allowed individuals to remain socially independent, discouraged saving for the future (necessary for the development of abstract thought and hence the literary and fine arts), and thus limited intelligent discourse.

It is easy to see how the geodeterministic model leads the casual observer to see an argument of social superiority implicit in the geographically preferred society or identity group of the author. While Toynbee's analysis appears to explain the geodetermined surety of the rise of Europe and the domination of European culture, innumerable similar theories can be found in opposition. Malcolm X, for example, argued that climatic harshness made the Caucasian races cold and distant, harsh in their relationships with each other, and completely untrustworthy.[37] The advantages of a milder year-round climate in more southern regions allowed peoples of color to develop in a more socially oriented, family-friendly, and trustworthy manner. These arguments have been taken up by Leonard Jeffries, among others, and have spawned a notion of the division of humanity into 'sun' and 'ice people'.[38] Europeans, 'cold' by nature, are independent and distrustful, while Africans and other peoples of color are antithetically congenial, family-oriented and supportive. Whether intended or not, these arguments will always lead some adherents to justify the superiority of their own group on bioevolutionary grounds.

Unique to the geodeterminist milieu is Frederick Jackson Turner's thesis that the character of societies and political institutions is based on their proximity to frontiers.[39] One of the many advantages of this argument is that it does not imply racial or cultual superiority, as any individuals or peoples on or near the frontiers have certain geodetermined advantages. His proposition is argued from two directions. Frontier peoples and states of necessity have a type of dynamism thrust upon them as they struggle to overcome their environments, and engage in direct combat/competition with frontier groups of other peoples. Individuals at the center or core of the state, not directly challenged by the dangers and lack of amenities at the frontier, will not develop to their full potential. Not only are the frontier people challenged to succeed by their environment, the frontier tends to attract individuals who are risk-takers. This group of explorers, entrepreneurs, the desperate, and occasionally the criminal elements of society, are dynamic individuals who are motivated, capable, and assured. Using this thesis, Turner asserted that it was the US position on the New World frontier that so quickly transformed it from minor colony to world power. Even within the frontier state, the dynamic element of growth was always at its expanding edge.

With just these brief examples, some preliminary projections of the character of spacefaring states and societies can be conjectured. We must begin our speculation from the premise that outer space is an extraordinarily harsh and inhospitable environment. Human civilization cannot be expected to emerge there; it must be highly evolved before even the attempt at entry, much less colonization, can be made. The first foray into the astrodetermined effects of space exploration must start from the unique combination of hyper-frontier hypotheses and inhumanly harsh environments. What kind of people can be expected to go there? What characteristics will they hone, and which will they prize in their companions? What kinds of cultures and governing institutions will arise naturally, and how will they in turn affect future expansion into space?

In the near term, we can look at the results of Antarctic exploration and space station habitation already attempted. The individuals who go to these analogous locations are highly educated, rigorously trained and psychologically screened for mental toughness and decision-making skills, and very physically fit. They are the best and brightest of our pilots, technicians, and scientists. They are rational, given to scientific analysis and explanation, and obsessed with their professions. While in the confined and remote habitats of either space station or modern high-tech igloo, they value the companionship of those they work with. Living in such close proximity they must be tolerant of the views and opinions of others, but exacting in their acceptance of procedure and professional expertise, for they will rely on the actions of their few comrades for their very lives. Any mistake could mean death. Competence becomes their measure of social value. In this situation they form extraordinary personal bonds. They see themselves as having shared experiences that no one but another of their ilk could truly understand. They are a superior subset of the larger group from which they spring.

Emphasizing and solidifying this observed subgroup fragmentation in the longer term, the most salient feature of the space environment, beyond its incredible inhospitality, is the vast distance between conceivable points of interaction. These distances will drastically limit *direct* human-to-human *cultural* interaction. For example, spacefarers can be expected to quickly develop specialized jargon, colloquialisms, and gestures to facilitate cooperation as they share in experiences that cannot be adequately described to Earth-bound associates. Groups clustered in disparate outposts will quickly adapt to their distinct environments, developing habits, traits, and idiosyncrasies most efficient for their peculiar environments and for their unique functions.

As already noted, and especially as true colonization efforts get underway, only the most physically and mentally fit members of the sponsor state/society will be sent to explore and exploit space. They will be the most capably endowed (or at least the most ruthlessly suitable, as the populating of America and Australia via penal colonies such as Georgia and Botany Bay so aptly illustrate). The radically desolate environment of space will challenge these selectively culled pioneers, continuously honing their specialized capabilities and radically altering their social relationships. It is not unreasonable to suspect that over time these selectively culled individuals will fancy themselves superior to those members of the society they left behind.

Should long-term colonization efforts be realized, these selectively recruited and experientially hardened groups can be expected to establish competent, dynamic, and powerful social and political associations, initially structured in accordance with hierarchical military organization or under the strict conformity of martial law. Unlike the harsh historical frontiers of Earth, where an enterprising and hardy soul could live and prosper alone (in the United States this frontier independence contributed to the nurturing of political liberalism), survival in space will require not only the cooperation of all individuals, but continued full and active participation by everyone. Government structure in these circumstances can be expected to take the form of a rigid if not wholly coercive militocracy, at least in its early stages. Duty and sacrifice will be the highest moral ideals. Advancement to the top of the political ladder can be expected to be based on the most rigorous standards of competence.

Such a political system could even threaten the sovereignty of terrestrial governments. Some on Earth would consider the space-generated political system a utopian one to be transferred whole to perceived corrupt and inefficient terrestrial governments.

This kind of enlightened despotic takeover has terrestrial parallels already. In several twentieth-century examples, including Mexico, Nigeria, Pakistan, and Turkey, military coups have been greeted by the population at large as a relief, a welcome return of order and rule of law in a state that has become irreparably corrupt and inefficient. New junta governments promise a return to more traditional institutions as soon as the crisis is over, but the damage is done. Society is conditioned to expect external corrections when needed, and is ill prepared to find solutions within the extant political framework. Should a general feeling of governmental mistrust – based on inefficiency, incompetence, or perceived timorousness in dealing with critical issues – become pervasive, that society may look outward to its extra-terrestrial heroes for assistance. Should the space colonists recognize the potential for increasing their Earth-based financial and resource support, they may look quite favorably on requests to act as champions of the people to claim Caesarian control. Should this rather far-fetched scenario not play out, it is not hard to imagine other structural causes of enmity between on- and off-worlders. The more independence naturally asserted by future space colonizers, the greater the efforts to rein them in politically by their terrestrial controllers. As with all such efforts in the human experience, it will be resented.

It will not be just political and ideological differences that separate those who live in space and those who remain terrestrially landlocked. Physical differences between spacefarers and the Earth-bound will emerge, and be exacerbated over time. James and Alcestis Oberg have carefully described the requirements anticipated in space exploration, and make a convincing case for the rapid evolution and adaptation of humans in space. Among the earliest physical changes, for example, is an overall 'puffiness' of the body as blood circulates evenly in zero gravity (instead of pooling with the tug of gravity). The change is so dramatic that Soviet Cosmonaut Valeriy Ryumin, reporting from the Mir space station, said that: 'seen in a mirror, [our faces] were difficult to recognize'.[40] Zero gravity additionally contributes to bone loss and muscular atrophy. The condition becomes so severe that astronauts and cosmonauts returning to the surface of the Earth after only a few months stay on space stations cannot walk without assistance. Breathing is labored, and these returning heroes must recline to conduct interviews. These significant short-term changes can only be intensified by the increased time frame of long-term space exploration and to the heavy exposure to cosmic radiation that is unavoidable. These regular and heavy doses of radiation will mutate genes more quickly and more dynamically than common exposure in the protected cradle of the Earth's atmosphere. Dominant mutations in successive generations will be different than those on Earth, too, because the environment the species is attempting to overcome is different. These changes can only be forecast wildly, but that they will be significant seems assured.

The vast distances, long travel time between inhabited outposts, physical and psychological changes expected to occur, and limited direct cultural interaction, will increasingly lead, on the grander scale, to the fragmentation of political authority as humanity spreads outward from the Earth. Individuals who are years from Earth and subject to stringent and unique living conditions will eventually believe that Earth-bound citizens, whose experiences are increasingly out of touch, can no longer adequately represent their interests. The farther from Earth the facility, the longer it will take to send and receive communications traffic. Immediate decisions will have to be made, and those who can make them effectively and decisively will be natural leaders. Despite efforts at strict electronic control by Earth authorities, self-governing or semi-autonomous political entities can be expected to emerge on – then command – every location that is conceptually separable. The size of the body will not matter, so long as it is self-sustaining. Planets, moons, asteroids, and large space stations will all develop a singular political authority. In time, the space-state system may come to resemble the ancient and Renaissance city-state systems of the Greeks and Italians, with a myriad of independent and unique governing units sharing a common history, past culture, and a formal common language. The teachings of Thucydides and Machiavelli may be more appropriate to this age than the modern federalist leanings of Kant and Publius.[41]

The astrodeterminist influence is not limited to space colonies and off-world speculation. It clearly has an impact on terrestrial states. For specific projections regarding the impact of astropolitics on global politicomilitary development, the eloquent and sophisticated expressions of German social historian Otto Hintze are theoretically illuminating.[42] Hintze described a relationship between reliance on *classes* of weaponry and military organization, based on the juxtapositions of natural resources and political boundaries, and the structure of government. The influence of a national reliance on sea power, for example, allowed for by geographic fortune, prompted the development of a specific kind of decentralized (conceptually liberal) government with a greater degree of individual freedom. To the contrary, reliance on land power, necessitated in continental states surrounded by other land powers, led inevitably to a more centralized or authoritative government with an emphasis on performance of individual duty and subordination to the state. The argument is reminiscent of the previous Thucydidean-derived expository on liberal Athens and conservative Sparta. The particular examples for Hintze were the naturally protected liberal seafaring states of post-Enlightenment England and the United States, and the more vulnerable authoritarian continental states of Europe, especially Prusso-Germany. The pertinent question to be posed in this line of thought is, what kind of government can be expected in a post-Cold War state relying heavily on space power for its security?

The critical difference between naval and land military power, it seems reasonable to aver, is in their ability to project force and to occupy territory. Though Hintze does not deny the notion directly, there is nothing inherently democratizing about boats, nor authoritarian about boots. Rather, navies are excellent tools for outward force projection, but have very limited capacities for occupying and garrisoning territory. Land forces, especially infantries, are strongest in prepared defense roles and are the historical force of choice for occupation and control of territory/population missions. The latter role is virtually indistinguishable from civil police authority employed for internal oppression. It is this facile transference, from external military defense to internal political protection, that is so conducive to authoritarian government and makes ground forces so historically anti-democratic.[43] This oversimplification can be only broadly generalized. Numerous other factors are necessary for specific projections of how a military force will impact political institutions.[44] Nonetheless, the generalization is useful, and intriguingly heuristic. Hintze did not envision the political impact of air and space forces, but we can make some extrapolations based on his arguments.

Space forces have the theoretical potential for maximal power projection (as platforms for kinetic or laser energy weapons or with mass-destruction payloads; see Salkeld and Karras for now classic early assessments[45]) but virtually no near-term capacities for terrestrial occupation. As such, a state reliant on space forces for the bulk of its defense could be expected to have a more democratic or liberal character than it otherwise would, following the analogy of the navy-reliant state. Air forces, too, should be more liberalizing than armies, but the ability of air forces to inject troops into hostile areas and their requirement for erecting and maintaining numerous staging bases, makes them an arguably less democratizing/liberalizing structural variable than space forces, and perhaps even than navies. In addition, the *direct* support that air forces can provide to armies to enhance civil pacification further limits their democratizing/liberalizing influence. Even without weapons in space, as is the current precarious condition, space-based military support missions enhance the capacities of land, air, and sea forces to accurately engage and destroy targets worldwide. The inference that space forces or a space-reliant military would necessarily enhance liberal democratic government is thus compromised. Still, the inability to occupy territory or (currently) inject troops into territory and act directly in a police role means that the Hintzian paradigm should hold, and such states will have a more liberal character.

Yet a further projection for the Space Age seems prudent. Perhaps the more pertinent issue is the prevalent focus of current military space missions. They are not for territorial occupation and pacification, but they are clearly appropriate for police-state control. Intelligence surveillance and information gathering, a legitimate tool of military operations engaged in external war making, is also a customary tool for internal law enforcement operations. If the high-technology capacities of space-based intelligence support satellites are transferred to domestic police activities, potential for abuse is clearly present.[46] Just as satellites act as a battlefield force-multiplier, in the role of civil oppression, they can be equally effective, and equally repressive.

GEOSTRATEGY AND ASTROSTRATEGY

The direction and tenor of geodeterminist theories in the realm of astropolitics is not here definitively declared and is open to much speculation. The intent is simply to identify heuristic parallels. Traditional grand geostrategy, which adapts emerging technologies to practical knowledge of the face of the Earth, is not so provisional or ambiguous. It is the most intuitively applicable of the primary categories of geopolitical theory to the realm of outer space and the most pivotal to this text. In order to clarify the parallels, and to prepare and animate the astropolitical model described in Chapter 3, a brief survey of informing historical geopolitical grand strategists is essential; the following made significant contributions in their eras, and continue to extend their influence in the age of astrostrategy.

The influence of emerging *technologies* on geography, in essence the practical shrinking of the Earth, is the foundation of the geopolitical strategists' thought. An early proto-geostrategist who fully grasped this relationship was German economist Friedrich List. Edward Earle Mead writes: 'The greatest single contribution that List made to modern strategy was his elaborate discussion of the influence of railways on the shifting balance of military power.'[47] List recognized that the full incorporation of this new transportation technology would fundamentally alter the political relations of the major powers. He saw a national rail network as the cement of German unification, changing the strategic position of Germany from beleaguered battleground of Europe to a defensive bulwark operating with the advantages of interior lines. Before the railroad, Germany had to maintain separate armies in east and west (and occasionally south). With the railroad, military power could be transferred quickly from front to front as needed. Germany's potential enemies could not similarly move Russian armies quickly to France, for example, and Germany would realize the advantages of economy of force. The military importance of rail power that List described in 1833 was overwhelmingly validated with the north's victory in the American Civil War, and most emphatically so in the spectacular German success in the Franco-Prussian War. Ultimately, List's early views became the foundation of the rail-dominated 'timetable strategy' of World War I.[48]

Rail power has no clear parallel to space power with the exception that, as a new transportation and information technology, space asset deployment surely has the potential to alter the political and military relationships of the traditional world and regional powers. In a sense, control of a global space network gives the previous advantages of interior lines – quick redeployment of military assets, efficient monitoring of all fronts, and not insignificantly, a nationalistic sense of unification – from what has traditionally been seen as a classic exterior line position. This is an ongoing debate in the emergence of communications and information 'spatial environments', which may soon attempt to engage the cyber-realm in similar geopolitical terms. Here, the distinction between the classic interior lines position, as provided by proponents of a high-capacity fiber-optic communications network, and what is viewed in this analysis as the new astropolitical dominance of a space-based electromagnetic network, highlights the value of a neo-astro/geopolitical debate. Fiber optics provide enormous data-transmission capacity but limit the user to hardwired access. Space communications are more expensive and require much higher maintenance, but do not limit the user location nor the target coverage. Fiber optics are potentially more secure (arguable, as they can be tapped into at any point) but can be targeted for disruption by conventional materials (simply cut the line). Space-based communications require sophisticated encryption techniques for security, and can be limited by electronic jamming, but currently they are extremely secure physically. Finally, a central switching station can control fiber optics, and it is this capacity that has major Hintzian ramifications for the state.

An authoritarian state would much prefer a land-based, fiber-optic network for transmitting data and information than a broadcast one. All information passed could be routed through a central screening station, and even the Internet could be scrupulously monitored. A space-based transmission network could not so easily be constrained, and information dispersion would be impossible to control. Such a network enhances the military forces of democratic states, whose missions are outward in focus and require force projection support. A fiber-optic support network would be extremely useful for a military that is set for point defense, inwardly focused with a primary design of territorial occupation, and maximized for a secondary police support role.

Sea power predates rail power most assuredly, and advocates of strong navies were evident long before List, but the first true *geostrategic* (global-scale) advocate of sea power was the American naval officer Alfred Thayer Mahan. Mahan believed maritime power was the key to great power status, and that this power was to some extent geodetermined. His monumental maritime studies, published under variations of the title *The Influence of Seapower Upon History*, were enormously popular, and his ideas influenced US, British, German, and Japanese foreign policy.[49]

Mahan began his argument with the premise that a state endowed with geographic position allowing for both the concentration of naval forces and, when appropriate, their dispersion, was paramount in the modern state power equation. Having an opinion similar to List's, Mahan saw that the ability to quickly retract forces for defense of the state and then move them out to prosecute offensive action was the characteristic of such naval powers as ancient Athens and contemporary Britain that allowed them to rise to dominance in their respective eras. Of course, in order to press this capability, the maritime state must be endowed with a suitable 'frontier' seaboard, studded with 'numerous and deep harbors' combined with ready access to the open ocean, and 'a population proportioned to the extent of the sea-coast which it had to defend'.[50] In the realm of astrostrategy, Chapter 3 will show there are analogies to a suitable frontier 'coast' in space, and that instead of harbors, the space-faring nation must be endowed with (or have access to) effective land-based launch, monitoring, and control sites.

Such advantageous physical features alone would not ensure the seafaring state had the tools necessary for naval dominance, however. The character of a nation's people must also be specially endowed. They must, at the very least, be appreciative of the value of sea-based activity, if not wholly immersed in it. They must be commercially aggressive, rational profit-seekers who recognize the potential bounty of sea trade, and who through hard work and persistence will achieve wealth from it.[51] This maritime citizenry will form the peacetime commercial fleet, gaining the skills and experience necessary to make a vast national reserve for mobilization in conflict, and at all times supporting through their taxes and other contributions the vibrancy of the sea-based national enterprise. The government, too, must be outfitted with appropriate institutions and political office-holders ready and able to recognize and take advantage of the state's position and attributes. Such a national character is evident in the potential for success in space endeavors as well. All spacefaring nations have attempted to tap into a national fascination with space exploration, if not directly manipulate their populations with promises of vast profit and adventure. The citizenry of the spacefaring state must be willing to sacrifice earthly comforts for unspecified gains in the exploration of the unknown, be committed to scientific endeavors and willing to hand over a large share of their income to the taxes necessary to support expensive long-term space projects, have a great interest (bordering on fetish or worship) in space developments and advances, and be tolerant of unavoidable failures, mishaps, and setbacks. With an energized and psychologically prepared populace, the inevitable tribulations necessary to enter into and then dominate space are bearable.

Mahan further saw the sea as a 'wide common, over which men may pass in all directions, but on which some well-worn paths [emerge for] controlling reasons'.[52] These controlling reasons were predicated on the efficient movement of goods, and the geography of the Earth provided natural corridors of trade. The state that could control these corridors would realize such enormous commercial benefits that through its subsequent wealth it would dominate other states both militarily and politically. Crucial to his theory was a discussion of *chokepoints*, globally strategic narrow waterways dominated by point locations. It is not necessary, Mahan argued, for a state to have control of every point on the sea to command it. In fact, such a strategy would be worse than useless. The military force required would drain every scintilla of profit from trade, not to mention every able-bodied seaman more usefully engaged in commerce. Instead, a smaller but highly trained and equipped force carefully deployed to control the bottlenecks of the major sea lanes would suffice. These bottlenecks were easy to spot on a global map, and Mahan identified seven of them: the straits of Dover, Gibraltar, and Malacca, the Cape of Good Hope, Malta, the Suez Canal, and the St Lawrence Seaway. Later geostrategists would expand the number to include the Panama Canal, Tsushima, the Skaggerak, and the Cold War 'GI–UK gap' (the ocean narrows between Greenland, Iceland, and Britain) among many others. Naturally, a competitor state could avoid most of these chokepoints by simply 'sailing the long way around' them, but in doing so the inefficiencies of lost time and additional fuel consumption would make goods less competitive commercially, and could be the difference between winning or losing the war where timely troop deployments are critical. Thus, control of these few geographically determined locations would guarantee dominance over global military movement and world trade to the overseeing state.

For the United States, Mahan advocated the establishment of naval bases at strategic locations (including Hawaii, the Philippines, and some Caribbean islands) and the construction of a canal linking the Pacific and Atlantic Oceans. He further asserted that the United States should follow the imperial model of Britain, which had prevailed in its hegemonic struggle with France because it had funneled its resources into sea power. Britain's rise to dominance was assured for two primary geopolitical reasons. First, as an island nation Britain did not have to incur the expense of maintaining a large land army so long as its navy was adequate for coastal defense, and second, because it had an unimpeded ability to concentrate its naval forces in defense. To many military strategists of the period it appeared that France had a material geopolitical advantage in that it possessed excellent access to both the Atlantic Ocean and Mediterranean Sea, then the world's two richest regions of maritime trade. France was stymied, however, by its dual needs to maintain an enormous land army to defend itself from hostile encroachments (draining off resources that could have been spent in maritime activities) and to split its maritime force between the two naval operations areas. Because it did not have control of the critical chokepoint (Gibraltar) that linked the Atlantic and Mediterranean, France could not concentrate all of its naval capacity when necessary in war. It needed two complete, expensive, independent – and therefore numerically deficient – fleets.

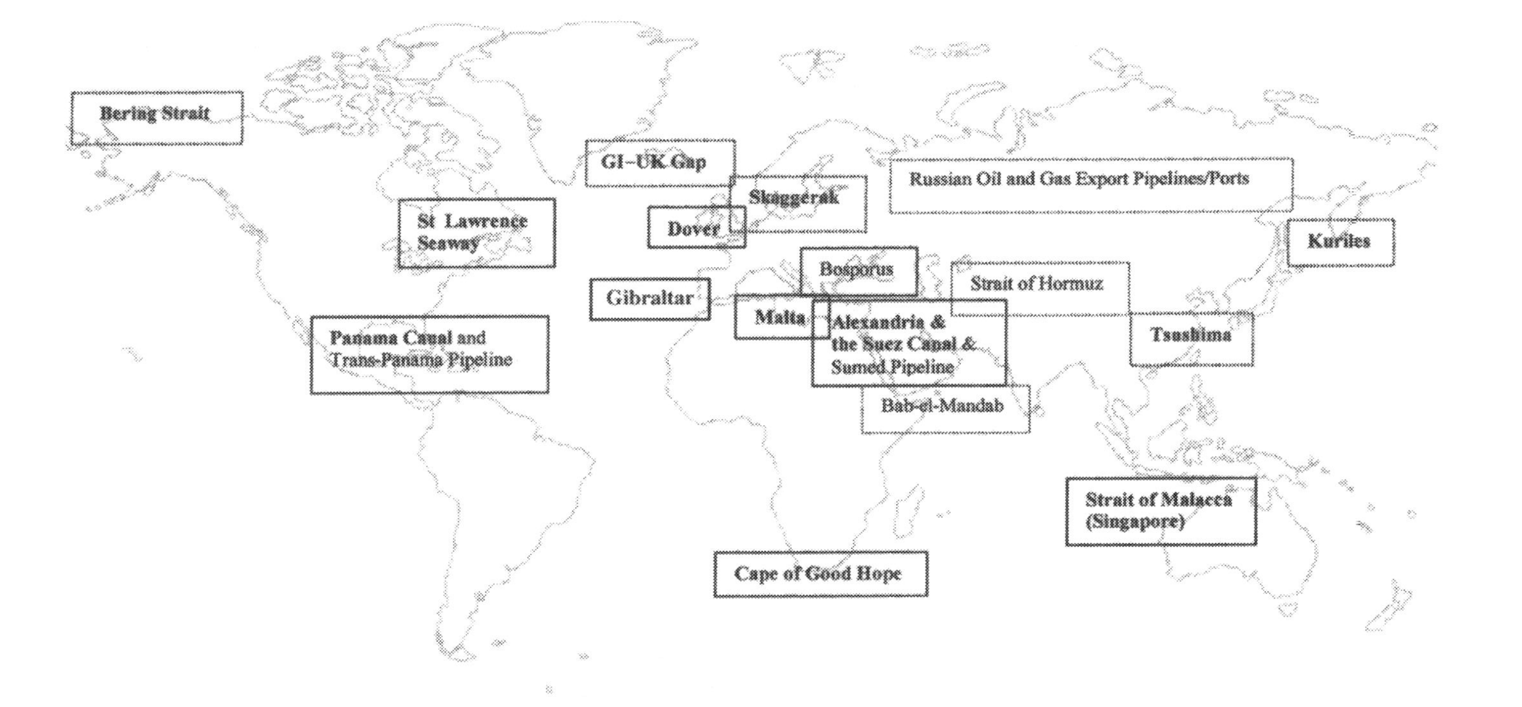

Figure 2.2: Mahanian, Cold War, and oil commerce chokepoints

Note: Mahanian chokepoints: Dover, Gibraltar, Malta, Alexandria, Suez Canal, Strait of Malacca (Singapore), St Lawrence Seaway
Cold War chokepoints: GI–UK Gap, Tsushima, Bering Strait, Kuriles, Denmark (Skaggerak)
Oil chokepoints (US Energy Information Administration): Bab-el-Mandab (Yemen), Bosporus (Turkish Straits), Strait of Hormuz, Russian Oil and Gas Export Pipelines/Ports, Strait of Malacca, Suez Canal and Sumed (Suez–Mediterranean) Pipeline

At the time, Mahan observed that the United States had both the British advantage of inaccessibility and the French problem of maintaining separate fleets. Its relative military isolation across the vast oceans – Canada and Mexico were neither serious nor imminent threats – had allowed it to develop industrially and commercially without the enormous and economically inefficient expense of a large land army to protect itself. Its potentially lucrative and dominating ready access to both Atlantic and Pacific Oceans was mitigated, however, by the time-consuming chore of a practical circumnavigation of the globe – all the way around the South American continent – in order to join the forces of the separate fleets. Therefore, the United States had to maintain fully independent and functionally redundant Atlantic and Pacific fleets to adequately defend its coastline, and these forces could be combined only at great national peril. For this reason, to follow the British precedent of constructing the Suez Canal to link the Mediterranean and Indian Ocean navies, Mahan advocated in the strongest possible terms a US-controlled canal across the isthmus of Panama.

Mahan's analysis was brilliant and convincing. If a *natural* chokepoint did not exist, it was possible and obviously beneficial in some cases for the forward-looking state to create one, and in the process eliminate a source of potential weakness. Moreover, this particular undertaking would alter the world's existing trade routes. Asia to Europe trade could be as efficiently accomplished through the US-dominated route as through the existing trans-African ones. Not only would world power relations be tipped in favor of the precociously emerging United States, it would force the then-isolationist tendencies of the public and politicians to change to internationalist ones, for a trans-Panamanian canal would immediately bring the 'interests of the other great nations, the European nations, close along our shores'.[53]

Mahan believed that the United States had luxuriated in its vast internal resources for too long. So many material goods, so much new land had been available as Americans followed their manifest destiny to settle the continent that the United States had not heretofore needed to involve itself in world affairs. But the days of practical autarky were coming to an end, and it was past time for the United States to take its place among the great powers. The altered geopolitical reality necessitated by the artificial change of an isthmus canal would force the United States away from its internal focus and out of its international slumber. In this complicated world of diplomatic intrigue, if it were to retain control of its political destiny, the United States would have to build and maintain a strong and responsive navy.

Today, with the demise of the Cold War, the United States has the luxury of reducing its land, sea, and air forces, and channeling monies and efforts saved into its space activities. Whether it will do so voluntarily remains to be seen, and in the current political climate increased funding to space is not only dubious, but it must compete with perceived domestic spending priorities.

For activists in either camp, the budget is seen as a zero-sum game; more money for me looks like less money for you. Still, while the ideological battle continues, the funding commitment issue may be spiraling out of the control of domestic preferences. The United States may find itself unable to avoid its newfound international space responsibilities and global commitments, many of which may not have been foreseen. For example, the United States military's Navstar/GPS navigational satellites were deployed to enhance its military power, as a force-multiplier, in the jargon of the military. The subsequent utility of these assets to global commercial navigation, communication, and above all commerce, has made them an indispensable world asset. The United States military now finds itself in the curious position of having to maintain a network of satellites that contributes billions of dollars to the world economy, and should it fail to be maintained, would have global civilian negative ramifications.[53] The creation and maintenance of global space-based communications and navigation systems, clearly a modern parallel to artificial technological chokepoints as the world becomes increasingly reliant on these assets, has brought the interests of other states 'close along' our (astropolitical) shores. The United States must be ready and prepared, in Mahanian scrutiny, to commit to the defense and maintenance of these assets, or relinquish its power to a state willing and able to do so.

Finally, Mahan argued for a guided national subjugation effort in support of the coming global role of the United States. He advocated the establishment of overseas bases at specific intervals to act as coaling and repair stations. The range of ships and natural interests of the state geographically determined their spacing. Without these bases, US war and trade ships would 'be like land birds, unable to fly far from their own shores'.[55] Two of the bases advocated were Hawaii and the Philippines, crucial to US control of the Pacific trade routes. A network of carefully placed stations could guarantee that US trade and war ships would never be out of range of a friendly depot, hence never at the mercy of foreign largesse for their success. In similar fashion, the astrostrategist should advocate the establishment of colonies or outstations for space exploration and exploitation. These stations could be used to stockpile fuel and other resources (especially life suport and spare parts), and could extend the life and range of space enterprises. These bases will all be astrographically and technologically determined (see model output in the next chapter).

Britain's rise to power came, Mahan believed, because 'she had exploited her location across the sea routes' of Europe.[56] Since the efficient movement of goods and capital in the nineteenth century was a factor of sea capacity, the nation or nations that controlled the most modern navies and the world's critical chokepoints could dominate the lanes of commerce, and thus the economic lifelines of an increasingly interdependent globe. A modern astrostrategist can and should make similar arguments. In space there are specific orbits and

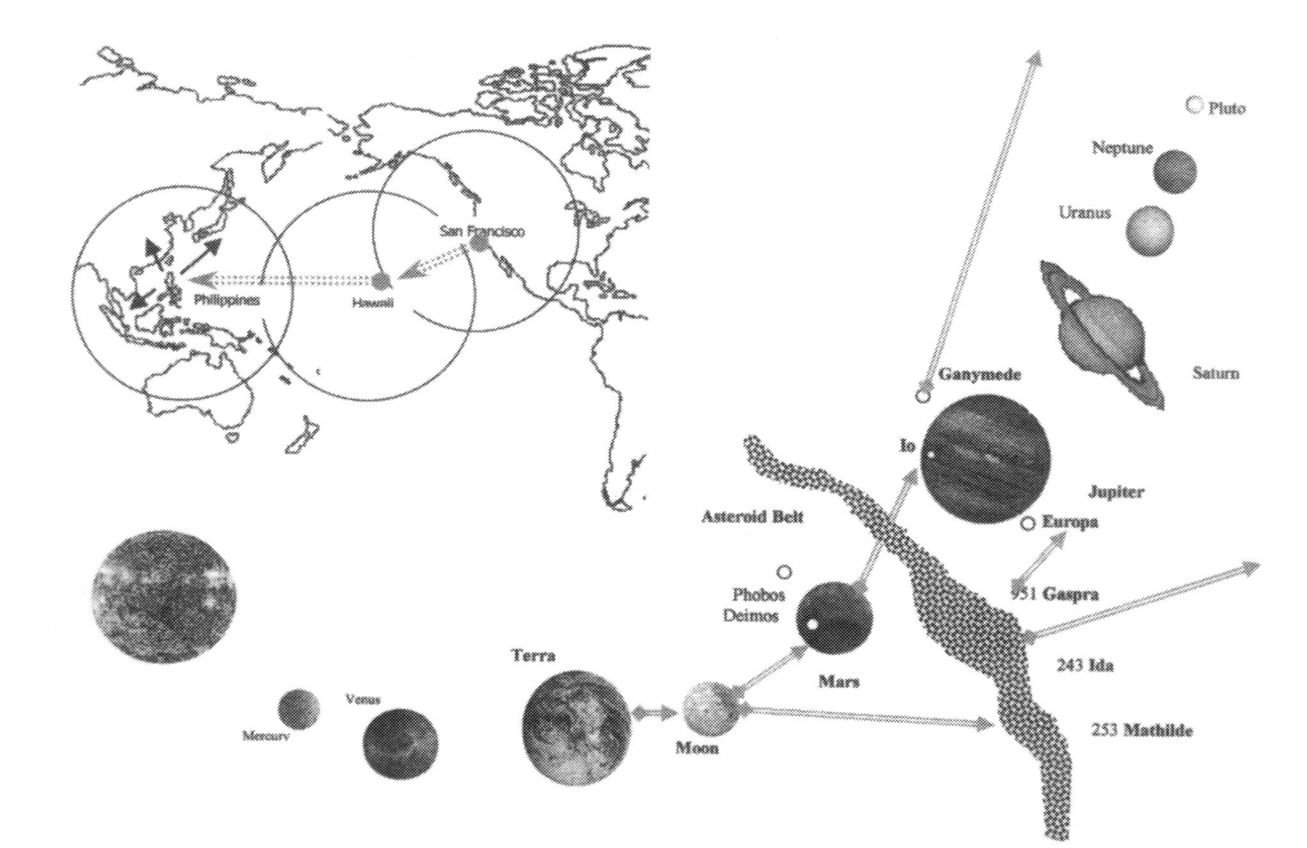

Figure 2.3: Mahan's Pacific strategy and Cole's 'stepping stones' to space

transit routes that because of their advantages in fuel efficiency create natural corridors of movement and commerce. Space, like the sea, can potentially be traversed in any direction, but because of gravity wells and the forbidding cost of getting fuel to orbit, over time spacefaring nations will develop specific pathways of heaviest traffic. Each of these pathways, identified later in the astropolitical model as Hohmann transfer orbits, can be shown to have or to be in themselves critical chokepoints. The state that most efficiently occupies or controls these positions can ensure for itself domination of space commerce and, ultimately, terrestrial politics.

Mahan's influence was and is extraordinary, but the most memorable of the geostrategists was undoubtedly Britain's Sir Halford Mackinder. Mackinder acknowledged the historical importance of sea power on the rise and demise of the great powers, but foresaw the end of naval dominance with the advent of the railroad. This emerging capacity would allow the efficient consolidation of the enormous Eurasian landmass, an area he referred to first as the *geographic pivot of history* and then as the world's *heartland*.[57] This huge potential state would form an impregnable land power that could not be defeated from the sea. In time, the vast natural resources of the heartland state would allow it to gain access to the sea and to construct a navy that, for sheer numbers alone, could overwhelm the peripheral sea powers. Inevitably, the world would be a single empire ruled from its natural core.

The key dynamic was the change in transportation technology, and the importance of military mobility. When the horse was domesticated and bred to allow for the unnatural weight of a rider, the primacy of cavalry emerged.[58] Add to this the development of the stirrup, which for the first time provided horse-mounted soldiers with the leverage necessary to give a lance or sword thrust the same striking power that infantry warriors could achieve on foot, and the medieval dominance of chivalric knights and the central steppe 'hordes' was assured. Grand improvements in sailing technologies allowed the seafaring states of Europe to encircle the central heartland and efficiently patrol its borders, shifting power to and fro as necessary to contain the potential of the mighty interior. With the advantages of the new maritime technologies, the efficiency and speed of sea movement effectively canceled the prior cavalry-based advantage of interior lines enjoyed by the Tatars and other notable steppe raiders. The advent of steam power and its application to both the railroad and waterborne transportation had the counterintuitive effect of initially accelerating this naval dominant condition, as the first short-range railroads and river steamboats simply fed goods and supplies that were hitherto inaccessible into coastal ports for oceanic commerce.[59] As the railroads grew to transcontinental scope, however, Mackinder saw that the balance of power was shifting back again to land, specifically to the heartland.

Mackinder's worldview divided the globe into three primary regions: the Eurasian core that comprised *heartland* or pivot area; the *inner crescent* made

Figure 2.4: Mackinder's worldview

up of the marginal regions around the heartland's periphery (including Western Europe, the Middle East, Indian subcontinent, and most of China); and the *outer crescent*, those regions separated from the heartland and inner crescent by water (including the entire Western Hemisphere, Britain, Japan, and Australia). Each area had a geographically determined role in global affairs. More convincingly, the theory seemed to validate Britain's accepted role as the 'balancing' state in the nineteenth-century multinational diplomatic classic balance of power era known as the Concert of Europe. Via deft and often clandestine back-stage political maneuvering, the British ensured that none of the great powers of its era would gain enough power to dominate the others. It was a bold, though heavily criticized strategy, as Britain forged and broke alliances as needed to preserve its notion of political equilibrium in Europe.

Until the railroad, sea power's advantage was its virtual monopoly on force projection over the world's most efficient trade routes. Railroads, Mackinder reasoned, would fundamentally alter the global equation and allow the land-based powers of Eurasia to regain the dominance they held when cavalry reigned supreme. Mackinder believed the history of civilization was in fact a cyclical tale of alternating dominance by land and sea powers, and that a change to land dominance was currently underway. The heartland, impervious to deep power projection from the sea and endowed with the resources necessary to build a monolithic military force, eventually would consolidate under a single state that could conquer the world. The outer crescent powers were natural allies who could retard the development of the heartland power by maintaining strict control of the sea and encouraging continuous warfare among the fragmented heartland and inner crescent states to prevent them from turning their capacities outward. Absolutely critical to the outer crescent states was the preemption of the formation of a powerful eastern European state, the presumed gateway to the heartland. Mackinder saw the flat, open northern plain as a natural highway to the vast potential of the heartland. It had to be kept fragmented at all cost, for: 'Who rules East Europe commands the Heartland. Who rules the Heartland commands the World Island. Who rules the World Island commands the World.'[60]

Crucial to Mackinder's strategy for Britain was the notion that if a state desired control of global affairs but could not physically occupy the critical keys to geodetermined power, *then it must deny control of those areas to its adversaries.* To the astrostrategist the parallel is all too obvious. The vast potential resource base of outer space is presumably so enormous, effectively inexhaustible, that any state that can control it will ultimately dominate the earth. To many of his contemporaries, in contrast, Mackinder's theories appeared overly simplistic and one-dimensional, and contained significant discrepancies and shortfalls. But they were not ignored, and follow-on geopolitical theorists both positively modified and negatively criticized them.[61] Dutch-born Nicholas Spykman faulted Mackinder on two primary points: (1) he overemphasized the potential power of the heartland, and (2) the dynamic between land power and maritime power was oversimplified. After 1920, when he came to the United States, Spykman began to believe that the United States, not Britain, would have to accept the mantle of leadership and become the balancing state in modern world politics. As early as 1942, when his basic argument from *America's Strategy in World Politics* was published on the front page of the *New York Times*, Spykman maintained that the concern of the United States should be with the end of the then ongoing conflict, and the resultant peace.[62] The complete defeat of Germany would not be welcome if it had the effect of swinging the European balance of power irrevocably to the Russians. Spykman slightly modified Mackinder's model. He called the Eurasian landmass the *world island*. He then identified the edges of the world island, essentially those Eurasian states that had ocean access, as the *rimland*. The rimland was vulnerable to both land and sea power and so by necessity must rely on both types of forces for survival. World power balances were, according to Spykman, influenced by the alliances *within* the rimland and *among* rimland and heartland/outer crescent powers. For the most part, Spykman's was only a revision of Mackinder's theory. In imitation, he even replaced the now famous Mackinderian dictum with his own: 'Who controls the Rimland rules Eurasia. Who rules Eurasia controls the destinies of the World.'[63]

Harold and Margaret Sprout criticized Mackinder for his reliance on a faulty perception of the world based on the distortion of Mercator map projections.[64] Hans Weigert (among many others) felt Mackinder's theories were rendered quickly obsolete as he failed to account for the growing influence of air power.[65] Robert Strausz-Hupé complained that both Mahan's and Mackinder's theories were overly deterministic, and preferred to downplay geography's role in the status of strategic influence.[66] The fact that criticisms and modifications continue to be made attests the power of Mackinder's theories, however. As recently as 1990, Saul Cohen modified the basic model to account for 'gateway states... uniquely suited to further world peace ... in geopolitical regionality'.[67] Gateway states are 'located largely along the borders of the world's geostrategic realms and its geopolitical regions', including the Baltic states in East Europe; Tibet, Kashmir, and North Burma in South Asia; and Quebec in North America.[68] These states could be the flash points for future war, but more likely, in his view, because of the recognized precarious positions in the geopolitical environment by statespersons of the great powers, they will be the globally managed start points for a lasting peace.

The previous discussion shows the rich body of theoretical literature devoted to geopolitical thought, which makes its precipitous decline after World War II all the more curious and noteworthy. Geopolitics is perhaps the most adept body of international theory when it comes to dealing with *systemic* change, and geostrategists have been remarkably prescient in their ability to project the effects of a specific new technology on the extant state system. In the twentieth century, the pace of technological change was breathtaking, and the geostrategists weighed in all along the way. H.G. Wells, for example, was one of the earliest to recognize the coming revolution in military doctrine and tactics with the arrival of the combustion engine and the automobile, and was able to heavily influence British strategy prior to World War I. Of note is Wells's description of the impact of the 'land ironclad', a mobile fortress that was much larger than, but essentially the harbinger of, the modern armored tank.[69] The impact of the land ironclad, he prophesied, would do more than change the way battles were fought; it would restructure the military forces that employed them. Defensive trench positions would be nullified. The mass armies the world then had would dwindle, becoming smaller and more professional as the training required for soldiers to master the skills necessary to apply the new technologies became a lifetime effort. States that failed to adapt would quickly find that large-scale drafts of foot soldiers would be ineffective against the land ironclads, and would quickly decline in state and military power. Wells's projections turned out to be inaccurate, as the giant land ironclad (as large as a battleship) was never deployed. But the logic was consistent with armored warfare as it eventually developed and overcame the defensive-dominant trench warfare practices of the day. In his theorizing, Wells became last century's first advocate of geostrategic change due to the arrival of a new technology. Many others followed, most of them enamored with the growth of air and then missile power.

The first of these was Giulio Douhet, an Italian Air Marshal who wrote extensively of the coming air power revolution in modern warfare. Though his vision was far-reaching, even he didn't recognize the full impact of this new dimension on the battlefield. Douhet insisted, for example, that 'aerial bombardment can never hope to achieve the accuracy of artillery fire'.[70] Despite the fact that aircraft were essentially unimpeded by the Earth's surface features (a critical change in the evolution toward astropolitics), they were limited in their operations by critical *air operations routes*, which required precisely located takeoff and landing fields and effective maintenance and repair facilities at major hubs. Douhet identified three of these air routes for Italy, one along the Po Valley and two more along the east and west coasts of the peninsula.[71] Douhet insisted warfare maps should portray these routes along with overlays of concentric circles, or range arcs, identifying the operational ranges of deployed aircraft at terrestrial bases.

US Army Air Corps General Billy Mitchell accepted Douhet's view that air bases represented vital centers of military operations, and believed his role was to extend theory into practice.[72] Mitchell professed that in the new Air Age Alaska had surpassed Panama as a strategic focus for the United States, since aircraft based in this region could maximize their radius of action against potential foes.[73] His bombastic and irascible personality eventually got him court-martialed (for conduct unbecoming an officer), but Mitchell was

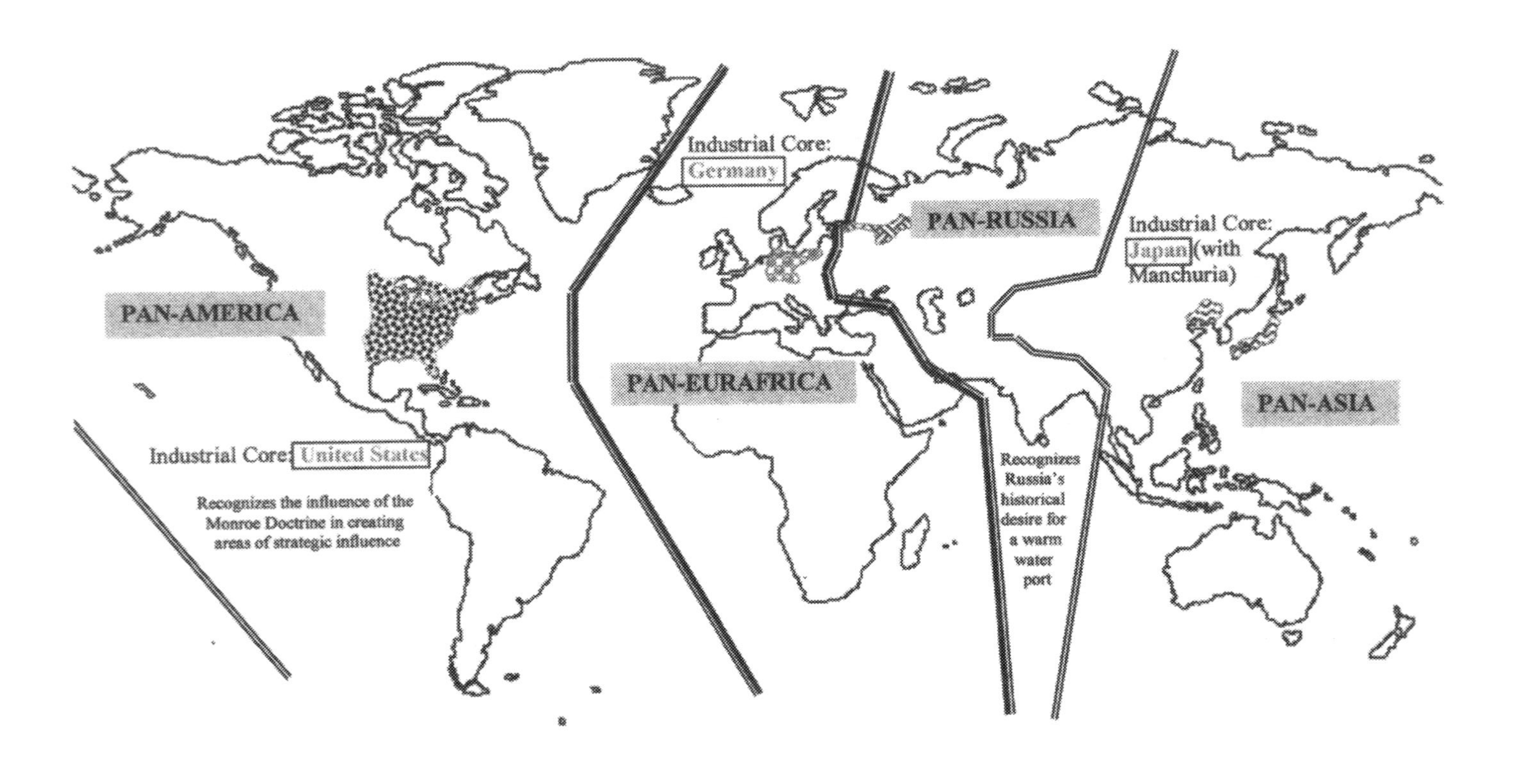

Figure 2.5: Geopolitik superstates

posthumously revered in the United States Air Force for his foresight, when events and the course of World War II seemed to prove many of his assertions.

Russian-born Alexander De Seversky was a practical engineer (he invented the first fully automatic bombsight) and a businessman (he founded Republic Airlines), but is best known for his powerful advocacy of a massive commitment to air power as the backbone of US strategic defense. De Seversky was the first geostrategist to use an azimuthal equidistant map (a polar view which limited the distortions of traditional Mercator projections) to show how physically close the Eurasian landmass is to North America.[74] By drawing air range arcs over the United States and USSR, he identified uncontested regions as *areas of dominance* and regions of overlap as *areas of decision*.[75] De Seversky's influence was widely persuasive, and became the policy foundation for the construction of the DEW (Defense Early Warning) radar line across northern Canada and Alaska to monitor former Soviet Union strategic forces.

As the Air Age gives way to (or at least coincides with) the Missile Age, much work is being done on the geopolitics of nuclear war. Lawrence Freedman points out that the lack of actual nuclear campaigns has not inhibited the development of nuclear strategy.[76] The first theorists considered nuclear weapons simply bigger bombs for established strategic bombing uses. Political and economic centers now become legitimate (and with missiles, highly vulnerable) targets of military planning. With the devastation apparent with Hiroshima and Nagasaki, theory quickly became politicized. The cutting-edge strategists devoted their efforts not to winning wars, but *avoiding* them. The technology became one that was uniquely paradoxical. No nation that could afford nuclear power could afford not to develop nuclear weapons. But once deployed, no nation could afford to use them.

As US dominance of the geostrategic realm took hold, Colin Gray asserts that the notion of balance of power became strained. Americans had never been comfortable, he argues, with the amoral necessity of separating foreign and domestic policy in a world of hostile states. The 'sustaining myth' of US superpower is that the United States is 'blessed and divinely commissioned' to transform the world in its own image, and the horror of nuclear power had been opportunely placed in its benevolent hands.[77] Perhaps only Americans, sure in their righteousness, could have developed the nuclear strategy of paradox so fittingly and simply called MAD (Mutually Assured Destruction), alternately praised as the strategy of deterrence that prevented World War III and reviled as the psychologically cruel and horrific 'balance of terror' that frightened two generations of the Cold War. MAD was the perverse logic that spawned 'contingently irrational' academic discussions of 'doomsday machines', 'launch on warning' (LoW) of attack, 'mad boat captain' scenarios, and 'nuclear brinksmanship' strategies that held the world hostage to superpower demands.[78]

To summarize the entire panoply of counterintuitive nuclear theorizing in support of MAD is impossible in this framework. It is necessary, however, to understand the conflicting, even diametric forces that contribute to *Astropolitik*. To illustrate the span of competing nuclear theory, and to extend nuclear theory to the realm of outer space, three of the most perplexing dilemmas in the use of nuclear weapons are discussed: centralized versus decentralized control, the logic of the First Strike Advantage (FSA), and counterforce versus counter-C³I (Command, Control, Communications, and Intelligence) strategy.

The first issue centers on physical control of weapons operations. The desirability of quick and assured response to deter a nuclear first strike necessitates decentralized release authority and quick, relatively simple prelaunch procedures. On the other hand, the calamitous risk of premature or imprudent use of holocaust-scale weaponry demands tight centralized control and time-consuming, redundant-verification pre-launch procedures.[79] This dichotomy of means has been described as a positive versus negative control option, as a 'perversely interlocking' choice between increased or decreased capacity to gather information, and as a preparation for war initiation versus war termination ('there is no military point in deploying safety devices that so complicate a weapon's firing sequence that it may fail to function when a legitimate need arises and authorized permission is given for its use', and, on the other, 'C³I structure must also facilitate war termination').[80] The options appear totally diametric, and a compromise solution may never be fully satisfying. Nonetheless, during the Cold War the United States (and probably the Soviet Union) attempted to straddle the fence, employing various control strategies for differing nuclear forces. Control varied by three broad categories: (1) weapons deployed outside the United States not under the sea – generally tactical nuclear weapons; (2) air and missile forces under the Strategic Air Command (SAC); and (3) the Navy's sea and submarine-based weapons.[81] Weapons in the first category are the most tightly controlled, since they are most susceptible to accidental use or misuse, conventional or terrorist attack, and hostile government action. A surprise attack would probably render them useless, as release authority for these weapons would have to be predelegated.[82] The SAC Commander had authority to raise readiness and to independently launch his bomber force to prevent its destruction on the ground. However, authority for bomber or ICBM (intercontinental ballistic missile) counterstrike was withheld prior to confirmation of hostile attack, and was precariously dependent on fragile communications systems. Navy assets of the third category had the least centralized control because of their unique communications requirements and relatively safe operating environment.[83] Insurance against premature or accidental launch was maintained by a positive control system in which 'three to five officers, including the Captain' had to simultaneously perform enable and launch procedures.[84]

Ideally, tight control should be practiced in peacetime, providing the maximum assurance of safety. In a crisis or war situation, control is released to multiple decision centers and pre-launch procedures would be relaxed. This dual system has two primary faults. First, coupling the dissemination of control with rising international tension clearly could serve to increase the possibility of inadvertent war – tightly coupled systems 'are notorious for producing overcompensation effects'.[85] The military response to heightened world tension is to heighten readiness.[86] As readiness increases, tensions increase, producing a spiraling decision matrix that can take on a life of its own, complete with full tautological rationality. Second, tight control during peacetime increases vulnerability to surprise attack. In a pure 'bolt from the blue' surprise attack on Washington, it is doubtful the President could escape.[87] Even if the Commander-in-Chief were able, miraculously, to get aboard the Advanced Airborne National Command Post (AABNCP), the disruptive nuclear environment could frustrate any attempt to control a retaliatory strike.[88] Though most analysts, military and civilian, are confident that a surprise attack is highly improbable, the sheer improbability of the event increases its probability of success.[89]

In outer space, assets that are farther from control centers will of necessity receive less control than assets in near Earth orbit, due to communications time lags. For manned space, the distinction is more critical. Emergencies cannot be addressed with multi-minute electromagnetic delays due to distance or electromagnetic shadows due to planetary and solar interruptions. This increased autonomy for manned missions will have short-term astropolitical effects and longer-term astrodeterminist ones. For military platforms, the logic holds. Spacecraft with military missions, especially unmanned ones (for example, the proposed 'Brilliant Pebbles/Brilliant Eyes' kinetic kill vehicles envisioned in the Strategic Defense Initiative's (SDI) anti-missile shield) will of necessity work in a threat environment that may preclude constant monitoring and contact. The probability that a computer or other mechanical error will cause an unauthorized or unintended malfunction/unauthorized attack increases in accordance with Murphy's Laws the less the system is under direct control. To provide increased autonomy increases the potential for unauthorized or disastrous uses of the platform, while on the other hand increased control increases the response time to deal with genuine emergencies or crises.

The second issue for study is drawn from the obvious maxim that the side striking first receives an incomparable military advantage. FSA is so compelling that analysts routinely pointed out the value of a 'preemptive' attack in the event that one power suspects the other of preparing a first strike.[90] In nuclear combat, the luxury of striking first guarantees the aggressor the use of any or all weaponry, the advantage of full, uninterrupted C³I for coordinating the attack, and a full range of target selection. Moreover, it is always possible that the victim would opt not to retaliate, and instead sue for peace. Such a fanciful vision is one of the few scenarios that allow for nuclear victory. Another possibility is that the first strike would leave the victims so weakened they could not retaliate, even if they wished to do so.

Studies of vulnerability have long shown C^3I to be the weak link of nuclear deterrence, leaving the guaranteed retaliatory capacity of nuclear forces less potent in fact than in theory.[91] During the Cold War, the United States and Soviet Union took different approaches to limiting command vulnerability. The former relied on mobility and human redundancy, whereas the latter relied on hardened bunkers and anti-ballistic/anti-air defense systems. Still, C^3I is subject to a variety of direct and collateral nuclear damage, including explosive blast, nuclear radiation, thermal radiation, electromagnetic pulse (EMP), Transient Radiation Effects on Electronics (TREE), and radioactive fallout. Additionally, C^3I is vulnerable to conventional warfare – military overrun/direct attack with conventional weapons; unconventional attack, such as sabotage and terrorist action; radio electronic combat including jamming, interception, and deception; and miscellaneous dangers to include natural phenomena, human error, and equipment failure. [92]

The terrain of space is essentially the unseen topography of gravity wells and electromagnetic emissions. Vulnerabilities in space forces will be categorized as in orbit (direct attack on spacecraft), on the ground (vulnerability of support facilities including launch and control, production, and monitoring sites to nuclear, conventional, or guerrilla attack, and espionage), and in electromagnetic transit (specifically the control up and data down links to disruption, jamming, and interception of data streams). The full ramifications of these vulnerabilities are discussed in greater detail in Chapter 6. For now it is enough to make the analogy that realist nuclear theory and *Astropolitik* are enmeshed, and the latter is an outgrowth of the former.

Finally, in discussing comparable analyses, C^3I's vulnerability makes it a prime candidate for first-strike targeting. Disabling an enemy by destroying the ability to control the weapons at its disposal is counter-C^3I, or, more colorfully, decapitation. Targeting the weapons themselves is a counterforce strategy – to maintain the analogy, dismemberment. A dismemberment attack is desirable because, in theory, it would eliminate the enemy's ability to retaliate, but would leave in place an authority structure which is capable of negotiating terms of surrender. A decapitation attack is desirable because, in theory, it would eliminate the enemy's ability to coordinate or even commence a retaliatory strike. The C^3I structure is vastly more vulnerable than nuclear weapons in hardened bunkers or on mobile platforms on the ground, in the air, or under the sea, however. A complete loss of C^3I is therefore more likely than a complete loss of forces. The major drawback of the decapitation strategy is that if the enemy were able to retaliate, via a launch-on-warning or launch-under-attack tripwire command structure (the 'doomsday device'), there would be no legitimate government authority with which to negotiate war termination. The result could be global suicide.

The dichotomy is generally associated with selective escalation and massive retaliation. The latter requires no battle management and the former is heavily taxing on C^{3}I systems. Given the extraordinary number of nuclear devices available today, a massive strike probably could not eliminate a nuclear power's entire nuclear force. In this age of overkill, even a few bombers and submarines spared from the initial salvo could cause unacceptable devastation to the aggressor in a second-strike retaliation. The C^{3}I structure, if preserved intact, could direct those remaining forces to the most efficient and destructive (and potentially appropriate) retaliation. Eliminating the C^{3}I structure would require fewer missiles, and would leave a larger retaliatory force. Without guidance, these weapons would be spasmodically (and massively) unleashed on targets of opportunity, most likely population centers.

Herein lies the greatest paradox. In order to increase options, enhance flexibility in targeting, allow for controlled escalation and de-escalation, and provide for the possibility of war termination before global catastrophe, the initiator and retaliator must agree or conspire not to attack the other's command and control infrastructures.[93] Both sides realize the need to 'spare the enemy's [C^{3}I] so that authorities can reach political agreement and military control in order to terminate the conflict'.[94] Nonetheless, 'command vulnerability encourages decapitation attack', and the all-or-nothing gambit encourages surprise attack.[95] General Robert Herres, former Commander of US Space and Vice Chairman of the Joint Chiefs of Staff, wrote, 'Imagine the incentives during crisis for launching [an] attack that might annihilate the national leadership and devastate command structures before they could recognize an attack was even coming.'[96] Verl Stanley and Phillip Noggio concur that C^{3}I warfare 'makes it possible to seize the tactical initiative, cripple the enemy's command and control system, and thereby defeat his forces'.[97]

Given the possibility that even a limited sortie of nuclear weapons is an attempt at decapitation, and with full understanding of the FSA advantage, the nation under attack has very few options.[98] If one assumes that both sides are evenly matched in terms of destructive capability and each side's intelligence and warning networks would detect any hostile missile attack, analysis suggests only two options: surrender or massive retaliation. If the victim gives up, the war is over. If the victim decides to absorb the attack, the risk of losing C^{3}I and the ability to launch a coordinated or in-kind response is too great. The optimum recourse is to launch as many weapons as possible in a retaliatory strike before control of them is lost. The aggressor, aware of the victim's quandary, cannot logically launch a limited first strike. Knowing that massive retaliation is a distinct possibility, the aggressor must attempt to destroy as much as possible of the enemy's retaliatory capacity in the first blow, thereby limiting any second-strike damage that may be forthcoming. Logically, since the victim cannot respond with a limited retaliation, and, knowing this, the aggressor cannot rationally initiate nuclear war with a limited strike, limited nuclear war is not possible. This is not to say limited nuclear war is inconceivable, it is to say that it will always be preempted by general war. MAD logic is impeccable.

The dilemma of tight versus loose control cannot be solved; at least it has not been solved here. The dilemma only adds to uncertainty in the nuclear environment. Tight control could lure an opponent into attempting a surprise decapitation strike. Loose control is a dangerous mess, and it is only a matter of time before an accidental or unauthorized launch tests the tolerance of the superpowers. Neither strategy decreases the likelihood of war. If that notion translates into a pessimistic inevitability, then the side that strikes first has the advantage, and FSA places a hair trigger on the arsenals. The logic of decapitation suggests first strike should be against enemy C^3I, but if the strike is successful, there may be no one left to negotiate surrender. The war may never terminate. Ultimately, given the probability of massive retaliation in any nuclear conflict scenario, limited war is not a practical possibility.

It is therefore not logical to design a C^3I system for survivability and endurance. It is also self-defeating. Such a C^3I system, perceived by its owners to be effective, would remove the requirement for guaranteed retaliation, and thus *decrease* the logic of deterrence. An enemy might be more tempted to try a decapitation attack based on the rational assumption that, with the tripwire removed, a successful anti-C^3I barrage would indeed render retaliation improbable. Improved crisis and wartime C^3I, by increasing the potential for controlling response, decreases the credibility of deterrence since it forces a rational decision-maker to order the irrational act of nuclear retaliation.[99] An enhanced C^3I system capable of extended battle management would be an irresistible target. Since a decapitation strike would inevitably lead to general, not limited, war, to build such a system is not cost-effective. Deploying an expensive C^3I system designed for a war that will never be fought, and that by its very existence increases the potential for the war that *could* be fought, is a bad option.

Astropolitics contains all of the classic elements of geostrategy just outlined. List's logistical transportation net, Mackinder's pivot area, Mahan's chokepoints, strategic narrows, and lanes of commerce, Douhet's and Mitchell's vital centers and avenues of attack, DeSeversky's spherical modeling, and the multitude of nuclear theorists' contrary logic all have counterparts in outer space. Before completing the transfer of these ideas to the astropolitical model, a final line of geopolitical thought must be considered for inclusion. At the very least, it cannot be ignored.

ORGANIC STATE THEORY, *GEOPOLITIK*, AND *ASTROPOLITIK*

Geodeterministic theories perhaps inevitably led to the exploration of a political theory of natural selection. As such, they fall into the general category of

Social Darwinism, replete with the misquoted theory of survival of the fittest. Once perverted, this transforms the individual or group from having a natural capacity for dominance to having a moral *duty* to dominate.

Friedrich Ratzel, nineteenth-century geographer and biologist, was heavily influenced by the work of Charles Darwin. In his classic *Political Geography,* he compared the state to a living organism and made a biological analysis of government.[100] The organic state analogy was not new with Ratzel, Machiavelli made similar analogies almost 400 years earlier, but Ratzel's observations were far more systematically defined. Ratzel's most notoriously influential work was *Der Lebensraum* (literally translated as 'Living Space'), in which he claimed organisms adapted to the space they occupied.[101] In what was clearly a Darwinist notion, Ratzel claimed that human culture groups, *acting* as organisms, attempted to colonize the space around them. If successful, they expanded their living space, or area of domination. Whether he intended it or not, German political theorists would adapt the idea of *Lebensraum* as the scientific basis for a racist plan of imperialism.[102]

Rudolf Kjellen, a Swedish political scientist, carried the analogy to its extreme, and declared unequivocally that the state *was* an organism. *Geopolitik* was one of five components, or 'organs' of the state, that included: *Kratopolitik,* the government structure; *Demopolitik,* the population structure; *Sociopolitik,* the social structure; *Oekopolitik,* the economic structure; and *Geopolitik,* the physical structure.[103] Kjellen insisted the dynamic state would grow and consume the weaker states around it. In doing so, the state achieved *autarky,* or national self-sufficiency. Ultimately, he believed, only a few large states would remain. One of these superstates, the greatest of all would be a European composite controlled by Germany.

For astropolitics, the analogy seems suitable. A common perception of humanity's reach for the stars is that it is simply the next logical advance of the evolution of species. Mankind has filled and dominated the biological niche that is Earth and must now expand beyond these confines and spread to the cosmos. Whether the impetus is survival from ourselves (escape to another habitable place before we ruin this one with environmental or nuclear holocaust), overpopulation (the biological safety valve of space colonization), wealth maximization (the search for ever-cheaper raw materials and abundant energy), or a new interpretation of manifest destiny, humanity's push toward the stars is portrayed as inevitable. Indeed, evolution may naturally reach its own economy of scale. One possible vehicle for manned space exploration, self-contained mobile ecosystems designed for multigeneration long-distance travel, is an abstract magnification in the evolution of life. I.M. Levitt and Dandridge Cole have argued that this kind of concentration of living organisms is the next evolutionary step beyond multicelled organisms.[104] With the soon-to-be-realized mapping of the human genome, combined with startling advances in the process of miniaturization, an alternate model can be envisioned. Strands of human DNA with incubating material can be sent to every star system conceivable. Upon reaching its final destination hundreds of millennia hence, a sensor looking for the most suitable environment guides the micro-pod to landing and begins the process of creating new humans. The analogy here is more flora than fauna, as the human colonization of space might better resemble the broadcasting of spores.

Organic state theories seem to lead unavoidably to notions of Social Darwinism, more so even than the geodeterminist ones discussed earlier. The argument follows along the lines that states or peoples who are capable of expanding, not only will do so, they *ought* to do so. They owe it to themselves and to the rest of the world. Ability to expand is *prima facie* evidence of naturally mandated political and social superiority, implying an absolute *right* to expand. Such reasoning can lead to abuses of power.

A state that successfully colonizes in outer space will undoubtedly extract pride from the accomplishment and probably will realize enhanced resources, spinoff technologies, and military power as well. If it uses that accomplishment, or the increase in wealth it can expect from so doing, as a normative justification for dominating or oppressing others, then the dictums of *Astropolitik* are invoked. To illustrate, a geopolitical tangent that carried the outputs of geostrategy and organic state theory to *one* logical conclusion was Professor General Karl Haushofer's School of *Geopolitik*. Adherents combined geopolitical determinism and geostrategy to create a unique form of *applied* geopolitics that ultimately became the embodiment of plans for a new German empire in Central and Eastern Europe that was *destined* to expand as far as its inevitable military power allowed.[105] For Haushofer and his disciples, *Geopolitik* was the 'master plan' of German resurgence, the manual that foretold 'what and why to conquer, guiding the military strategist along the easiest path to conquest'.[106] Although Haushofer attempted to legitimize his school by collecting veritable mountains of pertinent data, and in 1924 founded the academic monthly *Zeitschrift für Geopolitik* to profess the new *science* of geopolitics, his contributions were hardly scientific.[107] The failure was in collecting data to conform to a preestablished hypothesis rather than to test it. Physical traits that corresponded to Germanic peoples were *a priori* evidence of superiority. If Germans had higher foreheads than, say, Slavic people, then higher foreheads were clearly signs of superior intelligence. If, as it turned out, Africans had larger head circumference on average than Germans, then head circumference was not associated with intelligence. If German women were on average larger than Asian women, this was clear proof of their physical robustness and superior mothering/nurturing capacity.

The *Geopolitik* School was primarily geared toward awakening the forces of nationalist expansionism in the German populace via a propaganda campaign emphasizing Kjellen's notion of *Lebensraum*; literally, biological living space. *Lebensraum* in this view was a curious mixture of national mythology and pseudoscience.[108] It dictated that the state, as the *living* representative of its collective population, required space in order to thrive. So long as the state-organism expanded, it was healthy. If it ceased vigorous expansion it was bound to wither and die.

In this formulation, the German school was unable to project a *permanently* peaceful condition of global, autarkic superstates as Kjellen had done. Eventually, the superstates would clash and only one would survive – most likely the German-led state because of its natural resource abundance and preferred geographic position. For its part, the extreme version of *Astropolitik* must conclude that the state ultimately filling the biological niche that is Earth must continue its expansion or grow weak and susceptible to the internal diseases (social unrest, political fragmentation) that infect it. The healthy world-state will spill over into outer space and continue its *physical* expansion.

Geopolitik became the vessel of proof that the German nation and the German peoples were the geographically preferred successors to the Eurasian landmass. Should a parallel vision ultimately permeate the social theories of space exploration, *Astropolitik* could easily be perverted into a cosmic manifest destiny for human domination of the stars. We must remain ever wary of such powerful and emotive demagoguery.

Haushofer may have been personally uncomfortable with racist theory, but his 'confused fatalism acted directly on Hitler through [his] pupil Rudolf Hess. Germany was called on to claim the mission of world leadership in the interest of preserving the [German] race'.[109] Hess had stirred the future Fuhrer with a prize-winning essay, which he wrote as his *Geopolitik* master's thesis, entitled 'How Must the Man be Constituted Who Will Lead Germany Back to Her Old Heights.'[110] Indeed, certain passages in Hitler's *Mein Kampf* appear directly inspired by Haushofer through Hess.[111]

Not inconsequentially, Haushofer's students based their plan for world domination on the basic tenets of Mackinder's dictum. Domination of Eastern Europe would provide Germany with access to Russia. Control of Russia would provide access to the vital Heartland. With the resources of Russia feeding the voracious industry of Germany, the fall of Western Europe was assured. World or global domination, the final logical step, was not in the immediate plans of the German school, however. Following Kjellen, these adherents of *Geopolitik* projected the rise of five roughly equivalent superstates, each controlled by the dominant culture in that sphere. These states would be located in Europe, North America, and Central, East, and South Asia. Germany was expected only to dominate and control the Eurasian superstate. In the final analysis, the Eurasian region was the most amply endowed of the five. Since the German people and culture were the products of this favored region with characteristics that made them physically, intellectually, and morally superior to all other races – Germano-Europe's power would naturally outpace that of the other regions. In classic Social Darwinian fashion, the lesser regions would be consumed. But this was a matter for later generations. To make the theory more palatable to Germans and (somewhat) less threatening to non-Aryans, the later ambitions of world domination were downplayed.

Of note, *Geopolitik* panregionalism may have been heavily influenced by nineteenth-century US foreign policy. The German plan was in fact publicly referred to as 'a Monroe Doctrine for Europe'.[112] Reversing the intent of Monroe, who argued against the intrusions of outside influences in the Americas, the German adherents of *Geopolitik* increasingly claimed the right of non-interference from outsiders in their imperial ambitions in Europe. These Haushoferians claimed that just as the US had a natural right to dominance in its natural sphere of influence, Germany should legitimately claim and defend its own geopolitically determined rights and territories.

With the defeat of the Axis powers, *Geopolitik* and, for the most part, geodeterminist theories of state power were thoroughly discredited. The line of geopolitical reasoning here identified as geostrategy continued to flourish, however, and the advocates of new technologies have continually made modifications to popular or practical geostrategies. It is on this basis, the tremendous practical value of incorporating new technologies into the logic flow of the geopolitical paradigm, that an ongoing effort to restore geopolitical thought to academic respect is ongoing.

NOTES

1. A common misuse of the term, somewhat justified by the input received from the nightly news on television. I once heard a national anchor begin a report on allegations that Russian President Boris Yeltsin was ill, possibly from a drinking problem, with, 'In geopolitical news tonight …'.
2. D. Deudney, 'Geopolitics and Change', in M. Doyle, and G.J. Ikenberry (eds), *New Thinking In International Relations Theory* (Boulder, CO: Westview Press, 1997), pp. 93–9.
3. Ibid., pp. 99–100.
4. M. Glassner, *Political Geography* (New York: J. Wiley, 1993).
5. G. Parker, *Western Geopolitical Thought in the Twentieth Century* (New York: St Martin's, 1986), p. 1.
6. See particularly C. Gray, *The Geopolitics of the Nuclear Era: Heartland, Rimlands, and the Technological Revolution* (New York: National Strategy Information Center, 1977); *Maritime Strategy, Geopolitics, and the Defense of the West* (New York: National Strategy Information Center, 1986); *The Geopolitics of Superpower* (Lexington, KY: University of Kentucky Press, 1987); and 'The Influence of Space Power upon History', *Comparative Strategy*, Vol. 15, No. 4 (1996), pp. 293–308. See also P. O'Sullivan, *Geopolitics* (New York: St Martin's Press, 1986). Some theorists focus on the antithesis of war – peace – when applying geopolitical principles to their work. See, for example, D. Deudney, *Whole Earth Security: A Geopolitics of Peace* (Washington DC: Worldwatch Institute, 1983).
7. H. Mackinder, *Democratic Ideals and Reality: A Study in the Politics of Reconstruction* (New York: Henry Holt, 1919), p. 190.

8. Numerous titles exist. Those identified here include Sun Tzu, *The Art of War*, transl. S.B. Griffith (Oxford: Oxford University Press, 1972); N. Machiavelli, *The Art of War*, translated E. Farneworth (New York: Da Capo Press, 1990); H. Jomini, *The Art of War*, translated G.H. Mendell and W.P. Craighill (Westport, CT: Greenwood Press, 1972); and C. von Clausewitz, *On War*, transl. J.J. Graham (New York: Barnes & Noble, 1956). A solid overview is provided by M. Van Creveld, *The Art of War: War and Military Thought*, ed. J. Keegan (New York: Cassell, 2000).
9. See M. Hawkins, *Social Darwinism in European and American Thought, 1860–1945: Nature as Model and Nature as Threat* (Cambridge: Cambridge University Press, 1997). Although he does not use the term, E.O. Wilson's remarkable wide-ranging book, *Consilience: The Unity of Knowledge* (New York: Vintage/Random House, 1998), discusses the epigenetic foundations of such a notion (see Chapter 7, 'From Genes to Culture', pp. 136–77).
10. Excellent sources are A. Dorpalen, *The World of General Haushofer* (New York: Holt Rhinehart, 1942) and V. Veit, *The German People: Their History and Civilization from the Holy Roman Empire to the Third Reich* (New York: Alfred Knopf, 1946).
11. R. Mellor, *Nation, State, and Territory: A Political Geography* (New York: Routledge, 1989).
12. H. Wiegert, *Principles of Political Geography* (New York: Appleton-Century-Crofts, 1957).
13. S. Brunn and E. Yanarella, 'Towards a Humanistic Political Geography', *Studies in Comparative International Development*, Vol. 22, No. 2 (1987), pp. 223–38.
14. Deudney, 'Geopolitics and Change', p. 91.
15. Thucydides, *History of the Peloponnesian War*, ed. and transl. R. Warner (New York: Penguin, 1954). A recent overview edited by R. Strassler, *The Landmark Thucydides: A Comprehensive Guide to the Peloponnesian War* (New York: Free Press, 1996), is an excellent companion text.
16. A. Ferrill, *The Origins of War: From the Stone Age to Alexander the Great* (London: Thames & Hudson, 1985), pp. 91–4.
17. R.E. Dupuy and T. Dupuy, *The Encyclopedia of Military History: From 3500 BC to the Present* (New York: Harper & Row, 1970). Hans Delbrück plainly asserts the primacy of cavalry is 'a factor contributing to the development of a patrician class' (see H. Delbrück, *History of the Art of War: Within the Framework of Political History*, Vol. 1, transl. W. Renfroe (Westport, CT: Greenwood, 1975), p. 256).
18. For a fuller discussion of the role of military force structure on political institutions, see E. Dolman, 'War and (the Democratic) Peace', *Citizenship Studies*, Vol. 4 (2000), pp. 117–48.
19. Ferrill, *Origins of War*, p. 99.
20. C. Quigley, *Weapons Systems and Political Stability: A History* (Washington, DC: University Press, 1983), p. 271.
21. Ibid., p. 276.
22. Ibid., p. 273.
23. See A. Snodgrass, 'The Hoplite Reform and History', *Journal of Hellenic Studies*, Vol. 97 (1977), pp. 84–101.
24. W.G. Forrest, *A History of Sparta: 950–192 BC* (London: Hutchinson, 1968), pp. 55–7.
25 This observation is evident in the 'uncommon superiority of the knights over bourgeois and peasant infantry before the latter are trained and accustomed to being grouped together in tactical units', Delbrück, *History*, Vol. I, p. 257.
26. J.K. Anderson, *Military Theory and Practice in the Age of Xenophon* (Berkeley, CA: University of California Press, 1970), p. 13.
27. Quigley, *Weapons Systems*, p. 281.

28. Y. Yadin, *The Art of Warfare in Biblical Lands: In Light of Archaeological Study*, Vol. I (New York: A. Knopf, 1963), pp. 134–5.
29. Also called the Vulture Stele, see T. Watkins, 'The Beginnings of Warfare', in J. Hackett (ed.), *Warfare in the Ancient World* (New York: Facts on File, 1989), p. 20.
30. R. O'Connell, *Of Arms and Men: A History of War, Weapons, and Aggression* (Oxford: Oxford University Press, 1989), p. 36.
31. J.S. Morrison and J.F. Coates, *The Athenian Trireme: The History and Reconstruction of an Ancient Greek Warship* (Cambridge: Cambridge University Press, 1986).
32. Quigley, *Weapons Systems*, p. 299.
33. Based on a calculation of 200 rowers per trireme, with a maximum of 500 Athenian triremes in service at the height of the Peloponnesian Wars.
34. S. Andreski, *Military Organization and Society* (London: Routledge & Keegan Paul, 1954), p. 69.
35. I. Khaldûn, *The Muqaddimah: An Introduction to History*, transla. F. Rosenthal (Princeton, NJ: Princeton University Press, 1989): 49–70.
36. A. Toynbee, *A Study of History* (Oxford: Oxford University Press, 1956).
37. See A. Haley and Malcolm X, *The Autobiography of Malcolm X* (New York: Ballantine, 1964), pp. 162–8.
38. See L. Jeffries, *Dr Jeffries Speaks: War Against the Black Race* (New York: A&B Books, 1998). Criticism of Jeffries' work can be found in S. Howe, *Afrocentrism: Mythical Pasts and Imagined Homes* (London, Verso, 1999).
39. F.J. Turner, *The Frontier in American History* (New York: Holt, Rinehart & Winston, 1962).
40. J. Oberg and A. Oberg, *Pioneering Space: Living on the Next Frontier* (New York: McGraw-Hill, 1986), p. 17.
41. The latter pseudonym refers to James Madison, Alexander Hamilton, and John Jay, anonymous authors of *The Federalist Papers*.
42. O. Hintze, *The Historical Essays of Otto Hintze*, ed. and transl. F. Gilbert (New York: Oxford University Press, 1975). For a compatible argument, see also A. Vagts, *A History of Militarism: Romance and Realities of a Profession* (New York: W.W. Norton, 1937).
43. The phalanx analogy described earlier fits this paradigm. Although clearly a ground force, in implementation it is not useful for occupying or pacifying territory. Its supremacy reigns on the battlefield only. In defense of point locations such as cities, the soldiers are removed from their tactical formation and dispersed.
44. E. Dolman, 'War and (the Democratic) Peace', p. 123.
45. R. Salkeld, *War in Space* (Englewood Cliffs, NJ: Prentice-Hall, 1970); and T. Karras, *The New High Ground: Strategies and Weapons of Space Age Wars* (New York: Simon and Schuster, 1983).
46. For a similar exposition of these views, see E. Dolman, 'Military Intelligence and the Problem of Legitimacy: Opening the Model', in M. Manwaring and A. Joes (eds), *Beyond Declaring Victory and Coming Home* (Westport, CT: Greenwood, 2000); also published with minor revisions as 'US Military Intelligence and the Problem of Legitimacy', *Journal of Small Wars and Insurgencies*, Vol. 11 (2000), pp. 26–43.
47. E.E. Mead, 'Adam Smith, Alexander Hamilton, Friedrich List: The Economic Foundations of Military Power', in P. Paret (ed.), *The Makers of Modern Strategy: From Machiavelli to the Nuclear Age* (Princeton, NJ: Princeton University Press, 1986), p. 254.
48. See B. Tuchman for the best exposition of this view, *The Guns of August* (New York: Macmillan, 1962).
49. Mahan's influential body of work in this period includes *The Influence of Seapower Upon History: 1660–1783* (Boston, MA: Little, Brown, 1890); *The Influence of Seapower Upon History: The French Revolution and Empire, 1793–1812* (Boston, MA: Little,

Brown, 1892); *The Interest of America in Seapower, Present and Future* (Boston, MA: Little Brown, 1898); *The Problem of Asia and Its Effect Upon International Politics* (Boston, MA: Little, Brown, 1900).

50. Mahan, *The Influence of Seapower* (1890), pp. 35, 44.
51. Ibid., pp. 50–9.
52. Ibid., p. 25.
53. Ibid., p. 33.
54. This phenomenon was pointed out to me by M. Jennison in, 'The "Civil"-ization and Internationalization of Satellite Navigation', a paper presented at the *Sixth Biennial Conference on the Law Relating to National Security Activities in Outer Space*, in Colorado Springs (March 1994).
55. Mahan, *The Influence of Seapower* (1890), p. 83.
56. J. Keegan, *The Price of Admiralty: The Evolution of Naval Warfare* (New York: Viking, 1989), p. 110.
57. First in H. Mackinder, 'The Geographical Pivot of History', *Geographical Journal*, 23, 4 (1904), pp. 421–44; the latter reference in Mackinder's widely read book, *Democratic Ideals*.
58. Mackinder, 'Geographical Pivot', p. 430.
59. Ibid., p. 434.
60. Mackinder, *Democratic Ideals*, p. 150.
61. Well synopsized in J. Dougherty and R. Pfaltzgraf, *Contending Theories of International Relations: A Comprehensive Survey*, 4th edn (New York, Longman, 1996), pp. 144–72.
62. Cited in B. Blouet, *Halford Mackinder: A Biography* (College Station,TX: Texas A&M University Press, 1987), p. 273.
63. N. Spykman, *The Geography of Peace* (New York: Alfred Knopf, 1944), p. 43. See also N. Spykman, 'Geography and Foreign Policy', a two-part series in the *American Political Science Review*, Vol. 32, No. 1 (1938), 28–50 and in Vol. 32, No. 2 (1938), pp. 213–36; and *America's Strategy in World Politics* ([1942] Hamden, CT: Archon, 1970).
64. H. Sprout, 'Geopolitical Hypotheses in Technological Perspective', *World Politics*, Vol. 15 (1963), pp. 187–212; and H. Sprout and M. Sprout, *The Ecological Perspective on Human Affairs: With Special Reference to International Politics* (Westport, CT: Greenwood Press, 1979).
65. H. Wiegert, 'US Strategic Bases and Collective Security', *Foreign Affairs*, Vol. 25, No. 2 (1947), pp. 250–62.
66. R. Strausz-Hupé, *Geopolitics: The Struggle for Space and Power* (New York: Putnam and Sons, 1942).
67. S. Cohen, 'The World Geopolitical System in Retrospect and Prospect', *Journal of Geography*, Vol. 89, No. 1 (1990), pp. 2–10.
68. Ibid., p. 10.
69. H.G. Wells, 'The Land Ironclads', *Selected Short Stories* ([1901] Harmondsworth: Penguin, 1958), pp. 85–112. See also H.G. Wells, *Anticipations of the Reaction of Mechanical and Scientific Progress Upon Human Life and Thought* (New York: Harper, 1902).
70. G. Douhet, *The Command of the Air*, transl. D. Ferrari ([1921] New York: Coward, McCann, 1942), p. 62. See also P. Meilinger, 'Giulio Douhet and the Origins of Airpower Theory', in P. Meilinger (ed.), *The Paths of Heaven: The Evolution of Airpower Theory* (Maxwell AFB, AL: Air University Press, 1997), pp. 1–40.
71. Ibid., pp. 88–90.
72. A. Hurley, *Billy Mitchell: Crusader for Air Power* (Bloomington: University of Indiana Press, 1964): 81–3.

73. W. Mitchell, *Winged Defense: The Development and Possibilities of Modern Air Power – Economic and Military* (New York: Putnam, 1925).
74. A. De Seversky, *Victory Through Air Power* (New York: Simon & Schuster, 1942); see also A. De Seversky, 'The Twilight of Seapower', *American Mercury*, Vol. 52 (1941), pp. 647–58; and P. Meilinger, 'Alexander P. de Severskey and American Airpower', in P. Meilinger (ed.), *The Paths of Heaven: The Evolution of Airpower Theory* (Maxwell AFB, AL: Air University Press, 1997), pp. 239–78.
75. A. De Seversky, *Air Power: Key to Survival* (New York: McGraw-Hill, 1951).
76. L. Freedman, 'The First Two Generations of Nuclear Strategists', in P. Paret (ed.), *Makers of Modern Strategy: Machiavelli to the Nuclear Age* (Princeton, NJ: Princeton University Press, 1986), p. 735.
77. C. Gray, 'Strategy in the Nuclear Age', in W. Murray, M. Knox, and A. Bernstein (eds), *The Making of Modern Strategy: Rulers, States, and War* (Cambridge: Cambridge University Press, 1994), p. 581.
78. See E. Rhodes, *Power and MADness: The Logic of Nuclear Coercion* (New York: Columbia University Press, 1989), for an immensely thought-provoking overview.
79. T.K. Meyers, *Understanding Weapons and Arms Control: A Guide to the Issues* (Washington, DC: Brassey's, 1991), p. 104.
80. Respectively, P. Stares, *Command Performance: The Neglected Dimension of European Security* (Washington DC: Brookings, 1991), p. 3; M. Van Creveld, *Command in War* (Cambridge: Cambridge University Press, 1985), pp. 269–74; and D. Ball, *Can Nuclear War Be Controlled?* (London: Adelphi Papers, 1981), pp. 7–9.
81. P. Stein and P. Feaver, *Assuring Control of Nuclear Weapons: The Evolution of Permissive Action Links* (Lanham, MD: University Press of America, 1987), pp. 62–76; and Meyers, *Understanding Weapons*, pp. 101–4.
82. Donald Latham, Assistant Secretary of Defense for C3I, cited in T. Coakley, (ed.), *C3I: Issues of Command and Control* (Washington, DC: National Defense University, 1991), pp. 144–5. 'In our judgment, [one] errs on the side of safety, reasoning that I would rather not have the systems be able to work than just have an absolutely uncontrollable situation. In the case of artillery shells, if I couldn't get word through, they couldn't be used.'
83. Meyers, *Understanding Weapons*, p. 104.
84. Stein and Feaver, *Assuring Control*, p. 72.
85. P. Bracken, *The Command and Control of Nuclear Forces* (New Haven, CT: Yale University Press, 1983), p. 55. See also Stein and Feaver, *Assuring Control*, p. 62; and K. Gottfried and B. Blair (eds), *Crisis Stability and Nuclear War* (New York: Oxford University Press, 1988), p. 86; there is 'an obvious potential for friction as priorities shift'.
86. R. Garthoff, *Deterrence and the Revolution in Soviet Military Doctrine* (Washington DC: Brookings, 1990), p. 122. Garthoff cites Victor Kortunov, 'Disastrous Relapses into a Policy of Strength' (July 1980).
87. R. Betts, *Surprise Attack* (Washington, DC: Brookings Institution, 1982), p. 251.
88. Ball, *Nuclear War?*, p. 5.
89. D. Ford, *The Button: The Pentagon's Strategic Command and Control System* (New York: Simon & Schuster, 1985), p. 233. Ford cites a Pentagon source saying 'at least nine out of ten people in the military planning system – and I'm talking about the hawks – [feel] that strategic war wouldn't occur'. Bracken, *Command and Control*, p. 71, says a 'bolt-from-the-blue' attack has been so derided it is no longer given much credit. In such a setting, where defense planning has atrophied, 'it just might work'. More credibly, 'the vulnerability to surprise attack in peacetime increases because of the checks and balances intended to prevent accidental war'.
90. Gottfried and Blair, *Crisis Stability*, pp. 83–4; Bracken, *Command and Control*, p. 47,

'Soviet military exercises actually estimate the point that the United States issues orders to use nuclear weapons and then preempt before such an action can take place.'

91. Betts, *Surprise Attack*, p. 231. The author also correctly points out that this vulnerability may *increase* deterrent value. The enemy must assume that some low-level authority has been arranged in case of a confirmed nuclear attack to ensure retaliation. And on p. 252, 'Uncertainty is a prop to deterrence credibility.'
92. Meyers, *Understanding Weapons*, pp. 131ff; Ball, *Nuclear War?*, pp. 9ff.; and S. Cimballa, *Uncertainty and Control: Future Soviet and American Strategy* (New York: St Martin's Press, 1990), p. 160. For a fuller description of nuclear accidents, see J. Oberg, *Uncovering Soviet Disasters: Exploring the Limits of Glasnost* (New York: Random House, 1988), pp. 86, 240–4; G. Yost, *Spy-Tech* (New York: Facts On File, 1985), p. 108; and Bracken, *Command and Control*, pp. 49, 54–5.
93. L. Freedman, *The Evolution of Nuclear Strategy* (New York: St Martin's, 1981), p. 112, 'It takes two to keep a war limited.'
94. Garthoff, *Deterrence and Revolution*, p. 178.
95. Ibid., pp. 178, 185. See also B. Blair, *Strategic Command and Control: Redefining the Nuclear Threat* (Washington DC: Brookings Institution, 1985), p. 7.
96. R. Herres, 'Space-Based Support', *Defense '88* (November–December, 1988), p. 8.
97. V. Stanley and P. Noggle, 'Command and Control Warfare: Seizing the Initiative', *Signal*, Vol. 38, No. 8 (April 1984), p. 23.
98. Gottfried and Blair, *Crisis Stability*, p. 85, 'while there would probably be high confidence that the US is under attack, there would be but low confidence as to the nature of the attack'. Also, from Betts, *Surprise Attack*, p. 231, a single missile could be used to eliminate a national leader; in essence assassination by nuclear decapitation.
99. Bracken, *Command and Control*, pp. 163–5.
100. F. von Ratzel, *Politische Geographie: oder die Geographie der Staten, des Verkehres und des Krieges* (Munich and Berlin: R. Oldenbourg, 1903).
101. Cited in B. Blouet, '*Geostrategic Thought*', unpublished lectures (August 1994).
102. W. Smith, *The Ideological Origins of Nazi Imperialism* (New York: Oxford University Press, 1986), p. 146.
103. Glassner, *Political Geography*, p. 224.
104. See D. Cole and I.M. Levitt, *Exploring the Secrets of Space; Astronautics for the Layman* (Englewood Cliffs, NJ: Prentice-Hall, 1963).
105. A. Dorpalen, *The World of General Haushofer* (New York: Holt Rhinehart, 1942).
106. Strausz-Hupé, *Geopolitics*, p. vii.
107. Veit, *German People*, p. 246.
108. G. Sabine, *A History of Political Theory*, revised edition ([1937] New York: Henry Holt, 1950), p. 984; and Morgenthau, *Politics Among Nations*, pp. 158–64.
109. Veit, *German People*, p. 666.
110. W. Shirer, *The Rise and Fall of the Third Reich* (New York: Simon & Schuster, 1960), p. 48.
111. Ibid.; see also pages 177–85 in the R. Manheim translation of *Mein Kampf* (Boston, MA: Houghton Mifflin, 1943).
112. Sabine, *Political Theory*, p. 897.

3

Modeling the Astropolitical Environment

It has been suggested that the classical concepts of geopolitics, most of which are outlined in Chapter 2, are remarkably transferable to the *terrain* of outer space.[1] To be sure, the application of space technology is simply the latest in a logical line of techno-innovations in the continuing process of refining and resurrecting geopolitical theory. If indeed the resurrection and rehabilitation of geopolitics is a useful (if not yet altogether laudable) goal, then it requires at a minimum continuing political relevance. In this chapter the essential quality of classical geopolitics is captured, and its reach extended to the realm of outer space, a transition called astropolitics and, where appropriate, *Astropolitik*. If geopolitical theory developed for the Earth and its atmosphere can be transferred to outer space, then, *a fortiori*, the utility and value of its fundamental concepts and holistic design remain relevant, and are suitable for a set of revised or neoclassical geopolitical propositions.

The focus here is primarily on that variant of geopolitics called 'geostrategy', or the strategic application of new and emerging technologies within a framework of geographic, topographic, and positional knowledge. Without question, outer space has a distinct and definable geography, and much of the following rests on an exposition of its geographic characteristics. The remaining task, then, is to associate and extend existing geopolitical and geostrategic propositions to the described space model.

MODELING ASTROPOLITICS

Jean Gottman has argued that if the world were as featureless as a billiard ball, without terrain or topography, geopolitics could not have been posited.[2] Probably so, but with the perspective of scale gleaned from an outer space vantage, the Earth's terrain is relatively smoother than a billiard ball, and topographic features effectively disappear. Only the vast oceans interspersed with their continental juxtapositions remain. With this appreciation of scale, the important astropolitical features of Earth – or for that matter of any celestial body – are chiefly its mass (for determinations of gravitational pull), orbit, and relation to other space phenomena. Astropolitics is in this view the *purest* form of geopolitical analysis, converging entirely on elements of space and scale.

This grandest of all perspectives reestablishes one of the great achievements of the modern geopolitical theorists: the recognition that the study of politics cannot be nationally isolationist in its perspective. The Earth, to them, represented a conceptual unity. Without using systems terminology, they conceived of a single political arena. Each national unit was an integral part of the whole. State actions affected others, and states were in turn affected by the actions and reactions of those others. This holistic approach was a revelation in its day, and pushed the politicogeographic paradigm to lofty new heights.

Rather than reduce the importance of nation-states within the system, however, classical geopolitical theory has tended to amplify the centrality of national or regional rivalries. By manipulating knowledge of geopolitical characteristics, some states could hope to gain an advantage over others. At the very least, states could hope to prevent another from gaining advantages by blocking its efforts at control. The vision of astropolitics presented here reinforces those notions. The logic is so compelling that states wishing to remain sovereign must at a minimum prevent other states from gaining vital control of strategic space locations, pathways, and chokepoints. Before identifying these critical elements of astropolitics, to ensure a common ground for discussion, it seems prudent to describe briefly the physical properties and operating characteristics of outer space.

ORBITS AND ORBITAL MECHANICS

What appears at first a featureless void is in fact a rich vista of gravitational mountains and valleys, oceans and rivers of resources and energy alternately dispersed and concentrated, broadly strewn danger zones of deadly radiation, and precisely placed peculiarities of astrodynamics.[3] Without a full understanding of the motion of bodies in space, in essence a background in the mechanics of orbits, it is difficult to make sense of this panorama.

An orbit is the path of a spacecraft or satellite caught in the grip of gravity. Knowledge of orbits and orbital mechanics is vital for one primary reason – spacecraft in stable orbits expend no fuel. Thus the preferred flight path for all spacecraft (and natural satellites) will be a stable orbit, specifically limited to a precise operational trajectory. With this knowledge we can begin to see space as a demarcated and bounded domain.

The phenomenon that a satellite in orbit expends no fuel or energy is due to the fact that the satellite is constantly falling toward the body it orbits.

Consider the arc of a baseball as it is thrown, or better yet the path of a bullet fired from a gun aimed parallel to the Earth's surface (see Figure 3.1). The path of the bullet appears to arc downward toward the Earth until it hits the ground. The faster the bullet goes, the farther it will travel before being pulled to the ground by gravity. In the hypothetical case of a bullet traveling at 17,500 mph (just over 28,500 kph), the bullet would appear to fall toward the Earth at the same rate as the ground curves away, due to the spherical shape of the planet. Technically, the orbiting body is constantly falling (or is being pulled) directly toward the center of the Earth, but it never hits the ground.

An orbit is described first in terms of altitude (above the surface of the orbited body) and eccentricity (or variation in altitude). The highest and lowest points in an orbit are called the apogee and perigee, respectively (see Figure 3.2). Orbits are usually specified as circular, that is to say, of constant altitude with insignificant differentiation of apogee and perigee, or elliptical, of varying altitude and eccentricity. Once these parameters are established the orbit of the spacecraft can be envisioned as part of a flat plane passing through the

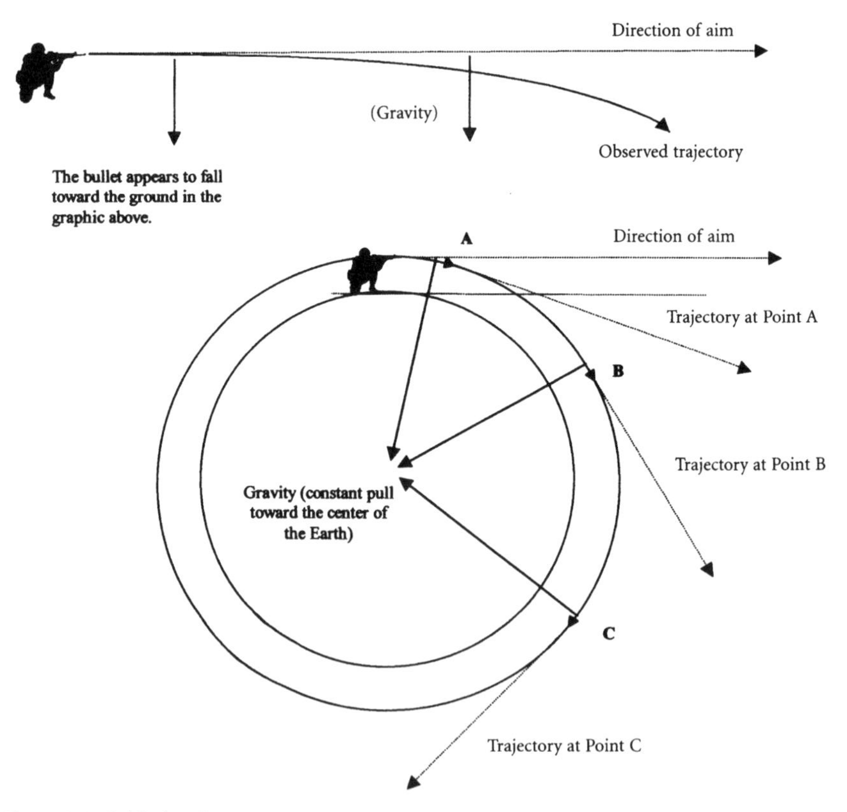

Figure 3.1: Orbital trajectory

center of the orbited mass. The time it takes for a spacecraft to complete one orbit is called its period. Additional useful details can be found by determining the satellite's inclination, the angle measured as the difference between the satellite's orbital plane and the orbited body's equatorial plane. The inclination tells us the north and south latitude limits of the orbit. It is also useful to know the orbital plane's position relative to a fixed point on the rotating body of the orbited mass. For the Earth, this point is the vernal equinox. The distance from it to the spacecraft's rising or ascending pass over the equator is called its right ascension. The points where an orbit crosses the Earth's equatorial plane are called nodes. If the orbit crosses the plane going from south to north, the node is the ascending node; from north to south, it is the descending node. The longitude of the nodes helps fix the orbit relative to the surface of the body it is circling.

As a rule, the higher the altitude, the more stable the orbit. This is simply because there is more interference from atmospheric density and gravitational fluctuations the closer one is to the orbited mass. Also, the higher the altitude the *slower* the spacecraft appears to travel relative to the body it orbits (relative orbital speed increases as the spacecraft spirals down the gravity well of the orbited mass). Higher orbits are not necessarily more desirable, however. Orbital differences can also signify a distinction in mission. Lower orbits are advantageous if a close or detailed view of the Earth is required, or a concentrated low-diffusion communications link is needed. Higher orbits provide a larger field of view, sacrificing detail for comprehension, and offer wider electronic accessibility. Circular or constant altitude orbits are generally used for

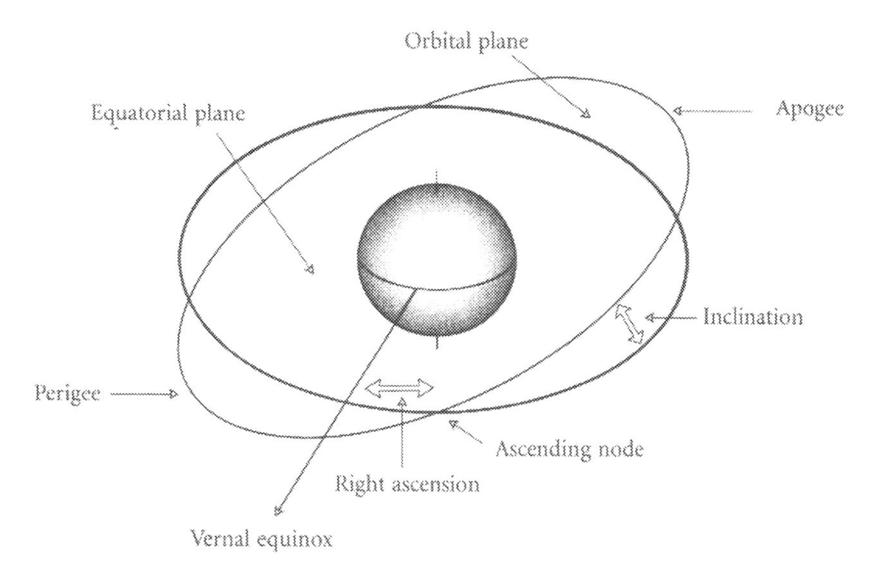

Figure 3.2: Orbital characteristics

spacecraft that perform their missions continuously, over the entire course of the orbit, while eccentric orbits usually signify that missions are conducted at critical points in the orbit – usually at perigee or apogee.

Ascension is also differentiated according to mission needs. The most vertical ascension orbit has a 90° inclination, which is perpendicular to the equatorial plane. This orbit is also called a polar orbit, meaning the spacecraft passes over the North and South Pole each complete orbit. The lowest inclination is 0°, which means the orbit is perfectly coincident with the equatorial plane. Inclinations below 90° are called posigrade orbits, meaning that the spacecraft tends to drift eastward on each orbital pass, while inclinations above 90° are retrograde, tending to drift westward. If the spacecraft's inclination is 0°, and its altitude is constant at 36,000 km, the spacecraft will appear fixed relative to a point above the Earth. This is called a geostationary orbit, and is the only orbit that has this fixed-point capacity. This orbit has extraordinary value for terrestrial acquisition of the spacecraft, as a tracking station or satellite dish does not have to move to maintain contact with the satellite. It is today undoubtedly the most commercially lucrative of the terrestrial orbits.

Orbits that are impacted by forces other than the constant gravitational mass of the orbited body have fluctuations in their natural movement. The orbit of an Earth satellite is never perfectly circular due to these fluctuations, which are called perturbations. The lower the altitude of a spacecraft, the more significant the friction caused by an encroaching atmosphere. As already mentioned, the effects of atmospheric drag are significantly reduced as periods (altitudes) increase. The effect is critical to space operations as satellites in a circular orbit with a period of less than 93 minutes require large amounts of fuel to make orbital corrections necessary to maintain spacing, distance, and velocity. Satellites in circular orbits with a period greater than 101 minutes are essentially unaffected by the atmosphere, and require relatively few attitude adjustments, as a consequence saving fuel and extending the useful life of the satellite. Orbits below about 160 km altitude (or an orbital period of 87.5 minutes) are theoretically possible, but not practically achievable due to accumulating atmospheric drag.

Perturbations also come from the bulge at the Earth's equator caused by the centrifugal force of its over 1,000 mph rotation, which causes the Earth's gravitational pull to be inconsistent. The Earth is actually flattened slightly at the poles and distended at the equator, a phenomenon that also creates small deviations in the flight path of a ballistic missile (one of the functions of geodetic satellites is to accurately measure the ever-changing oblation of the Earth – called spherical modeling – to increase the accuracy of intercontinental ballistic missiles [ICBMs]). Other perturbations, increasingly significant as one moves away from the Earth, are the gravitational fields of the sun, moon, and other celestial bodies, and the effects of solar radiation including solar flares, and the impacts of meteors and debris that strike the satellite at hypervelocity. Thus, no orbit is perfect and all spacecraft must have some fuel to occasionally make corrections. The useful life of a spacecraft is, for the most part, a function of its fuel capacity and orbital stability.

Given these parameters, currently useful terrestrial orbits can be clustered into four generally recognized categories based on altitude and mission utility (see Figure 3.3). The first encompasses *low-altitude orbits*, between 150 to 800 km above the surface of the Earth. These are particularly useful for Earth reconnaissance (military observation to include photographic, imaging, and radar satellites, and resource management satellites that can take a variety of multispectral images) and manned flight missions. These altitudes allow for 14 to 16 complete orbits per day. Manned flights generally have low inclinations to maximize spacecraft to control center contact, while reconnaissance flights generally have high inclinations to maximize coverage of the Earth's surface. Polar low-Earth orbits with a slightly retrograde inclination can be made to orbit in such a way that they are constantly above a sunlit Earth. This is extremely important for imaging satellites, and is all the more useful because the satellite can be made to stay above early morning or early evening regions. This creates long shadows helpful in identifying and determining the height of objects seen from directly above. Low-altitude orbits have the added advantage that satellites can be placed into them with cheaper and less sophisticated two-stage rockets. Orbits with a period in excess of 225 minutes (above 800 km) require at least a third-stage boost to achieve final orbit.

Medium-altitude orbits range from 800 km to 35,000 km in altitude, and allow for 2 to 14 orbits per day. These are generally circular or low eccentricity orbits that support linked satellite networks like the recently deployed – and

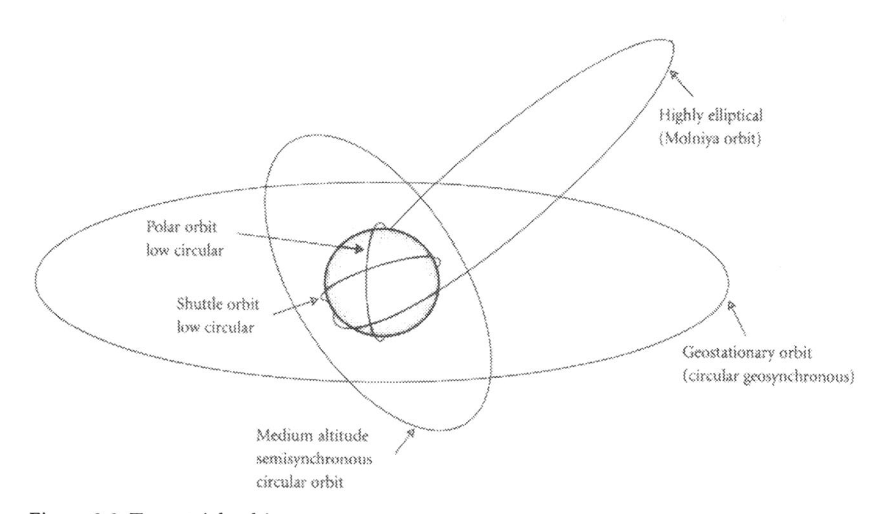

Figure 3.3: Terrestrial orbits

now possibly defunct – Iridium system from Motorola. Currently, navigational satellites such as the US GPS (Global Positioning Satellite, see Figure 3.4), that fix terrestrial positions through the triangulation of at least three satellites in view, dominate this orbit, though increasingly high-speed global telecommunications networks are envisioned in operation here.

High-altitude orbits, at least 35,000 km, provide maximum continuous coverage of the Earth with a minimum of satellites in orbit. Satellites at high-altitude orbit the Earth no more than once per day. When the orbital period is identical to one full rotation of the Earth, a *geosynchronous* orbit is achieved. Again, a geosynchronous orbit with a 0° inclination (placed directly above the equator) appears fixed in the sky from any point on Earth. This is called a *geostationary* orbit. Just three satellites at geostationary orbit, carefully placed equidistant from each other, can view the entire planet up to approximately 70° north or south latitude (see Figure 3.5, a satellite at geostationary orbit has a field of view of 28 percent of the Earth's surface). Since the satellites don't appear to move, fixed antennae can easily and continuously access them. Global communications and weather satellites are typically placed in this orbit.

For those latitudes above 70°, the advantage of long dwell time over target provided by a geostationary orbit is absent. This is simply because the limb or horizon of the Earth is not functionally visible. The angle of direct view is too oblique. One technique to overcome this deficiency is to use the fourth orbital category, the *highly elliptical orbit.* This orbit is described as highly eccentric with a perigee as low as 250 km and an apogee of up to 700,000 km. In theory, the Earth's gravitational pull extends about 900,000 km (one 166th of the distance between the Earth and Sun, about twice the distance between

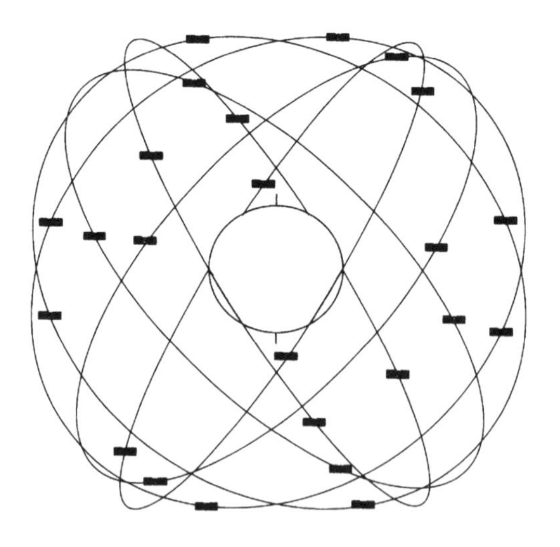

Note: 24 Satellites in
6 orbital planes
20,200 km altitude,
55° inclination

Figure 3.4: Linked network (NAVSTAR/GPS)

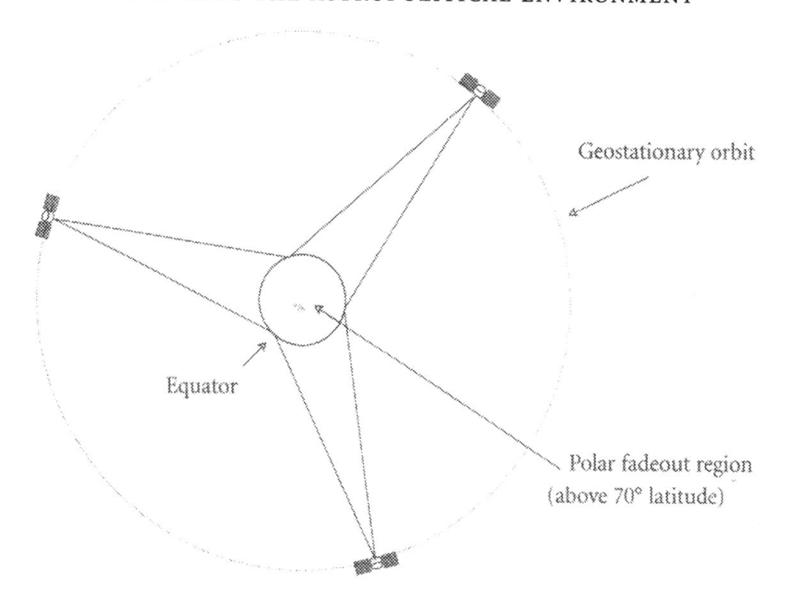

Figure 3.5: Geostationary fields of view

the Earth and Moon). Beyond this distance Earth orbits are not possible, as a spacecraft will eventually be drawn to another gravitational field.

Placed in a highly inclined orbit with apogee at 36,000–40,000 km, the satellite appears to dwell over the upper latitudes for several hours, making this a particularly useful orbit for communications satellites servicing Arctic and Antarctic regions. This apparent pause occurs because the speed of the spacecraft at apogee is only about 3,000 mph, while the speed at perigee is over 20,000 mph. At the great distance of apogee, the satellite appears to be barely moving relative to the surface of the Earth. When networked in the same orbit, one behind the other with equally spaced right ascensions, a minimum of three satellites can continuously access a single high latitude ground station. The Russians have made the greatest use of this semi-synchronous 12-hour orbit, and it is now routinely referred to as a *Molniya*-type orbit, after the Molniya series communications and weather spacecraft that use it (see Figure 3.6). A highly elliptical orbit with apogee at over 700,000 km can have a period of more than a month, and is especially useful for scientific missions that study comets, asteroids, solar and cosmic radiation, and other space phenomena.

With this essential exposition of orbital definitions and mechanics out of the way, an analysis of the terrain of outer space and the interaction of classical geopolitical theories can begin.

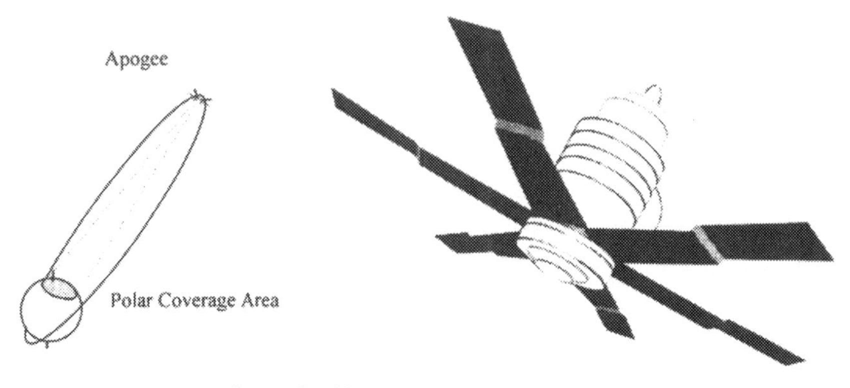

Figure 3.6: Molniya satellite and orbit

THE FOUR REGIONS OF SPACE

Halford Mackinder keyed his classic 1919 study of world power to the identification of distinct regions whose interactions defined the course of global history. History, he believed, could be understood as an alternating struggle between sea and land power. He projected that the nineteenth-century naval dominance of Britain would soon give way to a continental land-based power with the practical dominance of the new railroad technologies – unless, of course, the British actively prevented that dominance through balancing and other *Realpolitik*-style diplomatic techniques.

The key dynamic was the coming change in transportation technology, and with the inevitable rise of space transportation/exploration, a comparable division of the known environment into politicogeographic regions seems supported. So, following Mackinder's lead, astropolitics begins with a demarcation of the geopolitical regions of outer space (see Figure 3.7).

An assumption of this analysis is that the resource potential of space, like Mackinder's heartland, is so vast that, should any one state gain effective control of it, that state could dictate the political, military, and economic fates of all terrestrial governments. The Moon, for example, is rich in aluminum, titanium, iron, calcium, and silicon. Iron is in virtually pure form, and could be used immediately. Titanium and aluminum are 'found in ores not commonly refined on Earth, [and would require] new methods of extraction'.[4] Silicon is necessary for the construction of photovoltaic solar cells, an impressive and needed source of cheap energy. Abundant oxygen for colonies and fuel can be extracted from the lunar soil simply by heating it. Water from impacting comets is presumed to have collected in the permanently shadowed edges of craters. This near-Earth resource can already be exploited given current technology. The potential of the asteroids, planets and their moons, comets and meteors, and the sun can only be imagined. Access to these resources is possible only through the intervening regions between them and the Earth. The four distinct astropolitical regions of space are described here on the basis of physical properties.

(1) *Terra* or *Earth*, including the atmosphere stretching from the surface to just below the lowest altitude capable of supporting unpowered orbit. This is also known as the Karmann primary jurisdiction line, named after Theodore Von Karmann, the mathematician who first suggested its use. The inclusion of a terrestrial region is a critical concept for my model, and is a proper setting for space activities. Here the Earth and its atmosphere are the conceptual equivalents of a coastal area for outer space.[5] All objects entering from Earth into orbit and reentering from space must pass through it. It is on the surface of the Earth (*Terra*) that all current space launches, command and control, tracking, data downlink, research and development, production, anti-satellite activities, and most servicing, repair, and storage operations are performed. Terra is the only region or model that is concerned with traditional topography (continental forms, oceans, etc., see terrestrial basing below, p. 79) in the classic geopolitical sense, and is the transition region between geopolitics and astropolitics.

(2) *Terran* or *Earth space*, from the lowest viable orbit to just beyond geostationary altitude (about 36,000 km). Earth space is the operating medium for the military's most advanced reconnaissance and navigation satellites, and all current and planned space-based weaponry.[6] At its lower limit, Earth space is the region of post-thrust medium and long-range

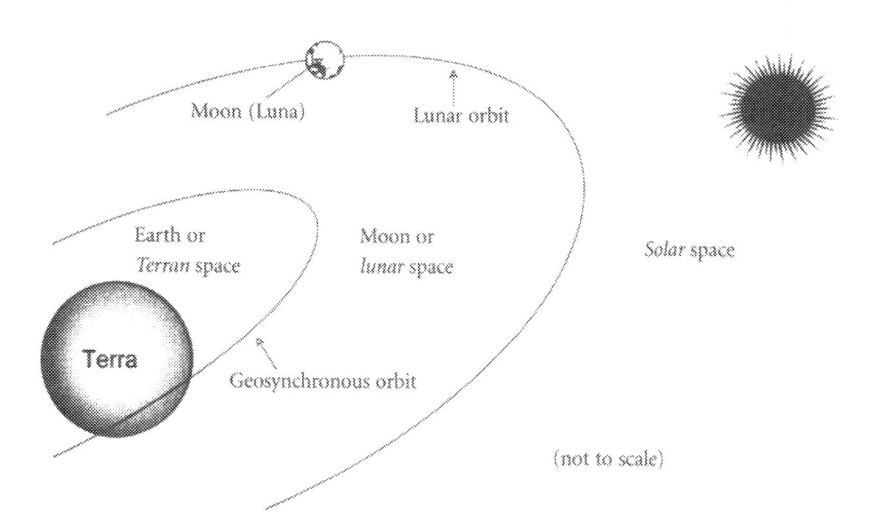

Figure 3.7: Four regions of space

ballistic missile flight, also called low-Earth orbit. At its opposite end, Earth space includes the tremendously valuable geostationary belt, populated mostly by communications and weather satellites.

(3) *Lunar* or *Moon Space* is the region just beyond geostationary orbit to just beyond lunar orbit. The Earth's moon is the only *visible* physical feature evident in the region, but it is only one of several strategic positions located there. Earth and lunar space encompass the four types of orbits described above, with the exception of the highly elliptical orbit with apogees beyond the orbit of the moon, currently used exclusively for scientific missions.

(4) *Solar space* consists of everything in the solar system (that is, within the gravity well of the Sun) beyond the orbit of the Moon. The exploitation of solar space will be treated quite briefly, as expansion into this region using current technologies will be quite limited. Nonetheless, the exploration of solar space is the next major goal for manned missions and eventual permanent human colonization. The near planets (Mars and Venus), the Jovian and Saturnian moons, and the many large asteroids in the asteroid belt undoubtedly contain the raw materials necessary to ignite a neo-industrial age. From an antiquated *Geopolitik* point of view, it also contains the *Lebensraum* for a burgeoning population on Earth.[7]

The vast resources of solar space represent the heartland equivalent of the astropolitical model. Earth space, like eastern Europe in Mackinder's design, is the most critical arena for astropolitics. Control of Earth space not only guarantees long-term control of the outer reaches of space, it provides a near-term advantage on the terrestrial battlefield. From early warning and detection of missile and force movements to target planning and battle damage assessment, space-based intelligence gathering assets have already proven themselves legitimate combat force multipliers. The most surprising and enduring contributions evident in the expanded military role of outer space technology, however, may have come from the previously under-appreciated value of navigation, communications, and weather-prediction satellites.[8] With its performance in the Persian Gulf, space warfare has emerged from its embryonic stage and is now fully in its infancy. All the industrially advanced states now recognize military space power as the apex of national security, and have tossed aside long-standing objections to military space programs as they eagerly pursue their own space infrastructures.[9] In future wars involving at least one *major* military power, space support will be the decisive factor as nations rely ever more heavily on the force multiplying effect of 'the new high ground'.[10]

With the growing importance of space technology on the modern battlefield, control of space becomes increasingly vital. The geo-/astropolitical mandates of space operations are now discussed in greater detail, beginning with

Earth and lunar space associations and ending with terrestrial basing requirements.

ASTROPOLITICAL CONSIDERATIONS FOR EARTH AND LUNAR SPACE

After the demarcation of space into astropolitically bounded regions, we turn to the 'wide commons' of Alfred Thayer Mahan, 'over which men may pass in all directions, but on which some well-worn paths [emerge for] controlling reasons', the aforementioned lanes of commerce and critical chokepoints of the open oceans.[11] Outer space, too, appears at first as a wide common over which spacecraft may pass in any direction, and to an extent this is so, but efficient travel in space requires adherence to specific and economically attractive lanes of movement, specific routes that are easy to project.

In the Age of Sail, wind and current – their appearance, prevalence, or lack thereof – were the determining factors in transoceanic travel. In rail travel, gradient is the determining limitation in transcontinental planning. In space, gravity is the most important factor in both understanding and traversing the topography of space. It dictates prudent travel and strategic asset placement. The unseen undulations of outer space terrain, the hills and valleys of space, are more properly referred to as *gravity wells*. Depiction of this terrain is difficult, but a two-dimensional portrayal is that of a weight sinking into a taughtly stretched sheet of rubber (see Figure 3.8). The more massive the body, the deeper the well. Travel or practical distance in space is less a function of linear distance than of effort or work expended to get from point A to point B. Traveling 35,000 km from the surface of the Earth, for example, requires 22 times as much effort as traveling a similar distance from the surface of the Moon, as the Earth's gravity well is 22 times deeper.[12]

In spacefaring terms, the important measure of work is the propulsive effort required to change a velocity vector, or the total velocity required to get from point A to point B. The total velocity effort (also called Δv or Delta V) is the key to understanding the reality of space travel and the efficient movement of goods. In another example of effective distance in space versus linear distance, it is much cheaper in terms of Δv to propel a spacecraft from the Moon to Mars (56 million km at the closest orbital point) than to propel the same spacecraft from the Earth to the Moon (just 385,000 km).[13]

> Thus the Δv to go from low Earth orbit (an orbit just above the atmosphere) to lunar orbit is 4100 m/s, which is only 300 m/s more than to go to geosynchronous [orbit, indeed] most of the effort of space travel near the Earth is spent in getting 100 km or so off the Earth, that is, into

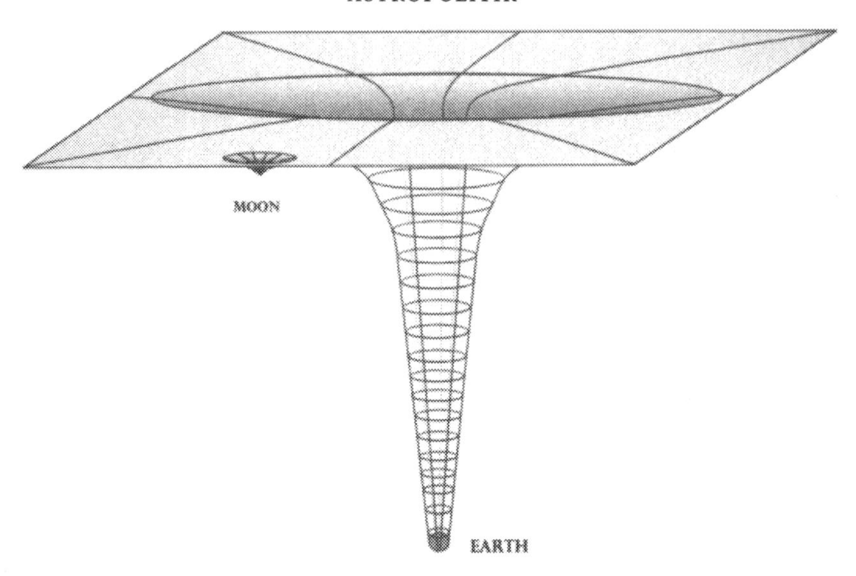

Figure 3.8: Earth–Moon gravity well comparison

> low Earth orbit. [More revealing,] to go from low Earth orbit to lunar orbit takes about 5 days, but requires less than half the effort needed to go from the Earth's surface to low orbit. [Thus,] certain points that are far apart in distance (and time) are quite close together in terms of the propulsive effort required to move from one to the other.[14]

The previous discussion of orbital mechanics has shown that a spacecraft in stable orbit expends no fuel, and is therefore in the most advantageous Δv configuration. The most efficient travel in space can then be envisioned as a transfer from one stable orbit to another with the least expenditure of Δv. Using this logic, in space we can find specific orbits and transit routes that because of their advantages in fuel efficiency create natural corridors of movement and commerce. Space, like the sea, potentially can be traversed in any direction, but because of gravity wells and the forbidding cost of getting fuel to orbit, over time spacefaring nations will develop specific pathways of heaviest traffic.

Orbital maneuvers can be performed at any point, but in order to conserve fuel, there are certain points at which thrust ought to be applied. The most efficient way to get from orbit A to orbit B (the proper language of space travel) is the *Hohmann transfer* (see Figure 3.9). This maneuver is a two-step change in Δv. Engines are first fired to accelerate the spacecraft into a higher elliptical orbit (or decelerate into a lower one). When the target orbit is intersected, the engines fire again to circularize and stabilize the final orbit. A

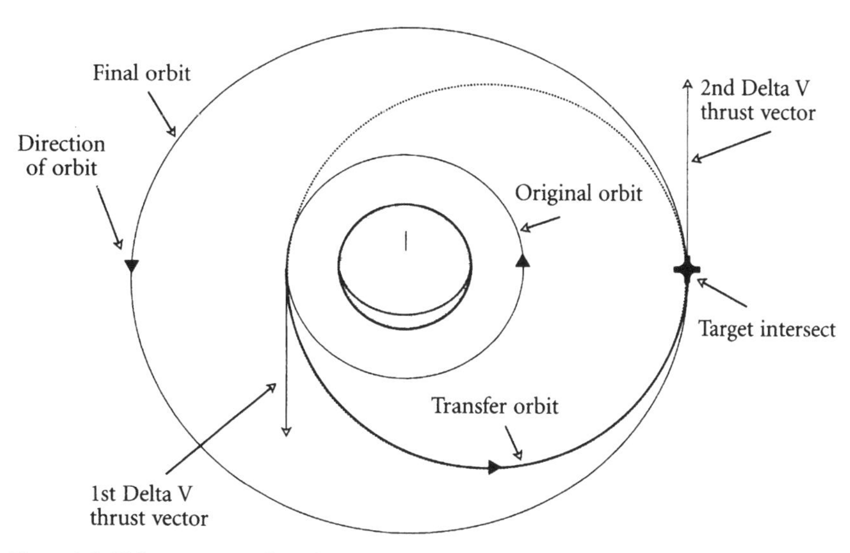

Figure 3.9: Hohmann transfer orbit

Hohmann transfer orbit is depicted from the Earth to geosynchronous orbit, but the same logic is used in all transfers including low-Earth orbit to geostationary, planetary movement, even interception of comets from Earth launch facilities. So-called 'fast transfers', in which the rules of orbital mechanics are ignored and a spacecraft simply expends fuel throughout its flight path, are of course possible, but require such an expenditure of Δv they will only be done only if fuel is abundant/functionally without cost, or if time is critical. This is the outer-space equivalent of sailing the long way round, however, and can make business unprofitable and military losses unacceptable. Given the vital necessity to conserve fuel and increase the productive lives of spacecraft, *the future lanes of commerce and military lines of communications in space will be the Hohmann transfer orbits between stable spaceports.*

Britain's rise to power came, Mahan believed, because it had exploited its location across the sea routes of Europe. A modern astrostrategist can and should make similar arguments. Mahan correctly observed that a prudent state not only could avoid garrisoning all the seas to dominate them, it would not even have to garrison the whole of the commerce lanes. Only the critical point locations along these lanes need be controlled. A small but highly trained and equipped force carefully deployed to control the bottlenecks or chokepoints of the major sea lanes would suffice. Control of these few geographically determined locations would guarantee dominance over military movement and world trade to the overseeing state.

The Hohmann transfer establishes the equivalent of the lane of commerce for space. Domination of space will come through efficient control of specific outer space strategic narrows or chokepoints along these lanes. The primary and first readily identifiable strategic narrow is low-Earth orbit itself. This tight band of operational space contains the bulk of mankind's satellites, a majority of which are military platforms or have military utility. This is also the realm of current anti-satellite (ASAT) weapons technology and operations, including the US F-15 launched satellite interceptor and the massive Russian proximity blast co-orbital ASAT. Within this narrow belt are the current and projected permanently manned space stations, and all space shuttle operations. Moreover, all the incomprehensible vastness of the universe can be accessed only by traveling through it.

At the edge of Earth space, beyond low-Earth orbit, lies the most obvious and discussed strategic narrow – the geostationary belt. This band about the equatorial waist of the Earth is the only natural orbit that allows for a stable position relative to a given point on the Earth. The geostationary belt has severe constraints on the number of satellites that can operate within it, however, due to the possibility of broadcast interference from adjacent platforms. This has caused it to be considered a scarce and precious *international* natural resource by *most* members of the international community. Nonetheless, in 1977, nine equatorial states asserted in the Bogota Declaration that national sovereignty extended upward, *ad just coloeum*, to geostationary altitude. The action is not dissimilar to the attempts of numerous coastal states to extend the limit of their internationally recognized territorial waters. In other words, the geostationary belt is considered the sovereign territory of those states directly beneath it, transforming an area routinely referred to as 'the common heritage of mankind' into a geopolitical conflict zone (see Chapter 4 for a complete discussion).

Mahan additionally advocated the establishment of naval bases at strategic point locations, including Hawaii, the Philippines, and several Caribbean islands, to act as fueling and resupply stations for the seafaring state's navy. The range of ships and natural interests of the state geographically determined their spacing. Without these bases, US war and trade ships would 'be like land birds, unable to fly far from their own shores'.[15] The notion is not fresh, and such staged basing is historically common, but its tendrils reach to outer space. Giulio Douhet's advocacy of a basing procedure predicated on new technology complements the Mahanian vision when transferred to space. Douhet wrote extensively of the coming revolution in modern warfare due to the fact that aircraft were essentially unimpeded by the Earth's surface features (a critical change in the evolution toward astropolitics with the gradually decreasing importance of topography). Air power was limited in its operations, however, by critical *air operations routes*, which required precisely located takeoff and landing fields and effective maintenance and repair facilities at major centers. Such bases should be considered critical for space control, and planets, moons, asteroids, and other heavenly bodies are obvious locations for 'way stations' or 'stepping stones' for space operations. But these may not be the most favorable point locations from a strategic perception. Another consideration based on Δv advantages must be taken into account.

The gravity well concept discussed above has important implications for military combat operations other than space transportation/logistics and way station location. In 1981, G.H. Stine wrote of the *energy* and *maneuver* advantages of high ground positions in outer space.[16] The first, energy advantage, is a firepower benefit because weapons placed higher in the gravity well gain the downward momentum – velocity in the power equation, velocity times mass – while kinetic energy weapons firing up the gravity well lose momentum, thus power. The maneuver advantage comes because spacecraft higher up in the gravity well have more time to observe and react to attacks than those at lower positions. Stine argued that true tactical and operational advantage in space would go to those who could dominate the top of the gravity wells, and the best positions were those that because of counterbalancing gravitational forces had no down well pull in any direction.

Perhaps the most intriguing point locations useful for strategic or commercial bases in Earth–Moon space are the gravitational anomalies known as Lagrange Libration Points, named for the eighteenth-century French mathematician who first postulated their existence.[17] Lagrange calculated that there were five specific points in space where the gravitational effects of the Earth and Moon would cancel each other out (see Figure 3.10). An object fixed at one of these points (or more accurately stated, in tight orbit around one of these points) would remain permanently stable, with no expenditure of fuel. The enticing property of libration points is that they maintain a fixed relation with respect to the Earth and Moon. In practice, owing to perturbations in the space environment including solar flares, orbital drift and wobble, and micrometeorites, only two of the Lagrange points are effectively stable – L4 and L5. The potential military and commercial value of a point in space that is virtually stable is highly speculative, but imaginatively immense. The occupation and control of these points is of such vital importance that an advocacy group called the L-5 Society was formed to influence national policymakers.[18]

One last phenomenon of the region that requires mapping and understanding is the location and impact of the Van Allen radiation belts, 'two donut-shaped regions circling the Earth inside the magnetosphere [that] trap charged particles and hold them. Spacecraft passing through the Van Allen belts are subject to damage. Astronauts passing through these areas risk [mortal injury]. Fortunately, they are well mapped and can be avoided.'[19] The inner belt first appears at about 400 to 1,200 km, dependent on latitude (see Figure 3.11). It extends outward to about 10,000 km with the deadliest concentration at 3,500 km. Anomalies in the belts put the lowest altitude at upper latitudes of the Southern Hemisphere, a particularly troublesome area for polar-orbiting satellites but easily avoidable by most manned flights.

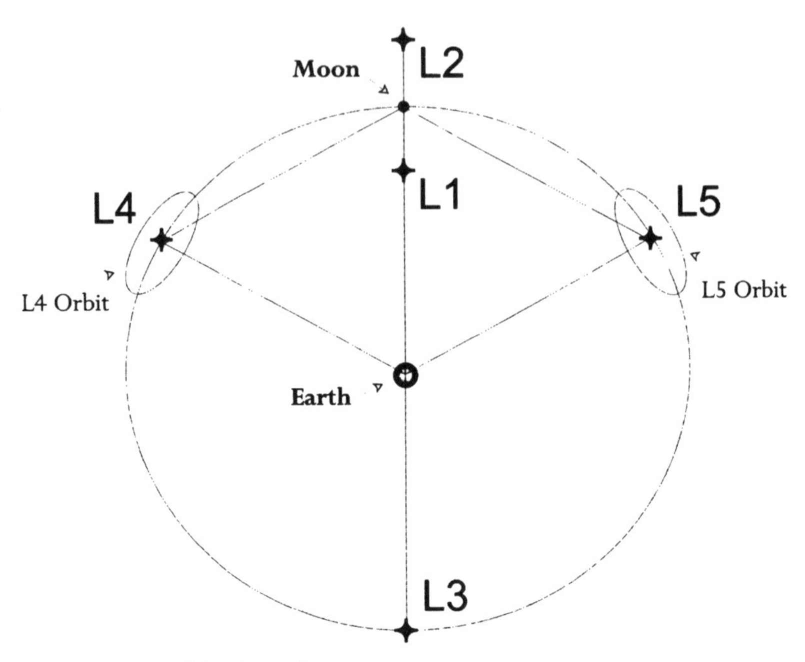

Figure 3.10: Lagrange libration points

The second ring begins near 10,000 km and extends up to 84,000 km, with deadliest concentrations at 16,000 km. The edges of the belts are relatively benign, thus a safe operating channel is evident between the two belts from about 9,000 to 11,000 km altitude. Of note, the outer belt is flattened to about 59,500 km in sunshine, extending to its maximum altitude in the Earth's shadow.

These few examples are just some of the many astro/topographical features of the currently exploited space terrain. Astropolitical analysis describes critical chokepoints in space as those stable areas including the planets, moons, libration points, and asteroids where future military and commercial enterprises will congregate. These are the coming ports of space, co-located with the valuable energy and mineral resources estimated to be there, or Mahan's, Douhet's, and Mitchell's way stations on the various Hohmann transfer routes to these resources.

ASTROPOLITICAL CONSIDERATIONS FOR *TERRA*

Earth is the current point of origin for all spacecraft and space-support operations. Ultimately, efficiency and economy will dictate that all essential

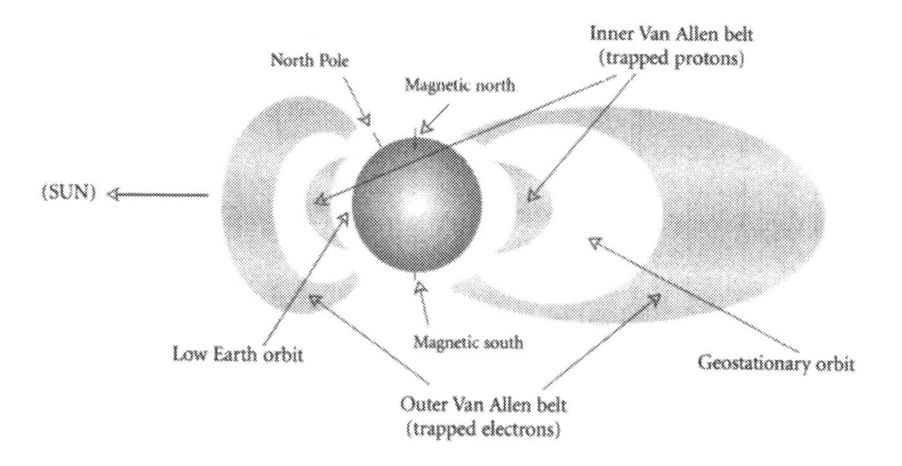

Figure 3.11: Van Allen radiation belts

space operations, including construction and launch, tracking and control, and various forms of space commerce will take place in space. For now, however, all of these functions are Earth-bound. When the day comes that these functions are performed off world, the vast population that feeds off the bounty of outer space will still remain, as will the governments that control space operations. The importance of *Terra* will not diminish, in the near term at least, nor will the necessity of political control. The astropolitical question, given the current realities, is simply where on Earth are the vital centers most efficiently placed?

We begin with launch center location in part because of its intrinsic relationship with orbital efficiency. The originating launch site of a spacecraft has a significant impact on its orbit. The equator, for example, has particular value as a launch site location, especially into geostationary orbit. This is because the spin of the Earth can be used to assist in the attainment of orbital velocity, and the relative velocity of the Earth's motion decreases from 1,670 kph at the equator to no relative motion at the poles. Since the minimum velocity necessary to climb out of the Earth's gravity well is just over 28,000 kph (mach 25), a launch vehicle heading due east along the equator would have to achieve a speed of just 26,400 kph relative to its launch point to achieve orbit. Conversely, a satellite launched due west along the equator would have to *add* 1,670 kph, and thus would need to achieve a velocity of almost 29,700 kph relative to its start point to place a satellite into orbit – a 3,300 kph difference. The fuel/Δv impact is plainly significant. In a real world example, a European Ariane rocket launched due east from the French Space Center at

Kourou, French Guiane, just 5° north of the equator, receives a 17 percent fuel efficiency advantage over a US rocket launched due east from Cape Canaveral, about 28.5° north of the equator. In perhaps a more powerful example, a Space Shuttle launched due east from Cape Canaveral has a cargo capacity of 13,600 kg. A Space Shuttle launched due west from roughly the same latitude (from the US Western Space Range at Vandenberg Air Force Base), can barely achieve orbit with its cargo bay empty.

Another factor of terrestrial launch basing is that the latitude of launch affects the inclination of the orbited spacecraft. Launches due east (90°) of Cape Canaveral will enter into low-Earth orbit at an inclination of 28.3°. Indeed, launches due east from any site on the Earth will have an inclination exactly the same as the launch latitude, given a two-stage direct insertion launch. Spacecraft do move from their original orbit, of course, and in the process change their inclinations (this is how the Shuttle places payloads into geostationary orbit, releasing them with an attached upper stage or bus). But the transfer costs additional fuel, fuel that had to be placed on the launching rocket, ultimately limiting payload weight or spacecraft lifespan. Launches on *any other azimuth* will place a satellite into orbit at *greater* inclination than the latitude of the site. Thus the launch site determines the *minimum* inclination (with a launch due east). A launch due west allows for the *maximum* inclination (in the case of the Cape, 151.7°, or 180° minus 28.3°). Launching due north or south will result in a polar orbit, that is, an orbit with an inclination of 90° relative to the equator.

The polar, sun-synchronized orbit is in fact one of the most important for military reconnaissance and weather imaging. A spacecraft placed into polar orbit passes over both the North and South Poles. If placed in a slightly retrograde motion (greater than 90° inclination), this configuration allows satellites to eventually fly over every point on the Earth, and to *remain in the sunlight at all times* – extremely important for satellite cameras that takes images in the visible light spectrum and for satellites that require continuous solar access for power. To place a satellite into a polar orbit, the most efficient launch azimuth is due north or due south.

Thus a space launch center that can send rockets both due east and either due north or south has distinct orbital efficiency advantages. Because rockets eject lower stages, and occasionally destruct in flight, it is further necessary that the launch sites have considerable downrange areas of open ocean or unpopulated landmass (at least 1,000 km). The optimum astropolitical launch points under these criteria are the northern coast of Brazil, the east coast of Kenya, and any of several Pacific islands east of New Guinea (see Figure 3.12). These locations are all sovereign national territory with astropolitical international importance.

There is at least one other critical feature of space launch centers that is based in astropolitical theory. Orbital perturbations degrade the stability of

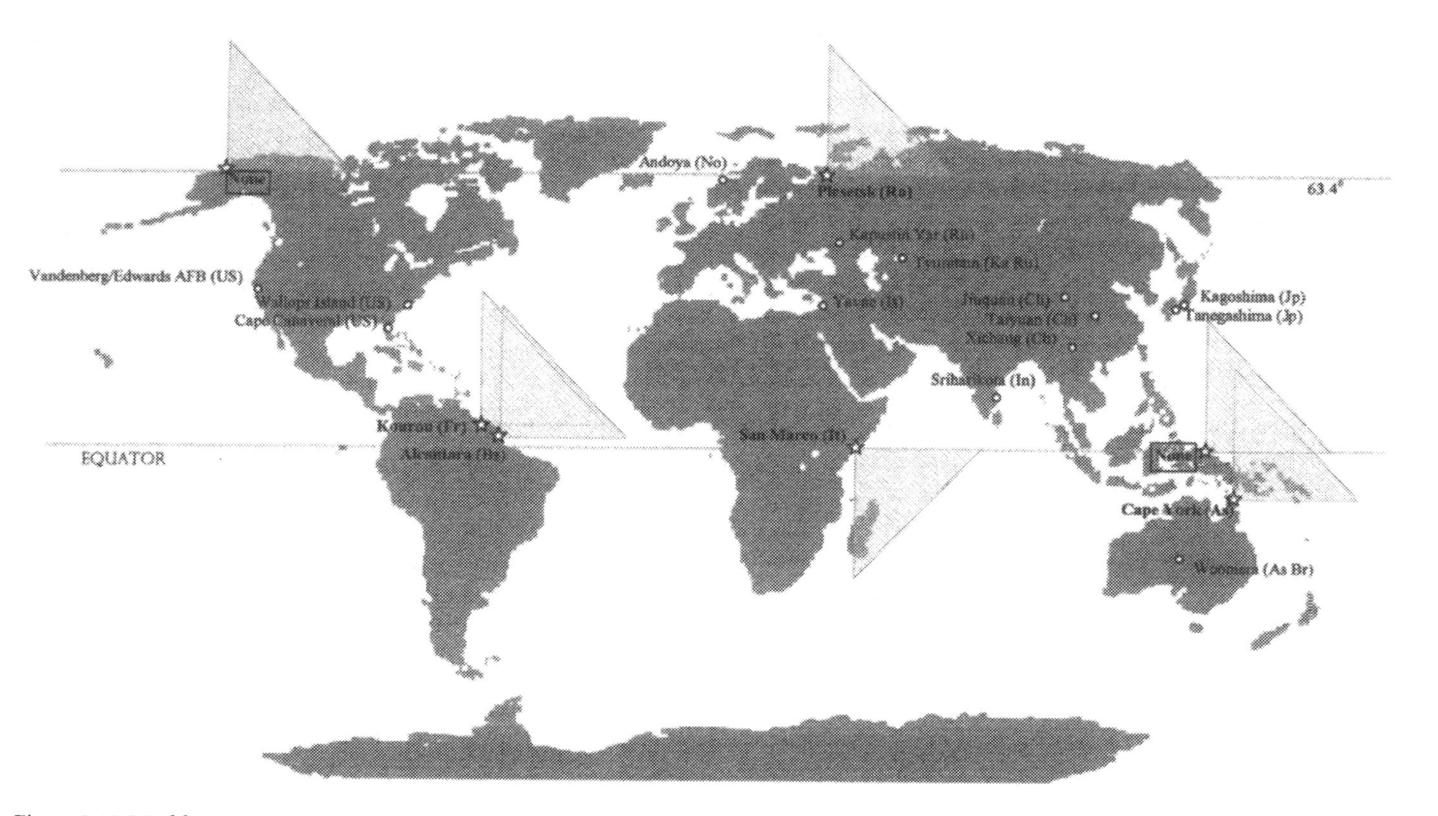

Figure 3.12: World space centers and Earth optimal launch points

all but two Earth orbits, requiring regular expenditures of Δv to restabilize them. The highly stable orbits are inclined at 63.4° and 116.6° relative to the equatorial plane. This means a satellite in orbit at either of these inclinations will remain stable with minimal expenditures of fuel, greatly increasing their useful lifetimes. More importantly, satellites operating in networks will maintain their proper spacing without continual orbital corrections. Satellites launched due east (maximizing the earth's rotational effects) from a space center at 63.4° north or south latitude will efficiently enter a 63.4° inclined orbit with a minimum expenditure of on-board fuel. Geolocations at 63° north with sufficient downrange capacity include northern Siberia, the east coast of Greenland, far north Canada, and most of Alaska (see Figure 3.12). The 63° south latitude intersects the Antarctic landmass, a cost-inefficient terrestrial location for a major spaceport. The most accessible of these areas are Alaska and northwest Siberia. Indeed, Russia's northern spaceport is efficiently located northeast of Moscow at Plesetsk, exactly 63.4° north latitude.

Finally, for the purposes of this book, a brief discussion of satellite *fields of view* completes the terrestrial survey but does not exhaust the astropolitical ramifications of Earth-centered placement. The important point here is that in order to control satellites in space, or to control the Earth from space, a global network of terrestrial contact points *or* a global network of interlinked satellites, respectively, is required. For several reasons, a state may wish to eschew the latter option. Satellite-linked networks are more vulnerable to Command, Control, Communications, and Intelligence (C^3I) interference than non-linked networks, and are especially worrisome for espionage satellites. Burst transmission and/or directed beam transmission from satellite to ground control is far more secure. Satellite-to-satellite C^3I linking is timelier, however.

Regardless of the control requirements of the satellite and/or network, space dictates the number of satellites needed for effective coverage. Physical limitations of orbital mechanics dictate that the only position in space that allows a satellite to maintain a constant position relative to the surface of the Earth is the geostationary belt. In order to optimize Earth access from geostationary position, a network of at least three satellites is necessary to view any point on the Earth between 70° north and south latitude (see Figure 3.5). Overlapping satellite fields of view are necessary to account for highly oblique lines of sight from the limb of the Earth, hence two satellites cannot effectively cover the globe. Even with three satellites, however, much of the Earth's territory cannot be reliably accessed. Terrestrial areas above 70° latitude routinely have transmission difficulties from satellites in geostationary orbit, especially in bad weather and during periods of heavy solar activity. These areas include much of Scandinavia, Russia, and Canada. They require an alternate or auxiliary network of three to six Molniya-type orbiting satellites for continuous communication.

In order to provide truly global coverage of the Earth from space, including the polar regions, in theory a minimum of just four satellites is required. Placed in precise 63.4° inclined supersynchronous (greater than 24-hour) orbits, one satellite can be in view from any point on the Earth at any time. Because these satellites are not fixed relative to the Earth's surface, terrestrial users would need the ability to track and acquire satellites as they move in and out of view, an expensive and time-consuming practice. Their use entails even more practical encumbrances. Satellites at super-synchronous altitude require large, heavy, high output transmitters to communicate with terrestrial users (due to physical distance). They are further unsuitable for some missions, such as high-resolution Earth imaging (again due to distance). For these applications, some satellites must maintain orbits closer to the surface of the Earth.

Conversely, in order to guarantee *continuous* communications with any *one* satellite from the Earth, at least three control stations spaced evenly around the Earth along the orbital plane are necessary for high Earth orbit and above altitude satellites (at inclinations of 63.4° or less, four or more for higher inclinations), and a minimum of 16 control stations for low-Earth orbit ones. This is why the United States maintains deep space-tracking stations in Australia and Spain (among other states), and Russia has kept a fleet of space-tracking and control ships deployed in international waters. Terrestrial control and data receive bases become less important as satellite networks become more common, however. Satellite-to-satellite electromagnetic linkage means that formerly dispersed functions can be conducted from virtually any site worldwide. That situation does increase vulnerability, however, by extending the command and control link and increasing the number of critical operations nodes.

As satellite orbits decrease in altitude, and increase in practical value, more satellites are required to maintain continuous global coverage. The Global Positioning Satellite (GPS) navigation system, which has an operational requirement for four satellites to be in view of any one point on the Earth at any given time (for accurate geolocation), requires 21 satellites to be precisely spaced in inclined semi-synchronous (12-hour) orbits at 24,000 km altitude. The Iridium commercial mobile communications network initially deployed a network of 66 satellites at 725 km altitude to ensure that at least one satellite is always in view.[20] The system offered state of the art global positioning and communications; the venture ultimately failed due not to technical problems, but to marketing failures.

The closer to the Earth, the more satellites are needed to provide continuous coverage. It is quite reasonable, however, to accept non-continuous or spot coverage of high-interest areas on a recurring basis. This is the function of intelligence-quality imaging satellites. These spacecraft can take higher detail pictures the closer they are to the target, a simple function of imaging resolution. The more detailed the picture, however, the less coverage of area (see Figure 3.13). Let us say, for example, that a camera can take a picture from

90 miles (145 km) altitude that would be so detailed as to distinguish facial features. The field of view would only be a few meters at best. The greater the detail, the less the field of view (think in terms of a variable zoom telephoto lens), and the more images needed to cover a large area. The more images there are, the more analysis is required.

Computer processing of raw data can speed the process, but it still requires a human analyst to interpret the images and make sense of the mass of incoming data. Hundreds of pictures can be generated in an hour from one imaging satellite, but it takes a human analyst several minutes (at least) to scan each image for useful or irregular information, even after the image has been

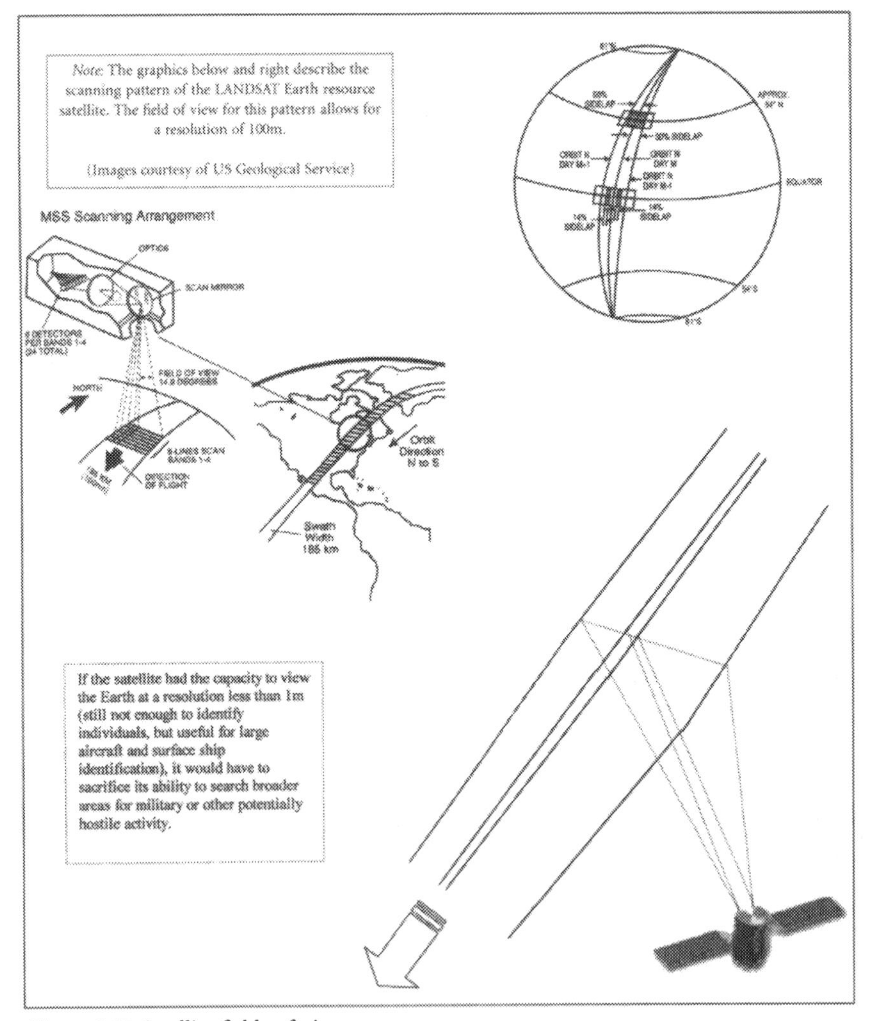

Figure 3.13: Satellite fields of view

machine processed and flagged for the same material. Once an image is identified as significant, it may take an analyst several hours to completely scan and correlate the information with other sources and to verify the intelligence accuracy on the image. For each imaging platform in orbit, hundreds of human analysts are necessary to fully exploit its capabilities.

This brings up a response to an interesting criticism of the intelligence community. With all its huge resources, why can't it find a specific individual (such as a dictator or an international terrorist) for targeting? If a license plate can be read from space (arguable, but an accepted assumption in order to respond to the question), why can't we find a particular person at a particular time with an imaging satellite (presumably so we could then launch a cruise missile at or dispatch an assassin to that location)?

The answer is relatively straightforward. The wider the field of view of the camera, the less detail in the image. The greatest detail, of course, comes from air-based platforms, to include aircraft and remotely piloted drones (they come physically closest to the target). These are also the most susceptible to enemy action, and the most obvious to the target. It is difficult to hide from a satellite that cannot be seen, much less shoot it down. In order to get an image resolution high enough to identify individuals and read license plates, the field of view can only be about 100 meters square (10 by 10 meters) or less. In order to point a camera so precisely, one has to know exactly for what one is looking.

Here is the problem. Saddam Hussein, for example, could be anywhere in Baghdad. At less than 6-inch resolution, not quite enough to identify someone through facial characteristics, it would be necessary to take over 16,000 pictures (with a field of view of 10m squared) to blanket the city. By the time analysts have had a chance to scan the pictures, even after machine processing, Hussein would be long gone. Essentially, one has to know where an individual *will be* in order to direct a space-based intelligence asset to look at that point at that precise moment. In other words, one needs intelligence to do intelligence. Electronic Intelligence (ELINT) collection satellites could possibly pinpoint a location, through an intercepted telephone conversation, say, and relay it to imaging satellite controllers in time to get a useful photograph, but that eventuality is based on luck. A reliable human agent (HUMINT) familiar with the dictator's schedule would provide much more time for satellite guidance and targeting preparation. High-tech imaging assets, then, are currently much better suited to real time identification of large equipment (airplanes, tanks, ships, industries, and infrastructure) and military units through broad area scans than individual persons. This is especially applicable to the traditional war scenarios against an enemy using modern equipment and tactics. Against guerrilla armies and non-traditional foes, which would be difficult to identify in wide-angle broad search techniques from space, and presuming communications for these groups does not enter into the electromagnetic spectrum, low-tech HUMINT may still be the most cost-effective instrument – if for nothing else than to key high-tech assets where and when to look.

This brief description has outlined only a few of the more salient astropolitical concepts. It is not an exhaustive list. The purpose is to combine sophisticated astronomical concepts with political theory in a manner that is heuristic. As space technology progresses, many of the above assertions will become dubious or even moot. New hypotheses will surface that have not yet been considered. However, the astropolitical dictum that control of certain terrestrial and outer-space locations will provide a distinct advantage in efficiency and will lead the controller to a dominant position in commercial and military power seems assured.

None of this analysis may matter if the ongoing moribund efforts to conquer space continue at their current lackluster pace. The likelihood of a golden age of space exploration seems remote given the current conditions. The following chapters veer away from the astropolitical model to describe the conditions and circumstances prompting the Cold War inspired entry of mankind into space. This compilation from the historical and legal record is used as the foundation of an argument to reinvigorate humanity's entry into outer space with a reintroduction of the motivator that began it all, national rivalry and self-interested competition. This time, however, the competition needs to be on an economic playing field, and not a nuclear war battlefield. If done properly, the tenets of *Astropolitik* can be invoked fruitfully.

NOTES

1. This chapter is adapted from my article, 'Geopolitics in the Space Age', *Journal of Strategic Studies*, Vol. 22 (Fall) 1999, pp. 83–106. Also included as a chapter in Colin Gray and Geoffrey Sloan (eds), *Geopolitics: Geography and Strategy* (London: Frank Cass, 1999), pp. 83–106.
2. J. Gottman, *Centre and Periphery* (Beverly Hills, CA: Sage, 1980), p. 1.
3. I am indebted to the many professionals at the Air Force Training Command's Joint Space Intelligence Operations Course (JSIOC) in Colorado Springs, who instructed me in orbital mechanics from 1986–90 when I took, and then had the opportunity to lecture in, their outstanding program.
4. T. Damon, *Introduction to Space: The Science of Spaceflight* (Malabar, FL: Orbit, 1989), pp. 180–2.
5. B. Smernoff, 'A Bold, Two-Track Strategy for Space', in U. Ra'anan and R. Pfaltzgraf (eds), *International Security Dimensions of Space* (Medfors, MA: Archon, 1984), pp. 17–31.
6. P. Stares, *Space and National Security* (Washington, DC: Brookings Institute, 1987), pp. 13–18. Stares presents a superior chronology of the process of space militarization in *The Militarization of Space: US Policy, 1954–1984* (Ithaca, NY: Cornell University Press, 1985).
7. For a more thorough exposition, see H. Herwig, '*Geopolitik:* Haushofer, Hitler, and Lebensraum', in Gray and Sloan (eds), *Geopolitics*, pp. 218–41.

8. Especially the case for Global Positioning Satellites, or Navstar/GPS. See M. Ripp, 'How Navstar Became Indispensable', *Air Force Magazine*, November (1993), pp. 46–9.
9. A. McLean, and F. Lovie, *Europe's Final Frontier: The Search for Security Through Space* (Commack, NY: Nova Science Publishers, 1997).
10. See T. Karras, *The New High Ground: Strategies and Weapons of Space Age Wars* (New York: Simon and Schuster, 1983).
11. A. Mahan, *The Influence of Seapower Upon History 1660–1783* (Boston, MA: Little Brown, 1890), p. 25.
12. M. Vaucher, 'Geographic Parameters for Military Doctrine in Space and the Defense of the Space-Based Enterprise', in Ra'anan and Pfaltzgraf (eds), *International Security*, p. 35. Vaucher's descriptive comes very close to the type of astropolitical analysis I am attempting here, and his work deserves extraordinary praise.
13. A. Wilson (ed.), *Interavia Spaceflight Directory* (Geneva: Interavia SA, 1989), p. 600. Formerly *Jane's Spaceflight Directory.*
14. NASA Web Site, 'Two Kinds of Separation in Space: Metric Distance vs Total Velocity Change (Δv)', *Space Settlements: A Design Study* (http://www-sci.nas.nasa.gov/Services/Education/SpaceSettlement/75SummerStudy/Table of Contents1.html).
15. Mahan, *Seapower, 1660–1783* (1890), p. 83.
16. G.H. Stine, *Confrontation in Space* (Englewood Cliffs, NJ: Prentice-Hall, 1981), pp. 58–9.
17. See D. Beason, 'What Are these Lagrange Points Anyway?', in J. Pournelle (ed.), *Cities in Space: The Endless Frontier*, Vol. III (New York: Ace, 1991), pp. 58–65.
18. The L-5 Society has since been absorbed into the National Space Society, where many of its former members are now primary officers.
19. Damon, *Spaceflight*, p. 40.
20. The Iridium constellation originally was to have 77 satellites, and was named after the 77th element on the Periodic Table. When the constellation was scaled back to 66 satellites at a slightly higher altitude, a name change to Dysprosium (Periodic Table element number 66) was not made, for aesthetic reasons.

4

Realist Visions: The Domination of Space

We, the United States of America, can be first. If we do not expend the thought, the effort, and the money required, then another and more progressive nation will. It will dominate space, *and it will dominate the world.*

James H. Doolittle (1959)[1]

Is the model of space presented in the preceding chapters a likely or even useful representation? Indeed, is it even plausible? The popular vision of the exploration of space, the image that captures public attention, is that of a cooperative effort by all humanity. It has certainly not been perceived in terms of the statist *Astropolitik* model, here associated with the harsh and competitive diplomatic doctrine of *Realpolitik*. But that latter mode undeniably was the vehicle that propelled mankind into space. Arguably, without the competition in space engendered by Cold War rivalry and latent geopolitical dictums, the world might still be in the space-flight development stage.

If a case for extending the long-established and powerfully explanatory geopolitical body of theoretical thought into the twenty-first century is to be made, then it must also be shown that at least some aspects of the geo/astropolitical paradigm have *already* been at work. For this reason, a condensed discussion of the most expansive period of space exploration in the brief history of space flight, the mid-Cold War period, is offered. As the story unfolds, it will become apparent that astro/geostrategic principles and *Realpolitik* diplomacy provided the impetus for spectacular outward expansion. In the process, a secondary set of tentative assumptions is derived from the theoretical and historical development of the model. These conjectures cluster around the hypothesis that without the re-establishment of a competitive, widely embraced, and recognizably astropolitical space regime (one that encourages space exploration on the basis of competition without confrontation), future growth in outer-space exploration is likely to be stunted. To help make the case, the rhetoric and reality of the Golden Age of Space Exploration is summarily described.

The rhetoric of harmony and cooperation that attends most popular accounts of humanity's entry into outer space simply belies the historical record. Despite an ongoing effort to make the cosmos an international commons (the so-called 'province of mankind'), expansion into near-Earth space came not as the accommodating effort of many nations joined as one, but rather as an integral component of an overall strategy applied by wary superstates attempting to ensure their political survival. The technique these combatants chose was classically Mackinderian. They established an international regime that ensured none of them could obtain an unanticipated advantage in space domination – for if any one nation did, the face of international politics might be changed forever.

Regimes are an important and evolving component of the post-World War II international environment, yet outside of academic political science they appear poorly understood. Stephen Krasner, who has done more to develop the notion and explain the relevance of regimes to the academic community, describes them as: 'Principles, norms, rules, and decision-making procedures around which actor expectations converge in a given issue area'.[2] The four characteristics are arrayed in a strict top-down hierarchy: 'Principles are beliefs of fact, causation, and rectitude. Norms are standards of behavior defined in terms of rights and obligations. Rules are specific prescriptions or proscriptions for action. Decision-making procedures are prevailing practices for making and implementing collective choice.'[3]

Straight to the point, regimes are perceived to structure extant political arrangements so as to enhance or facilitate negotiation, bargaining, and – ideally – cooperation. In this definition, regimes can be implicit or explicit, and the issue areas can be specified or limited. Krasner further notes the difference between regimes, which are intended to be lasting structures, and international agreements or treaties, which are *ad hoc*, often 'one-shot' deals. Over time, successful regimes can shape normative behavior through habituation. Expectations of future actions can be made predictable, and over time behavior changes.

Regimes are thus intended to be more than a substitute or expediency for short-term self-interest. They imply a continuing area of agreement and co-operation. Too commonly we mistake regimes for the functioning bodies and bureaucracies associated with them, and lose sight of the true regime as a process of cooperation. The World Trade Organization (WTO), for example, is not a regime. It is *part* of a regime, embodying the rules and decision-making procedures for structuring the international system along principles and norms associated with free-trade theory. For those who believe (in *principle*) that all states can gain from free trade, behavior should be guided by the *norm*, among several others, that tariffs and other trade barriers should be gradually reduced and ultimately eliminated. Within that mandate, the WTO is established. Moreover, since regimes by definition must encompass principles and norms, the utility function that is being maximized must embody some principle of obligation. The WTO is thus a set of rules and decision-making procedures established by a voluntary association of states working to make real the principles and norms of a liberal world free-trade system.

Likewise, the United Nations is not a regime in and of itself. It is the manifestation of a belief (*principle*) that national or individual state sovereignty can best be achieved through collective means (a permanent coalition opposed to aggression), structured within the *norms* of open negotiation and constant vigilance. Rules and decision-making procedures (international agreements and the physical presence of the United Nations as a negotiating, public forum) can be formulated in a variety of ways that comply with the extant principles and norms of a regime, and so changes or modifications in the agreements/institutions do not overturn – though they can seriously weaken – the regime itself. Changes in principles or norms, however, do require the acceptance or establishment of a new regime. Should the principle that all states are sovereign be revoked over time or by circumstances, the United Nations as an organization would crumble.

The regime for outer space as typified by international agreement and committee action has ostensibly been created on the overarching *principle* that space is the common heritage of all humankind, and on the *norms* that no nation should dominate there nor should large-scale military weaponry and activities take place there. These stated maxims have had the unfortunate effect of limiting post-Cold War space expansion, a theme to be taken up in detail in the next chapters. For now, the intent is simply to show how the apparently cooperative regime was constructed for the purpose of furthering competitive state policies.

The accepted rules and decision-making procedures of the contemporary outer space regime are summarily described in four multilateral treaties negotiated among the world's spacefaring nations through the diplomatic channels of the United Nations. These are the Outer Space Treaty (1967), UN Resolution 34/68 (1968), and the Conventions on Liability (1973) and Registration (1976) (described in full below, pp. 129–34).[4] Four additional agreements, the Limited Test Ban Treaty (1963), US/USSR ABM Treaty (1972), International Telecommunications Convention (1973), and the Convention on the Prohibition of Military or Other Hostile Use of Environmental Modification Techniques (1980), address military-specific concerns and complete the legal-institutional framework.[5] This arrangement is routinely hailed as a model of international accord. It is an extension of the most successful international agreements already in place, and has been a framework for subsequent treaties. Yet herein lies the paradox. The outer-space regime, widely recognized as the acme of global cooperation, is in fact the product of Cold War competition and national rivalry. How can this be, and if the argument is convincing, what difference does it make to the future of space exploration?

HISTORICAL PERSPECTIVE

Walter McDougall asserts that all the world's space programs were born of four great inventions: Britain's radar, Germany's ballistic rocket, and the United States' electronic computer and atomic bomb.[6] Not coincidentally, these inventions were the product of humankind's most destructive conflict – World War II. There is no embedded argument here that war or preparation for war somehow advances the spark of creativity. All of the *theoretical* work for these inventions had been accomplished well prior to the war. The simple truth is that it took the massive infusion of public monies and the national imperative for total victory that fueled that conflict to provide the format for their *practical* emergence. After the war, and although their potential utility for space exploration was evident to all who participated in the various programs, these inventions were not immediately applied to space applications, but instead to intercontinental ballistic missile (ICBM) development. The hot war was over and the Cold War was on.

The Soviet Union saw the need for ballistic missiles most keenly. The United States had acquired a dominant lead in atomic and nuclear weapons technology, evident with its four-year monopoly on atomic warheads from 1945 to 1949. More important from an early Cold War perspective, the United States also had deployed a large and effective strategic bomber delivery force with forward deployment at foreign bases situated so as to allow strikes deep within the Soviet Union, a capacity the Soviets simply could not match. Because of its technical lead in and heavy reliance on airborne strategic delivery capabilities in the late 1940s, with the exceptions of the Army's team of German V-2 missile scientists led by Werner von Braun and the Navy's low-priority Viking high-altitude research rocket program, there was nothing that could be termed a serious US space or missile effort.[7] In order to counter the US bomber threat and transcend the great distances that insulated North America from the rest of the modern world, the Soviets felt compelled to concentrate development efforts on an intercontinental rocket force.

What is more, because of their lag in warhead technology, the Soviets were determined to build massive rockets with the throw-weight necessary to transport their less advanced but much heavier yield nuclear arsenal to intercontinental range. Possession of atomic or nuclear weapons alone would not have been enough to bully the Americans if the United States did not believe the Soviets had a credible delivery capability.

In 1951, the United States began rethinking its reliance on air-breathing delivery systems. Phillip Klass identifies an Air Force-funded ICBM contract to Convair as including the first feasibility study recommending missiles as the primary delivery vehicle for the anticipated hydrogen bombs.[8] After six years of US threats, Soviet air defenses were becoming increasingly effective, and aircraft overflights correspondingly dangerous. It was only a matter of time before Soviet anti-aircraft technology would render the West's World War II-era bomber fleet obsolete. Pushing the decision along, in May of the same year, the US Atomic Energy Commission (AEC) validated the scientific feasibility of a hydrogen bomb. Just over two years later, the AEC announced the thermonuclear breakthrough. Laboratory tests indicated the latest bombs could be made small enough to permit a drastically reduced ICBM, and these smaller rocket requirements began to look increasingly attractive to the US military.[9]

When the Russians detonated their own thermonuclear device on 12 August 1953, just months after the US test, the Pentagon formed the Strategic Missiles Evaluation Committee (SMEC) to investigate the potential for ICBMs, given the new technology breakthroughs. In its first report in February 1954, this committee urged the fastest possible development of a strategic rocket program. Without an immediate and massive effort to secure an ICBM capability, the SMEC argued, the United States was in grave danger of being irreparably behind the Soviets by 1959–60.[10]

Despite the military and scientific communities' warnings, the Eisenhower administration refused to support priority development of ICBMs until 1955, when military intelligence confirmed that Soviet Intermediate Range Ballistic Missiles (IRBMs, up to 1,000 miles range) were operational, and that a longer-range missile would be deployed within a year.[11] This news was so disturbing that the National Security Council (NSC) recommended that the Air Force's Atlas rocket program be given the highest national priority. Even with immediate priority, most on the NSC believed the Russians would likely develop an operational ICBM two years before the United States, guaranteeing Soviet capacity for nuclear second strike operations. Such an outcome, if achieved, would strip the Eisenhower policy of Massive Retaliation for any Soviet transgression of much of its deterrence value.

Not that the doctrine of Massive Retaliation ever had much value as a practical deterrent. Eisenhower was a fiscal conservative who wanted to get the most bangs for the bucks the United States was spending on its nuclear arsenal. He also wanted to reign in the budget for conventional forces as much as possible. The doctrine of Massive Retaliation was his answer. He proposed that any transgression against the United States, no matter how slight, *might* be countered with massive nuclear punishment. The policy suffered from a lack of credibility so obvious that it eroded until it could not thwart egregious incursions, much less tiny ones. Would the United States truly risk global nuclear holocaust for a tiny incursion against its interests? In the end, the doctrine could not even deter the blockade of Berlin and the brutal suppression of Hungarian reforms that occurred under Eisenhower's watch. Still, Eisenhower clung to the policy, regarding himself as the master of political brinksmanship, uniquely qualified to pull it off.[12]

Eisenhower grudgingly agreed with the NSC's assessment in September 1955. The Atlas and Titan programs (from Martin Marietta) were given top national priority. In addition, two IRBM programs, Thor from Douglas Aircraft and a modified Redstone rocket called Jupiter from the Army's Von Braun team, were given the go-ahead for development. These shorter-range missiles were anticipated to be operational in advance of the heavier ICBMs, and if necessary could be deployed in Europe as a provisional measure to alleviate the looming 'missile gap'.[13] The truth behind the ominous Soviet 'gap', which took some time to develop, is an interesting story in itself, illuminating the power of international apprehension in domestic politics; to the extent that it existed at all by 1960, it was decidedly in favor of the United States. Nonetheless, the Democrats ran and won on the popular perception that the Soviets were far ahead in nuclear warheads and technology. In reality, the Soviets would not achieve parity until the mid-1960s. Interestingly, Vice-President Nixon, who knew the missile gap was not a fact but a projection, could not take that knowledge to the electorate because the sources of that information were classified. When Nixon did take office in 1968, the Soviet Union did in fact surpass the United States in both missiles and warheads. Nixon ultimately had to deal with the issue, but Kennedy never did.

It was this pattern of perceived military necessity shouldered for fear of the growing power of a potential enemy that ultimately drove the development of space programs. The same inventive breakthroughs that spurred development of the ICBM (radar for acquisition and guidance; heavy lift rocketry; electronic computers for precise targeting solutions, flight profiles, and earth modeling; and, of course, the atomic bomb) were found to have critical application to national space programs. The atomic weapon link is more obscure than the others, but it was indispensable to and spurred space programs for two reasons: (1) its enormous development and procurement expense, and (2) its wide-area destructive capability. Both factors made essential a long-distance delivery system that was virtually invulnerable to countermeasures. Although atomic-bomb-specific technology had little direct application to space development, it was the atomic weapon that provided the financial and military imperative for the procurement of rocket and satellite support systems.

As it turned out, the requisites for development of a successful intercontinental missile were in essence the same for development of a minimally competent space launch vehicle. The thrust capacity and sophisticated targeting and guidance systems required to place a heavy nuclear payload close to a target thousands of miles away are analogous to the capacities needed to place a satellite into precise orbit. Indeed, owing to the similarities of missile and space launch vehicle development, every successful national space launch program to date has its lineage based in a direct path to a ballistic missile development program. Virtually every early space launch vehicle was, and many current launchers are, simply adaptations of existing ICBMs. This holds for US, Soviet/Russian, British, French, Chinese, Italian, Indian, Brazilian, and Israeli efforts. Notable exceptions appear to be the Japanese and the European Space Agency (ESA), but even these can be found with a little effort to have adapted missile technology in their early space launch vehicle (SLV) designs. The Japanese, not having their own program, based their earliest SLVs on outdated US missile programs. The ESA adapted its Ariane SLVs on French and British SLVs, those in turn adapted from national ICBM programs.

Even though a missile development program puts a state on a path towards a space launch vehicle capacity, it does not guarantee that capacity. The reverse, however, constitutes a more powerful international declaration. A state that demonstrates a working space launch/orbital payload capability fully demonstrates the capability of an ICBM.[14] For this reason, many states have used the guise of developing a space launch capability when their true intention has been to develop an operational ICBM. In this manner, they skirt international sanctions in the transfer of ICBM technology, or at least paint for themselves a portrait of peaceful cohabitation with other states, via the acceptable pursuit of scientific – as to opposed to military – knowledge. Iraq and North Korea are clear examples. Both have modified Soviet medium-range SCUD ballistic missiles by adding a third (orbital boost) stage to the two-stage SCUD. Attempts by Iraq to place a small spacecraft in orbit using this vehicle failed in the late 1980s, and to date Iraq has not developed an intercontinental missile capability (confounded by international sanctions since Desert Shield). North Korea's efforts have been ongoing, and a 1999 launch of the No Dong SLV crossed the northern Japanese island of Honshu. The Koreans claimed they were testing a space launch vehicle for peaceful purposes.

By 1954, humankind's entry into space was no longer a question of if, but who would get there first, when, and how. McDougall reveals that Werner von Braun, working on the Army's advanced rocket program in Huntsville, Alabama, virtually begged to be allowed to use the Redstone (itself based on the German V-2 rocket design) to launch a satellite as soon as possible. In a 1954 report titled, 'A Minimum Satellite Vehicle', von Braun warned that the blow to US pride would be enormous if another nation successfully launched first. He requested just $100,000 to accomplish a satellite launch for the United States using existing facilities and technology.[15] The request was denied.

Not only was the hardware – via missile programs and facilities – available, the technical aspects of space flight and operations had long been accessible. Scientists and science-fiction writers, in 'a form of cultural anticipation', had conceived the theoretic framework and deduced the necessary mathematical equations.[16] For example, science-fiction writer Arthur C. Clarke wrote (tongue-in-cheek) in 'A Short Pre-History of Comsats, Or: How I Lost a

Billion Dollars in my Spare Time', that he 'gave away' the idea of geostationary orbit in a technical paper penned in 1945 for *Wireless World* magazine.[17] Everything, it seemed, that the scientists brought to fruition in the lab or on the drawing board, science-fiction writers including Jules Verne, H.G. Wells, Robert Heinlein, Isaac Asimov, and others, had already written about in marvelous detail a generation or more before.

Nor had the world's scientific 'rocketeers' been idle. The giants were Russia's Constantin Tsiolkovski and America's Robert Goddard, who pioneered rocket science; Germany's Werner von Braun, who led US efforts after World War II and is considered the father of the Saturn rockets; and Sergei Korolev, Stalin's chief designer and creator of Russia's massive, sturdy stable of dependable space launch vehicles. Though the evolution of Soviet rocketry is obscured by policies of deception and *maskirovka*,[18] making an accurate assessment of their historic capabilities difficult, von Braun may have been ready to build and launch a satellite aboard a modified V-2 as early as 1947. At any rate, by 1954, all the world's top rocket scientists declared themselves ready to place a satellite into orbit within six months.[19] Political considerations artificially constrained the initial deployment of the first satellite (outlined below), but when it finally came, it did so with a bang.

The launch of Sputnik on 4 October 1957 was 'truly a shot heard round the world'.[20] It 'acted as the starter's pistol in the Soviet–American race to place mankind on the moon', a race the United States would ultimately win.[21] Beyond that, it signaled the beginning of a race to build more missiles, more spacecraft, more weapons – in short, more of everything.[22] This was not the first salvo of the Cold War. Relations between Moscow and Washington had been steadily deteriorating. But as it cemented the notion that relations between the superpowers were accelerating from wary antagonism to all-out competition, Sputnik more crucially signaled to all the world that this new style of modern conflict had at stake more than just the classic balance of great powers. This new competition was different.

The space and arms races that began with the launch of Sputnik were destined to determine a global economic champion and establish the model of development for the world's emerging nation-states. This paradigm battle was clearly evident, and it acted as a catalyst to change two fundamental perceptions about the world. First, it now appeared to prove the Soviet contention that the command-economy model of the Soviet Union was superior to the US free-market model technologically. Economic superiority was touted as proof enough that the Soviets were also ahead socially and politically.

LIFE magazine, bellwether of the US mood in the late 1950s, stated flatly in its editorial pages that the national consensus was that the Russians had *caught and surpassed* the United States technologically – and would soon do so militarily and economically if the United States did not take immediate action. In an article titled 'Soviet Satellite Sends US Into a Tizzy', *LIFE* reported that, 'US rocket men were stunned. [They] could no longer deny the assertion of one Muscovite that, "America designs better automobile tailfins but we design the best intercontinental ballistic missiles and earth satellites."'[23] The following week, under the banner headline, 'The Feat That Shook the World', the editors harangued, 'It was becoming all too apparent Russian scientists were as good as any in the world – or better.'[24] Washington Senator Henry 'Scoop' Jackson was quoted: 'Russia has dealt a *devastating* blow to US prestige as the world's technological leader.'[25]

Even the US government expressed doubt. In their introductory note to National Security Council (NSC) Report 5814/1, issued 20 June 1958, the authors wrote, 'Perhaps the starkest [fact] which confront[s] the United States in the immediate and foreseeable future [is that] the USSR has surpassed the United States and the Free World in scientific and technological accomplishments in outer space.'[26] The event seemed to reaffirm the communist claim that the demise of capitalism was not only inevitable, but also imminent. It became the empirical basis for Soviet Premier Khrushchev's assertion at the United Nations, as he pounded his shoe emphatically on the table, that the Soviet Union would soon 'bury' the United States economically.

Second, and perhaps more important because it played upon the fundamental fears of modern humanity, the Sputnik launch brought home the realization that no person would ever again be safe from nuclear terror. *LIFE* amplified America's fears by stating, 'ominously, the launching seemed to prove that Russia's intercontinental ballistic missile is a perfected machine since it would take such a rocket to launch the satellite'.[27] The notion that 'Americans were settling into uneasy familiarity with the inarguable fact that Russia's moon was passing overhead four to six times a day' was presented in the context of an inevitable future confrontation, possibly even World War III.[28] Senator George Smathers is quoted in support: 'We can't afford to be second best; the stakes are our survival.'[29]

In fact, 'all hell broke loose'.[30] The technological and now apparent military superiority the Soviets were reveling in was more than just a slap to American pride (which it most painfully was). It was a direct and immediate menace broadcast with each successive orbit, on a precise 90-minute schedule. 'For the first time since 1814 the American homeland lay under direct foreign threat.'[31] The vast distances between continents were no longer a barrier. And what a perilous threat this was. Total nuclear devastation could happen to anyone, anytime, anywhere.

Truth be told, both these fundamental perceptions were in error. To maintain the race metaphor, the Soviets appeared to be comfortably in the lead, but the United States was just pacing itself. The United States was not behind the Soviet Union in any meaningful measure of national power, but it was politically and militarily imprudent to detail the many deficiencies of the Soviet system. In a cryptic comment to the press, however, Secretary of State

John Foster Dulles went so far as to suggest Sputnik would become 'Mr Khrushchev's boomerang'.[32] The Soviets began a race they were ill equipped to win. The shortcomings of their command economy were too many and too deep.

In retrospect, it seems Dulles was prescient. The misplaced perception that the Russians were broadly ahead may ultimately have cost them the Cold War. In the space race, Sputnik galvanized the US government and popular will at a level comparable to the Japanese bombing of Pearl Harbor 16 years earlier. Space was a race the United States could not afford to lose, and even the most technophobic isolationists reacted with patriotic fervor, ready now to sacrifice for the national interest. By 1969, the United States' true lead was evident in space. By 1989, it was equally plain in every other military, economic, and arguably social category, as the former Soviet Union suffered an ungracious demise. Even the scathing *LIFE* editorial, 'Common Sense and Sputnik', that followed the launch event, recognized this fact. Despite arguing that: 'It took [the Soviets just] four years to break our A-bomb monopoly[,] nine months to overtake our H-bomb[, and] now they are apparently ahead of us in intercontinental ballistic missiles', the editors warned that the Soviet Union was paying for its erstwhile supremacy on borrowed time and capital: 'The cost of this satellite is 40 years of deprivation by the Russian people ... Sputnik will not feed Khrushchev's subjects or cement the crumbling walls of his inhuman empire and irrational economic system.'[33]

As far as nuclear devastation was concerned, that fear had been overplayed, too – in one sense, because Americans had been for all intents and purposes vulnerable to atomic and nuclear violence since the bombing of Hiroshima, and from then on always would be. Knowledge cannot be unlearned, and when the destructive power of the atom had been unleashed, it could never be put back in the box.[34] In another, more sophisticated sense, the fears of global destruction were too arbitrary. The military value of nuclear power is optimally realized in the defensive/deterrence realm only, and then simply as a last resort. Its offensive power is equivocal. Why would the Soviet Union destroy the United States in a first-strike atomic attack? What would be left to occupy? Even if a winner could somehow be determined via a dismal and grisly body count in the millions, what kind of horrors would the victors inherit in the post-apocalyptic world? The result of the nuclear stalemate in the Cold War has been called the 'balance of terror' by some, and the *Pax Atomica* by others.[35] An uneasy peace resulted as neither side could find a profitable way to use the weapons they had spent billions to produce.

But they could transfer their national rivalries to the battle for ideological supremacy. In October of 1957, the United States appeared to be at a turning point in its history. The Soviet Union had just blasted away the barriers of science fiction by entering outer space, and popular opinion held that technical, military, and cultural subordination to the communist bloc might now be inescapable. The Soviets were first in space and looked prepared, with their presumed stockpile of huge *Vostock* launch vehicles, to dominate the newly breached region. US foreign policy had to meet the challenge of this enormous potential threat.

Thinly veiled public efforts at cooperation seemed to be the answer. Behind the scenes, American scientists worked obsessively to catch up to their antagonists, while US foreign policymakers were trying to convince or manipulate the Soviets into a public position of joint exploitation of outer space, as the aforementioned 'common heritage of all mankind'. If outward cooperation could not be achieved, military neutrality in space was vital. This new frontier, with its combat potential as the ultimate 'high ground', could provide any nation that dominated it with a crucial battlefield edge. In military jargon, space control could become a force multiplier. In geopolitical terms, it is recognized as a fundamental dictum that for any critical power factor a state cannot dominate; its highest priority should be to prevent domination of that factor by a potential enemy. An unflagging policy of global cooperation, in the view of the United States, should be outwardly (if somewhat disingenuously) pursued to deny such supremacy to any other nation.

It is impossible to aver that the whole of mankind's early efforts at space exploration were divisive and confrontational, if outwardly pacific. Truly cooperative efforts have emerged, if primarily at the epistemic community level of experts and technicians, and of space enthusiasts. If nothing else, through it all the space race has been a journey into a collective global consciousness.[36] The efforts of the superpowers brought humanity together through the opposing influences of a shared destiny and a mutual terror. Images of Earth, from a perspective that made it visible in its entirety, graphically portrayed the planet as a shared home. Melvin Kranzburg observed: 'Mankind's space programs have given visual content to what had previously been a vague abstraction: for the first time, everyone could see the earth whole, in its fragility and loneliness.'[37] Ecologic interconnectivity transcended national boundaries. The images were so powerful and compelling they monopolized the social propaganda of the era. The only politically correct perspectives of international relations in space were those dominated by terms such as 'common heritage' and 'province of mankind'. Space was an area to be shared by all peoples. By its very nature, no one person or state, nor group of persons or states, could lay claim to it.

The association of common ownership and fraternal exploitation do not entirely mitigate the competitive nature of society, however. Even where a common or social good is recognized as desirable, and the best means of achieving that good are publicly known, it remains unlikely that individuals will pursue the optimum acquisition of that good as desire for personal enrichment mathematically outweighs desire for group gain. While it is true that visions of humanity's common plight were popularized in the Space Age, they are not unique to it. The logic of a common heritage for space extends back into the legal traditions of antiquity, and the tragic failure of a truly cooperative regime to operate in such areas is a story perpetually retold.

RES COMMUNIS AND THE GLOBAL COMMONS

For those who would claim that subordination of individual goals to social ones typify humanity's entrance into space, the following description of the development of the space exploitation regime is offered as a refutation of that thesis. The theoretical enquiry requires an excursus into the nature of common, social, and public goods.

The institutional notions of common goods as we now understand them date back to Roman law and have been invoked as validation for a variety of competing viewpoints. Roman law held that certain resources were unsuited for ownership by individuals or governments, and they were so distinguished by the terms *res communis*, or a 'thing' (*res*) 'for everyone' (*communis*), and *res nullius*, or 'thing for no one'. *Res communis* was applied to the theoretically non-appropriable domains such as the air, sea, and sunshine – realms which could be jointly used, but which by their very nature dictated that no individual or state could stake a private claim upon them. *Res nullius*, by contrast, was exemplified by the perception of the birds and the fish. These resources were wild and free *in their natural state*, not subject to ownership until they had been extracted from nature and placed under the physical control of an individual. Under Roman law the concepts were distinct. By the dawn of the Space Age, the concepts *res nullius* and *res communis* had achieved an almost interchangeable status, one being freely substituted for the other, and the tenets of each being included in the descriptions of both. Walter McDougal distinguishes between *res nullius*, 'space as belonging to no one'; *res communis omnium*, 'space as the "heritage of all mankind"'; and *res commercium*, with space 'sovereignty and jurisdiction vested in the UN'.[38] Some authors also distinguish *res publicus*, or a thing 'open to all', while others incorrectly make no distinctions at all, for instance using the term *res nullius* exclusively to describe the classic state of the high seas prior to the 1958 and 1960 Law of the Seas Conventions.[39] The differences are more than semantic, however. *Res nullius naturaliter fit primi occupantis*, the ancient legal principle that a thing having no owner naturally belongs to the first finder, was to be problematic for applications to either public or private activities in outer space.[40]

The refinement of the international definitions of *res communis* and *res nullius* is an interesting case. Following the post-medieval rise of Europeans in world history, such internationalist jurists as Hugo Grotius and John Locke appropriated the concepts. Grotius concentrated his efforts on developing workable international laws for the unclaimed (and unclaimable) oceans.

Included among his many contributions was the notion of *innocent passage*: a concept that has been part and parcel of the freedom of the high seas customs for the last 500 years, and that had its philosophic foundation squarely in the Roman tradition of *res communis*.[41] Innocent passage held that any vessel, even military craft, had right of access to unmolested transit on the oceans (so long as no state of war existed between the nations involved, or intention to commit an act of war was pending).

For his part, Locke argued that the resources of the earth are by nature the communal property of mankind, since they are required by all for survival and are accessible to all who would possess them. Unlike the Roman *res nullius* concept, in which the resources belonged to no one, Locke insisted they belonged to all in the aggregate. However, once an individual had extracted the communal resources of the earth and 'admixed his labor to it', the thing became the private property of the laborer.[42] This alternative definition is distinct from but still complements the Roman notion of *res nullius*. It was here, nonetheless, that the old distinctions between *res nullius* and *res communis* became initially muddled. Defined terms of one overlapped the other. Freedom of access to the seas, for example, was fine so long as the resources therein were effectively *inexhaustible*.

By analogy, the sea was understood to be like the air one breathed: any individual could partake of it as much as he or she required and could never use it up, or use so much it was considered the detriment of others. This is, of course, the now classic two-part definition of common, public, or social goods as defined by Mancur Olson in *The Logic of Collective Action*.[43] In the case of the sea, and fishing in particular, the analogy became stressed. By the sixteenth century, extremely efficient mariners had the capacity to locally deplete existing resources to the detriment of latecomers. The solution offered by the dominant states – which to the less developed states of the day was no solution at all – was to *combine* the old Roman concepts. Since an aggregate definition (based on equal access for all, including innocent passage of military vessels, with absolute property rights assigned for *res nullius*-type resources extracted) was most advantageous to the premier seafaring states of the day (they had the most developed and efficient means to extract resources), and since those states could implement the policy with force if necessary, it was readily incorporated into the customary Law of the Sea. Scuttle and fishing rights, for example, were generally developed from this combined definition. From the sixteenth century through to today, *res communis* has traditionally been synonymous with freedom of the high seas.[44]

The logic of this modified definition of *res communis*, as it had been developed in the course of naval tradition, being officially applied to the realm of outer space was arguably reasonable. By analogy, space appeared to have more in common with the deep oceans than land or air, and in the 1950s the transition was acceptable to all potentially space-capable nations. The vast and untold resources of space would belong to those first finders who admixed their labor to the extraction thereof, and so the United States recommended that it be officially recognized and implemented by formal treaty in 1958.

The first protests against this standing definition of *res communis* came, not unexpectedly given Cold War antagonisms, from the Soviet Union – though for an unexpected reason. The communal definition of outer space, it was widely thought, *should* appeal to Soviet socialist sensibilities. For the communist traditionalists, however, *res communis* as it was now defined, was far too steeped in post-sixteenth-century capitalist heritage to be acceptable. The argument centered on the then-current communist doctrine of 'peaceful co-existence' versus the more traditional hard-line approach, which asserted that any capitalist-approved international law was by definition immoral, and therefore moot. Soviet law professor S.V. Molodstov argued:

> the sources of *res communis* are rooted in the teachings of Roman jurists on the law of property. They saw the bases for ownership in the thing itself, and ... deduced these bases from the character of the thing, and not from the relationships among people in the process of social production ... [in order] to justify the rule of exploiting the classes.[45]

The Lockean definition of ownership rights had by then transcended the old Roman criterion (that a thing's ownership was derived from its natural state or being), but the 'admixture' of labor principle described by Locke was still anathema to Molodstov because it conferred individual or private, not state, ownership. Failing to understand ownership as a social relationship between producers of wealth thus offers legal sanction to the exploitation of labor in capitalist commodity production.

Although Soviet traditionalists might have possessed the more consistent argument on ideological principle, Soviet reformers won the day, probably because they provided a better fit for Soviet national interest. Perhaps because the Soviets recognized that they themselves, like England before them on the seas in the heady days of empire, had a distinct advantage in the new realm of space under the capitalist definition of *res communis*. They were, after all, first on the scene and, in 1959, had an infrastructure (they believed) second to none. The perquisites that accrue to the first and most powerful (open exploitation and full profit) applied to them as well as to any capitalist government. No state could take better advantage of the West's *res communis* definition for national gain than they, and so the term as defined by the United States was formally accepted as a description of the status of outer space[46] – with this concession to the hard-liners: future negotiations would actively work to change the meaning of the term to make it consistent with contemporary socialist theory, specifically from a 'no-public-sovereignty' in outer space, to a 'no-private-property' provision.[47] The ultimate goal of the Soviets was to limit space exploration to the state, and to keep out private enterprise, which they feared would give the West a competitive edge. This ability to adhere to international convention when politically expedient was typical of the Soviet approach to foreign policy. To seek legal and policy principles associated with peaceful coexistence was not seen to be contrary to the actual disregard for international law (except in so far as that law furthered Soviet aims) propounded in standard socialist rhetoric.[48]

The next protest would come from the non-spacefaring nations, and is analogous to the protests of landlocked states when discussing exploitation of the oceans. As generally poorer and weaker members of the international community, states ill-equipped to develop a space program of their own naturally tended to decry the US–Soviet definition. Their argument was that since all humanity and therefore all states collectively 'owned' space (as the 'province of mankind'), all states should share equally in its bounty, *regardless of who admixes their labor.* In other words, the non-space-capable states expected an equal share of the profits, technologies, and resources from space development, without paying for or even participating in the effort of exploitation. In a shot to assuage the sensibilities of the increasingly vocal South, Brazil was allowed to insist on the inclusion of the provision in Article I of the 1967 Outer Space Treaty (OST) that requires all countries to share in the benefits of space 'irrespective of their degree of economic or scientific development'.[49] The fairness of the sharing was not further elaborated.

As profoundly unacceptable as the ratified concept of *res communis* was to Molodstov, this new definition caused a furor amongst the capitalist states. Concerned particularly with the Brazilian initiative, the concept was hotly debated in US Congressional Hearings on ratification of the OST. Senators Church and Gore repeatedly demanded assurances that the communications industry in particular was not subject to appropriation by developing countries under the Treaty definitions, and that the notion of common ownership was not in any way inferred.[50] Despite the equivocal wording of the Treaty, negotiators assured Congress that no participating nation had asked for equal shares of space resources dependent on their perceived needs, nor would the spacefaring nations have to turn over any percentage of the real profits of their ventures. Without these assurances, this seminal Treaty would not have been ratified.

The assurances since have rung hollow. The Less Developed Countries (LDCs, formerly called the 'Third World') have found the United Nations to be an excellent sounding board for their grievances, a forum that gives them disproportionate weight in international affairs relative to their economic and military strengths (though hardly relative to their populations). Through this medium, the LDCs were able to influence the draft of the 1979 Moon Treaty to include a new definition of *res communis* based on 'common *benefits*' for all. The Treaty states that 'equitable' – if not exactly equal – benefits shall be shared among all the nations of the Earth.[51] This definition is so problematic and antithetical to the Western contention that resources should become the property of the extracting state, that neither the United States nor any other spacefaring nation has ratified the Treaty, and future ratification seems unlikely.[52] Still, this new definition is gaining credibility, and has been partially implemented in the Treaty issued from the 1982 United Nations Convention on the Law of the Sea (UNCLOS III). The UNCLOS Treaty provides for high royalties and transfer technology from companies and states engaged in resource extraction from the deep sea beds so that all nations can benefit from the labor of a few.[53]

Roman law is not the sole basis for the popular notion of common property as it has been applied to space. Other significant precursors are evident. From British history, predating Roman occupation (though primarily from the period 200 years after the Norman Conquest in 1066 CE), comes the body of English Common Law, a heritage which was essential to the colonial experience of the United States and continues to influence contemporary US views of space law. Specifically, in England, *the commons* were local tracts of land set aside for use by all members of the community. From this localized communal heritage, the social concept of a common area or commons has increased in scope to include any area that is by its nature or by administrative decree for the use of all, including the atmosphere, the oceans, the Antarctic continent, wilderness areas, national parks, and outer space.

THE TRAGEDY OF THE COMMONS

The problems of *res communis* and the commons area stem from their joint use by all without restriction. Historically, common areas were so vast that their use was free and unregulated. Each could take from the commons all that he or she was able to. Unfortunately, as population pressure mounted, the resources of the commons began to deplete. Gradually, there was not enough where once there had been plenty. This description of the problem of the commons has been outlined in a famous article by Garret Hardin, the popular title of which, 'The Tragedy of the Commons', has been elevated in the social sciences to the stature of cliché.[54]

Hardin attempts to rebut Adam Smith's assertion that an 'invisible hand' acts to promote the common welfare in matters of community property. Smith's position, according to Hardin, was that if everyone does what is in his or her own best interest, in the aggregate everything will ultimately work out for the collective good. An individual 'who intends only his own gain [is] led by an invisible hand to promote ... the public interest'.[55] The logic was simple. If everyone in society tries to maximize his or her individual prosperity, over time the aggregate prosperity of the whole must increase. Of course, neither Smith nor his followers asserted this was invariably true, but, from a conceptual vantage in 1776, it no doubt seemed that nature would tend to seek an equitable balance in all things.

The rebuttal to Smith and the 'invisible hand' theory came in 1833, in a little-circulated pamphlet by amateur mathematician William Foster Lloyd. Hardin says it was Lloyd who coined the term 'tragedy of the commons' when he described a scenario in England in which all the members of a village shared a common pasture for their animals. In Lloyd's scenario, each individual (the 'rational herdsman', in modern parlance) seeks to maximize his or her own position by maximizing individual use of the common pasture. Explicitly each asks: 'What is the advantage to me of adding one more animal to my herd?' Since maintenance costs are stable on the common pasture, and the herdsman will receive all the benefit of the additional animal, this utility has a positive impact of nearly +1. The negative aspect is that the commons will be over-grazed, but all herdsmen who share the commons will share the loss. The negative utility to the individual herdsman who adds an animal is therefore only a fraction of –1, dependent on the number (x) of herdsmen (–1 divided by x).

Imagine that the commons is a pasture for cattle, and the value of each cow is based on weight. If the carrying capacity of the pasture is 100,000 lbs of cattle, and a grown cow weighs 1,000 lbs, then the pasture can sustain a herd of 100 cows. If there were 10 herdsmen, each would equitably have a personal herd of 10 cows. If the value of the cows is also based on weight, say £1 per lb, then each cow has a value of £1,000 and each herd a value of £10,000. If the rational herdsman adds one cow to his or her herd, making a herd of 11 cows, he or she alone would gain the entire value of the new cow, but would suffer only one-tenth the collective detriment of doing so. Remember that only 100 cows can efficiently graze on the pasture, based on its 100,000 lb carrying capacity. With 101 cows now grazing, the weight of all the cows would go down by approximately 0.01 per cent (1,000 lbs/101), or about 10 lbs each. With competition for grass keener, each cow now weighs about 990 lbs instead of its previous 1,000. Thus, the rational herdsman's 11 cows have a value of £10,890 (11 × 990) and the remaining 10-cow herds have an adjusted value of £9,900 (10 × 990).

The herdsman who has seen the value of his herd decline must rationally add one or more animals to make up for the loss, and the original profit maximizer will rationally counter by adding even more animals. Ultimately, rational herdsmen seeking to maximize their own gain will add so many animals to the common pasture that its carrying capacity will be destroyed, taking the herds and the prosperity of the herdsmen with it. This was all that Lloyd needed to explain the enclosure movement in Britain, and ultimately the urbanization of the country as herders squeezed out of their lands sought wages in industry. In time, the only way to save the commons was to destroy it. The pastures were subdivided and fenced off, so that a rational herdsman would gain 100 percent of both the advantage and the detriment of adding to the herd, and so would limit their assets to the carrying capacity of the land. It seems clear from this model that each individual attending solely to his or her own gain can *never* promote the public or common interest (when scarcity, not abundance, is presumed). Individuals are locked into a system that compels them to increase their individual herds to the ultimate demise of the community. They find themselves working harder and harder to obtain a diminishing rate of return from each animal, until suddenly the system collapses. Hardin laments: 'Ruin is the destination towards which all men rush.'[56]

Hardin's thesis is a rather bleak one. Humanity is prohibited from saving the commons through individual action, since, as men are natural maximizers (according to Hardin), 'it is mathematically impossible to maximize for two (or more) variables at the same time. This was clearly stated by von Neuman and Morganstern, but the principle is implicit in the theory of partial differential equations, dating back at least to D'Alembert (1717–1783).'[57] Because of these mathematical imperatives, we cannot expect technology to solve the problem of the commons; only artificial political organization and law can do so. The world is finite, and, without social restructuring, doomed to a dismal Malthusian future because of unchecked population growth and individual greed. Even the economic promise of an abundant new commons in outer space, he claims, will not alleviate this tragedy. Hardin implies that man in his natural state is simply not cooperative. He is an economic maximizer who will 'free ride' whenever the opportunity presents itself.

Since man is therefore incapable of self-regulation, the only solution is bureaucratic organization based in law. Government, with its monopoly on force and coercion, must step in and manage the commons for the benefit of all humankind. Friedrich Kratochwil points out that Hardin is guilty of a major policy oversight, as do most of his critics, by not exploring further the historical solution of dividing the commons into exclusive rights or private property zones: '...we can see how the assignment of such entitlements counteracts the fear generated by some types of generalized [prisoner's dilemma] situation, depicted in Hardin's "Tragedy of the Commons"'.[58] The failure to consider the logical approach comes from the assumption that common property is more desirable and just than private property, an assumption that is never challenged. This failure has impoverished the national space programs of Earth, and set them on an entropic course toward apathy and demise. I will return to the property solution, in Chapter 5, as a potential solution to the space exploration dilemma.

Beryl Crowe, in his response article, 'The Tragedy of the Commons Revisited', takes Hardin to task for some fundamental misconceptions. Crowe calls Hardin 'psychologically brave, but professionally foolhardy', in part because he offers an anti-technology message in a magazine devoted to technophiles, but mostly because of the failure to recognize the reality that natural and technical developmental factors have always moderated projections of gloom and doom. The 'population bomb' never detonated.[59] Oil reserves have not yet been depleted, although such was projected by far too many analysts. For example, Peter O'Dell and Kenneth Rosing as recently as 1980 predicted, based on mathematical models, the 'relative scarcity of oil after the mid-1980s'.[60] In a more excusable example, Harvey O'Connor predicted in 1962 that '*at the current rate of consumption*, ... the United States oil reserves would last until 1975, the Soviets' until 1990'.[61] More dramatically, copper, which in the early 1970s was to have become a precious metal through rarity, is now too cheap to justify most extractive mining methods. The telecommunications boom was supposed to have created such a need for copper that world reserves of the metal would soon be depleted. The advent of fiber optics and satellite communications has reduced the requirement for copper to such an extent that new estimates of reserves have grown to over 250 years.[62] It would certainly be a mistake to rely on technology to fix *any* misfortune the human condition can conceive, but to predict catastrophe based on straight-line projections of current growth rates is a flagrant analytical error. It can also be ultimately harmful to the analysts' position, fostering a type of rebound effect. When straight-line predictions inevitably fall short, public opinion generally hardens against conservation. When popular forecasts of doom based on catchphrases like the 'greenhouse effect' fail to materialize as predicted, these miscalculations will be cited as 'proof' by detractors that the problem is either unimportant or non-existent. Even Malthus, the father of population pressure doomsayers, believed that deer and humans were the only animals that would allow themselves to overpopulate to the detrimental collapse of their own species (a false assumption, but a widely believed and intriguing one).[63]

Crowe further argued that Hardin's solution, administrative management of the commons, was as problematic as free use. Since there is no 'monopoly of coercion'[64] in the international system – no 'common power to overawe' states, to draw from Thomas Hobbes – no single source of omnipotence focuses patterns of behavior in a selective manner. If such a monoply existed, a second and potentially more difficult problem is the one of reliance on the benevolence of the custodian (*Qui custodiet ipsos custodes?*, or 'who shall watch the watchers themselves?'). The essential nature of international relations and by extension the nationalist exploitation of outer space – that is to say, Hobbesian anarchy – is the realist justification for continuing confrontational power politics, despite the outward desire for mutual cooperation by virtually every state leader today.

Finally, while it may not be a miracle solution, technology can be a valuable tool in the battle against scarcity and the diminution of the commons, if nothing else, by monitoring the environmental impact of its use. Many of the problems of overgrazing and pollution are caused because a point of no return, or breakpoint, in the equilibrium of the commons ecosystem is reached before there is a clear recognition that a problem even exists. Unfortunately, the groups that tend to argue strongest for the preservation of international commons, the peace and ecology movements, have a tendency to view technology as part of the problem, and not as a major potential weapon for their cause. Daniel Deudney laments the failure of the various Green and peace movements in particular to seize a technologic initiative, 'in part due to their technophobic cultural values'.[65] The assets of space might be particularly suited to assisting in forming environmental policy. Multispectral imaging land resources satellites already contribute heavily to our knowledge of actual rainforest destruction, ocean warming, and ozone depletion.

Hence the debate over the use, regulation, and even the definition of the commons is at the philosophical root of outer-space regime development. The treaties describing the regime are based in notions of common property and equally distributed proceeds; reached, as I have already asserted, in an attempt to prevent distinct advantages going to potential enemies rather than as an altruistically cooperative effort to transform international relations. But the outer-space regime is not entirely without precedent. When attempting to draft and implement a regime, negotiating states looked toward past cooperative activities and existing regimes for reference and guidance. In the 1950s, those existing regimes were dominated by the transnational scientific efforts at exploration.

THE INTERNATIONAL GEOPHYSICAL YEAR AND THE FIRST SATELLITE

Where better to look for institutionalized cooperation than to the seekers of truth, to the epistemic communities of intensely impartial scientists? In part because of the commonality of its empirical nature – Kenneth Boulding has remarked that the periodical table of elements is the same in Russia as it is in the United States – and the often culturally transcendent character of its esoteric languages, physical and social scientists have a solid reputation for cooperation in the modern age that rises above the petty squabbles of diplomats and bureaucrats. At least, this is the perception on basic research. Scientific competition is as intense, secretive, and politicized as any other when it comes to breakthroughs, patent rights, and the prestige of the scientists involved. Yet more than just the ideological conviction of the scientific method is involved. Much of government policymaking today is dependent on the opinions and outlook of experts for projections and solutions to problems. No policymaker can be expected to be functionally knowledgeable on all international issues, from the inner workings of nuclear weapons and delivery systems to biological foundations for species preservation or disease prevention, or to complex protocol issues for treaty negotiation. For these reasons, scientific expertise and organization is relied upon to assist in the delicate negotiations between states, and scientists and epistemic communities are equivocally at the forefront of international cooperation.

It seems barely noteworthy, then, to acknowledge that the practical history of space flight began as part of the program for international scientific co-operation called the International Geophysical Year (or IGY, from July 1957 to December 1958). That is, until one delves into the fierce competition that drove this event. Dr James Van Allen, discoverer of the extensive and deadly bands of radiation around the earth that bear his name, and several of his colleagues conceived the IGY in 1950. It was envisioned as an extension of two previous international scientific cooperative efforts, the First and Second Polar Years (beginning in August 1882 and August 1932, respectively).[66] The two previous events were organized and carried out more by individuals than by governments, and were intended to provide both impetus to and attention on Arctic and Antarctic explorations.

Representatives of 66 countries, including about 60,000 scientists and technicians, participated in the IGY, and it was sincerely hoped that in following the lead of the preceding Polar Years, spectacular results could be achieved.[67] This was a significant majority of then-existing nations, and the organizers could be excused for thinking they had wrought an oasis of cooperation in the midst of Cold War entanglements. Even the People's Republic of China (PRC) initially participated, though it withdrew after a request by Taiwan to participate was granted.[68] This was but the first of a series of politicized confrontations that ultimately drove the event.

The objectives of the IGY included an outer space component because of a desire to study the upper atmosphere and solar–terrestrial relationships. For this reason, in 1954, four years after the original call for an international effort, scientists participating in the IGY Assembly in Rome recommended that an attempt be made to launch a small satellite in support of their goals.[69] Initial government responses from both the United States and Soviet Union had been unenthusiastic, but after officials of the IGY requested an attempt to be made to orbit a satellite, their interest was piqued.[70] The publicity and global popularity of the event could help spur space launch developments, and at the same time provide suitable cover for the underlying political and military needs both sought to gain from the conquest of space. After several studies confirmed the technical ability to do so, the United States announced on 29 July 1955 that it would try to launch a satellite during the IGY. Not to be outdone, the Soviet Union made a similar announcement the following day.[71]

This international event, the acme and future model of epistemic community cooperation intended to expand the frontiers of human knowledge, quickly degenerated into a global arena for international competition. According to Hugh Odishaw:

> Science itself became a peripheral consideration despite the language used in statements originating in both the Soviet Union and the United States. Perhaps government investments were too great to avoid capitalizing upon space feats, and the fact that only the United States and the Soviet Union had satellite capabilities heightened the competitive element.[72]

And this from Phillip Quigg:

> Although the IGY was conceived and directed by scientists and yielded rich returns in knowledge, the operation inevitably became politicized ... In the case of the United States, the National Security Council decided that the US effort would be second to none.[73]

Both the Soviet Union and the United States had concealed motives for planning a satellite launch during the IGY. The Soviet rationale was not difficult to fathom. The prestige of such an event would prove that the Soviet Union was a serious technologic competitor and a true superpower with hegemonic reach. Such public acknowledgment was sorely needed. Despite weekly reports touting the progress of Russian rockets, technical data from reentry studies, and medical tests on dogs launched to high altitudes, the Soviets suffered from severe credibility problems. Even when the Soviets published the planned operating frequency of Sputnik on 1 October, days before the historic launch, little attention was paid to them: '[I]t was just that few took them seriously'.[74] Along with the publicity and credibility, a launch during the international scientific event would present an image of the Soviet Union as a progressive and accommodating international partner.

On this side of the iron curtain, the United States' motives were at the time much more obscure, and were based on a need for strategic intelligence. In the 1950s, getting accurate information out of the Soviet Union was an extremely difficult endeavor. Eisenhower believed the tensions between the two states were based in part on the inability of either to accurately assess the other's military movements and stockpiles. He had already suggested a solution. International air law should be modified to permit 'innocent passage' of reconnaissance aircraft in order to gather vital information. The proposal was called 'open skies', and offered a reduction of international tension through the lessening of information asymmetry. In 1956, the United States was fixedly interested in Soviet ICBM progress, and so had commenced high-speed, high-altitude reconnaissance aircraft overflights of the Soviet Union. This action was extremely uncomfortable for the national policymakers, because it was in blatant disregard of international law.[75] Even so, the United States was willing to disregard convention because the potential value of the information was greater than the anticipated international outcry. Besides, the

Soviets could do nothing about it. Until 1960, when the Soviets shot down Gary Powers's U-2 spy plane with a surface-to-air missile, and airborne missions over the Soviet Union ended, the Americans were relatively safe in this mode of espionage. Still, the flights were clearly illegal under international law and never were intended to be a permanent solution for US intelligence needs. They were deemed operationally necessary at the time because of a dearth of alternative information on the subject. The long-term answer, according to RAND reports dating back to 1946, was satellite-based reconnaissance.[76]

For their part, the Soviets were unwilling to complain too strenuously – so long as the United States did not release the information they were collecting for public scrutiny. Despite what would become the clarion call of John F. Kennedy's victorious 1960 presidential campaign, that the Americans were woefully behind in the ever-widening 'missile gap', US military intelligence knew that the Russians were not as strong in atomic weaponry as their image portrayed. And the Soviets wanted to keep it that way.

To realize its long-term plans, the United States desperately wanted to have the prevailing notion of innocent passage as reflected in the law of the sea applied to outer space, and not to allow an upward extension of existing air law, in which territorial ownership extends upward, *usque ad coloeum* (as 'far as the sky'). By agreeing to launch a satellite as part of the cooperative IGY, it was hoped that the Soviets would not protest its inevitable overflight of their borders – a hope that could not be confirmed. The Soviets had long condemned any effort to pry beyond their borders, including the use of unmanned aircraft and balloons. The United States could not be sure of the Soviet reaction to their use of a satellite overflying their sovereign territory, but in the guise of an IGY event, as its purpose, there was hope the appropriate precedents could be established. As it turned out, the Soviets launched first. Initially, US policymakers were stunned, but their dismay soon turned to elation when they realized that the Soviet Union had unwittingly solved the overflight dilemma for them. It 'had no choice but to renounce its belief in unlimited "vertical sovereignty"'.[77] The Soviets had unwittingly placed themselves in a position where they could hardly argue the illegality of the trespass of their own Sputnik. Nonetheless, they managed to do so in backhanded fashion. Despite the fact that from the 1960s until its demise, the Soviet Union maintained by far the world's largest fleet of military satellites in orbit, it continued to publicly deplore the use of US espionage satellites, claiming they represented the aggressive, military use of space specifically prohibited under international space law. Their own satellites, they insisted, were of a peaceful, earth resource information gathering nature. Still, the inadvertent Soviet establishment of the principle of unimpeded overflight in outer space remains intact. 'Having argued necessarily for the legality of their [own] satellites, the Soviets had to deal with the hidden American agenda, the use of satellites for espionage and military support.'[78]

So advantageous did the launch of Sputnik ultimately become for the US space program that several analysts and commentators, including McDougall, have advanced the possibility that the Eisenhower administration and/or his top security advisors deliberately held back US progress on a satellite to *allow* the Soviets to launch first. The editor of Interavia's *Spaceflight Directory*, considered by many the bible of world space programs, claims that Werner von Braun was fully prepared to launch a satellite into orbit on a Redstone rocket in September 1957, fully a month before Sputnik.[79] Why an attempt was not made is unknown, but two reasons stand out. The first, already advanced, was that the Soviets would be unable to protest the overflights of US spy satellites and the dangerous U-2 overflights could be ended. The second is more far-fetched and has the ring of conspiratorial fantasy, but it is not implausible. Eisenhower and his advisors were undoubtedly aware of the public outcry that would ensue if the United States were not first in space. To the military strategists, such an outcry could be used much as Roosevelt turned the bombing of Pearl Harbor into a patriotic call for immediate and enthusiastic entry into World War II. In effect, Sputnik would be the public relations equivalent of a Pearl Harbor for the Cold War. The fact that it was not Eisenhower, but the Kennedy administration that called for the massive space build-up of the 1960s, certainly detracts from this theory.

The fevered superpower competition that appeared to find a safe outlet in space rivalry had reached a point where an international regime had to be enacted. Both sides had already compromised on and accepted the definitions of space commons that would anchor any recognized space regime, but the competition had only started. The specifics of the regime would have to come from legal precedent, and now the battle moved to which precedents were more advantageous to whom.

NOTES

1. My emphasis. Cited in the preface to Air Force Manual 6-1, *Military Space Doctrine* (Washington, DC: Department of the Air Force, 15 October 1982).
2. S. Krasner, 'Structural Causes and Regime Consequences', in S. Krasner (ed.), *International Regimes* (Ithaca, NY: Cornell University Press, 1983), p. 2.
3. Ibid.
4. See N. Goldman, *American Space Law: International and Domestic Issues* (Ames, IA: Iowa State University Press, 1988), p. 84, and D. Wadegoankar, *The Orbit of Space Law* (London: Stevens & Sons, 1984), p. 27.
5. 'Legal Principles Relevant to Military Activities in Outer Space', *Department of the Air Force* Office of the General Council, Memo dated 28 February 1994.
6. W. McDougall, ... *the Heavens and the Earth: A Political History of the Space Age* (New York: Basic Books, 1985), p. 6. This brief overview is no substitute for McDougall's book, which is still the best treatment of this subject.

7. D. Cox, *The Space Race: From Sputnik to Apollo, and Beyond* (New York: Chilton Books, 1962), pp. 40–1.
8. P. Klass, *Secret Sentries in Space* (New York: Random House, 1971), pp. 14–15.
9. C. Schichtle, *The National Space Program: From the Fifties into the Eighties* (Washington, DC: National Defense University Press, 1983), p. 41.
10. Klass, *Secret Sentries*, p. 16.
11. Schichtle, *The National Space Program*, p. 41.
12. For an excellent synopsis, see J. Gaddis, *The Long Peace: Inquiries into the History of the Cold War* (New York: Oxford University Press, 1987).
13. Schichtle, *The National Space Program*, p. 43.
14. See D. Deudney, 'Forging Missiles Into Spaceships', *World Policy Journal*, Vol. 11 (1983), p. 271.
15. McDougall, *...the Heavens and the Earth*, p. 119.
16. Ibid., p. 100.
17. T. Damon, *Introduction to Space: The Science of Spaceflight* (Malabar, FL: Orbit Books, 1989), p. 62.
18. Loosely translated, *maskirovka* means deception, but to intelligence professionals it has a much more subtle context. It includes the notions of misdirection and camouflage, all rolled into a tapestry of small lies. With *maskirovka*, just enough truth is revealed to lure the observer into a trap.
19. McDougall, *...the Heavens and the Earth*, pp. 20–62.
20. Harry Stine, a Martin Corporation executive quoted in *LIFE* magazine 21 October 1957, p. 35.
21. A. Wilson, *Interavia Spaceflight Directory* (Geneva, Switzerland: Interavia SA, 1989), p. 194.
22. R. Williamson, 'International Cooperation and Competition in Space', in D. Papp and J. McIntyre (eds), *International Space Policy: Legal, Economic, and Strategic Options for the Twentieth Century and Beyond* (New York: Quorum Books, 1985), p. 105.
23. 'Soviet Satellite Sends US Into a Tizzy', *LIFE*, 14 October 1957, pp. 34–5.
24. 'The Feat That Shook the World', *LIFE*, 21 October 1957, p. 21.
25. Ibid., p. 22. My emphasis.
26. Cited in P. Stares, *The Militarization of Space: US Policy, 1945–1984* (Ithaca, NY: Cornell University Press, 1985), p. 38.
27. 'Soviet Satellite', *LIFE*, 14 October 1947, p. 35.
28. 'The Feat', *LIFE*, 21 October 1957, p. 21.
29. Ibid.
30. McDougall, *...the Heavens and the Earth*, p. 132.
31. Ibid., p. 7.
32. Ibid., p. 295.
33. 'Common Sense and Sputnik', *LIFE*, 21 October 1957, p. 2.
34. J. Schell, *The Fate of the Earth* (New York: Alfred A. Knopf, 1982).
35. G. Snyder, 'The Balance of Power and the Balance of Terror', in P. Seabury (ed.), *The Balance of Terror* (San Francisco, CA: Chandler, 1965). The term *Pax Atomica* has now entered the common diplomatic discourse, see, for example, J. Duráo Barroso, 'The Transatlantic Partnership in the New European Security Context', *NATO Review* 9505-1 (Web edn), Vol. 43, No. 5 (September 1995), pp. 3–6; and M. Cioc, *Pax Atomica: The Nuclear Defense Debate in West Germany During the Adenauer Era* (New York: Columbia University Press, 1988).
36. George Hoover, US Navy Commander and veteran of Project Vanguard, the United States' first operational satellite, quoted in *LIFE* (27 October 1957, p. 22): 'I think this is the first step toward the unification of the peoples of the world, whether they know it or not.'

37. M. Kranzberg, 'The Top Line: Space as Man's New Frontier', in D. Papp and J. McIntyre (eds), *International Space Policy: Legal, Economic, and Strategic Options for the Twentieth Century and Beyond* (New York: Quorum Books, 1985), pp. 13–30. See also D. Deudney, *Whole Earth Security: A Geopolitics of Peace* (Washington, DC: World Watch Institute, 1983), p. 5.
38. McDougall, ...*the Heavens and the Earth*, p. 188.
39. The latter error is made by R. Keohane and J. Nye, *Power and Interdependence: World Politics in Transition* (Boston, MA: Little, Brown, and Company, 1977), p. 90.
40. J. Hickman and E. Dolman, 'Resurrecting the Space Age: A State-Centered Commentary on the Outer Space Regime', unpublished manuscript. Much of the legal interpretation and solution for the outer space regime is dependent on conversation and debate with Dr. Hickman.
41. Grotius's internationalism is expressed in Latin legal writings, foremost among them *De Jure Belli ac Pacis* (The Law of War and Peace). See C. Edwards, *Hugo Grotius, the Miracle of Holland: A Study in Political Thought* (Chicago, IL: Nelson-Hall, 1981), for an overview.
42. See W. Bluhm, *Theories of the Political System* (Englewood Cliffs, NJ: Prentice-Hall, 1971), p. 342; G. Robinson and H. White, *Envoys of Mankind: A Declaration of the First Principles for the Governance of Space Societies* (Washington, DC: Smithsonian Institution Press, 1985), p. 187; F. Thilly, *A History of Philosophy* (New York: Henry Holt, 1914), pp. 326–8; and G. Sabine, *A History of Political Theory* ([1937] New York: Henry Holt, 1950), pp. 526–9.
43. M. Olson, *The Logic of Collective Action: Public Goods and the Theory of Groups* (Cambridge, MA: Harvard University Press, 1965).
44. Robinson and White, *Envoys of Mankind*, p. 187.
45. Quoted in R. Crane, 'Soviet Attitude Toward International Space Law', *American Journal of International Law*. Cited in Robinson and White, *Envoys of Mankind*, p. 185. The referenced debate occurred during the Second Annual Meeting of the Soviet Association of International Law, February 1959.
46. McDougall, ...*the Heavens and the Earth*, p. 260.
47. Robinson and White, *Envoys of Mankind*, p. 191.
48. See H. Almond, 'Arms Control, International Law, and Outer Space', in U. Ra'anan and R. Pfaltzgraff (eds), *International Security Dimensions of Space* (Hamden, CT: Archon Books, 1984), pp. 221ff.
49. 'Statement by Ambassador Goldberg', in *Hearings Before the Committee on Foreign Relations*, United States Senate, 90th Congress, 1st Session, 7 March 1967 (Washington, DC: US Government Printing Office, 1967), p. 8.
50. Ibid., pp. 13, 28–30.
51. Article XI, paragraph 7(d), 1979 Moon Treaty. Reprinted in Goldman, *American Space Law*, pp. 217–25.
52. N. Goldman, 'Transition of Confusion in the Law', in Papp and McIntyre (eds), *International Space Policy*, p. 164.
53. Ibid.
54. G. Hardin, 'The Tragedy of the Commons', *Science* (13 December 1968), pp. 1243–8. The primary early challenge to this view was presented by B. Crowe, 'The Tragedy of the Commons Revisited', *Science* (28 November 1969), pp. 1103–7.
55. Hardin, 'Tragedy of the Commons', p. 1243.
56. Ibid., p. 1244.
57. Ibid., p. 1242.
58. F. Kratochwil, *Rules, Norms, and Decisions* (Cambridge: Cambridge University Press, 1989), p. 115.

59. P. Ehrlich, *The Population Bomb* (New York: Ballantine Books, 1968).
60. P. O'Dell and K. Rosing, *The Future of Oil: A Simulation of the Inter-Relationships of Resources, Reserves, and Use, 1980–2080* (New York: Archon, 1980), p. 23.
61. My emphasis. H. O'Connor, *World Crisis in Oil* (New York: Monthly Review Press, 1962), p. 271.
62. K. Boulding, *Human Betterment* (London: John Murray, 1985), p. 206.
63. T. Malthus, *An Essay on the Principles of Population* (1798) 6th edn (London: John Murray, 1826).
64. Crowe, 'Tragedy of the Commons Revisited', p. 152.
65. Deudney, 'Forging Missiles Into Spaceships', pp. 280–1.
66. D. Kash, *The Politics of Space Cooperation* (Englewood Cliffs, NJ: Prentice-Hall, 1967), p. 2.
67. A. Fruitkin, *International Cooperation in Space* (Englewood Cliffs, NJ: Prentice-Hall, 1965), p. 15.
68. Kash, *Politics of Space Cooperation*, p. 3.
69. H. Odishaw, *The Challenges of Space* (Chicago, IL: Chicago University Press, 1962), p. 110.
70. McDougall, *...the Heavens and the Earth*, pp. 59–60.
71. Ibid., p. 160.
72. Odishaw, *Challenges*, p. 111.
73. P. Quigg, 'Antarctica: The Continuing Experiment', *Foreign Policy Association Headline Series*, No. 273 (March–April 1985), p. 9.
74. McDougall, *...the Heavens and the Earth*, pp. 60–1.
75. Ibid., p. 117. 'Blatant violation of Soviet Air Space was a hit-or-miss means of espionage.'
76. Ibid., p. 113.
77. Ibid., 120.
78. Ibid.
79. Wilson, *Spaceflight Directory*, p. 194.

5

Shaping the Outer-Space Regime: Then and Now

The battle for national supremacy in space began in contentious diplomatic, legal, and scientific wrangling. These disputes were grounded in classical geopolitical imperatives. Still, the world needed a standardized and explicit regime. Common ground had to be reached in a political and commercial arena, the future value of which could only be widely speculated upon. Monitoring the activities of others was essential, to ensure that no potential antagonist could suddenly surge ahead in the technological and ideological battles sure to commence, if there were to be any hope that a future military confrontation could be contained. Reasonable expectations of future behavior had to be standardized if any rational diplomatic stance could be established.

The need for development of a written and explicit regime was patently evident, but the devil is in the details, and the first details were based on precedent. Specifically, what terrestrial precedents applied to the political and legal realms of outer space? More important, who would gain most from which applications and interpretations of those precedents?

AIR AND SEA LAW PRECEDENTS

Irvin White makes a compelling case for the evolution of space law from a basis in international sea and air traditions.[1] The formalized law of the sea, in fact, sets precedents for the bulk of international space law, with air law gaining an increasing share. Both bodies of international law originate in classic Roman law, sharing much of the logic of the previously discussed notion of common property, but there are significant differences in their institutionalization.[2] The bulk of air law, codified in the twentieth century in conjunction with rapid technological developments of the air, then jet plane, has developed primarily through bilateral treaties and multilateral conventions. Law of the sea, on the other hand, developed primarily by codifying existing customary and normative behaviors of seafaring states. The major classifications of issues common to sea, air, and space law are *delimitations, sovereignty, registration and liability,* and *innocent passage.* All are contentious.

Delimitations

The issue of delimitations is insufferably problematic for outer space. The question, simply put, is where does space begin? What defines the boundary of outer space? The points that land, sea, and air (essentially solid, liquid, and vapor) begin are clearly visible. Even in areas where they overlap, such as coastal regions and estuaries, they have been generally and readily definable. Yet no obvious natural geo/astropolitical barriers appear to exist for space. One of the primary complications involved in defining outer space lies in the curious international situation in which tangible benefits for any given definition are not yet unmistakably evident. We just do not know which of the many possible definitions of where space begins will advantage or disadvantage which states. Thus, states have preferred to set aside formal specifics until real value is determined.

This has left us with a working definition that may be murkier than no delineation at all. UN Ambassador Arthur J. Goldberg, US representative to the Outer Space Treaty Negotiations and advocate for ratification, testified before Congress that a strict definition of outer space was unnecessary. He was replying to a rather sarcastic question on the definition of outer space posed by Senator Hickenlooper, to wit, 'It just begins out yonder somewhere?' Goldberg replied, 'It reminds me of what my distinguished colleague on the Supreme Court, Potter Stewart – Justice Stewart – once said when wrestling with the question of what is obscene or pornographic. Justice Stewart said, "I can't define it, but I know it when I see it", and perhaps the same rule applies here. We know out yonder is outer space.'[3] Goldberg went on to point out that at the time of the Outer Space Treaty negotiations, a definition of what constitutes outer space was purposefully not discussed. This was because negotiators did not want the generally contentious issue to bog down the negotiations as a whole.[4]

Moreover, some analysts still maintain the notion that the boundary of space is of negligible importance, since aircraft and spacecraft operate in mutually exclusive arenas. Michael Allehurst states: 'The precise location of the point where air and space ends and outer space begins is uncertain but unimportant, because the minimum height at which an aircraft can fly is at least twice the maximum height at which aircraft can fly.'[5] Such an idea is increasingly primitive, as technology progressively blurs the distinction between the two realms. The planned National AeroSpace Plane (NASP), a horizontal takeoff and landing aircraft which will operate from SST class runways, will have the ability to enter orbital space from air space – taking passengers from New York to Tokyo in as little as 90 minutes.[6] The Germans and Japanese have similar aerospacecraft in the preproduction stage. The

1. Future Japanese lunar base (*Source*: courtesy of Japanese Space Agency NASDA)

2. Alfred Thayer Mahan
(*Source:* courtesy of United States Navy)

LGM-30 MINUTEMAN III LAUNCH

3. Nuclear triad
(*Source:* Minuteman III and B-2 courtesy of USAF; *Ohio* SSBN courtesy of the US Navy)

THE USS *OHIO* (SSBN 726)

B-2 SPIRIT STEALTH BOMBER

4. Japanese Space Launch Center Yoshinobu H-I Launch Complex, Osaki Range, Ranegashima Space Centre
(*Source:* courtesy of NASDA)

5. Kourou Space Launch facility ELA-3 Launch Complex at the ESA Space Launch Facility in Kourou, French Guiane.

(*Source:* photo courtesy of ESA)

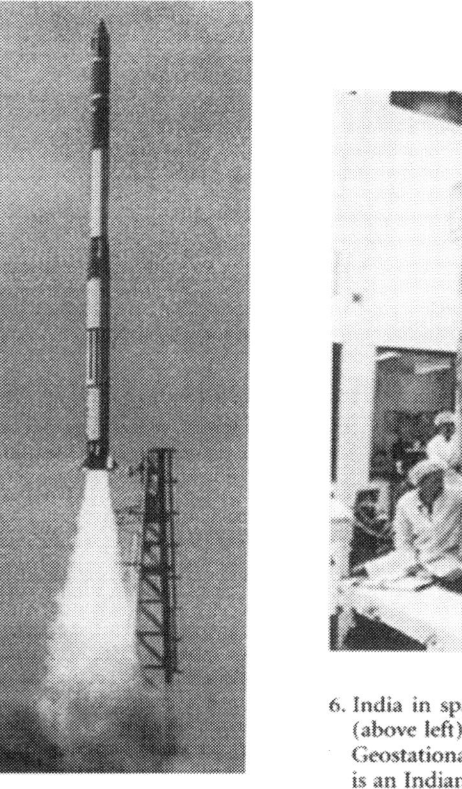

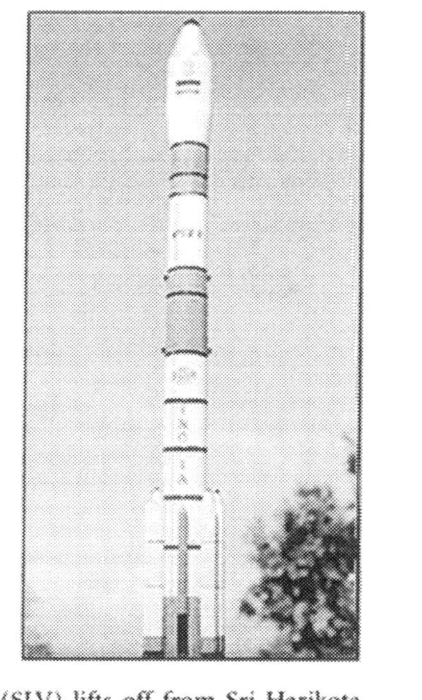

6. India in space. The first Indian Space Launch Vehicle (SLV) lifts off from Sri Harikota (above left). The third-generation Polar SLV (or PSLV, above right) will be followed by a Geostationary SLV (GSLV) capable of manned spaceflight operations. The satellite (center) is an Indian geostationary communications satellite, INSAT-1B
(*Source:* all photos courtesy of ISRO)

7. DSP satellite. Defense Support Program (DSP) satellites are part of North America's early warning system. From geosynchronous orbits, DSP satellites detect missile and space launches, and nuclear detonations. (*Source:* photo courtesy of Air Force Space Command)

8. Scud B short-range ballistic missile. *Note:* The Russian SS-lc Mod 1 (also called the SCUD B) is the most exported guided ballistic missile in the world. This is the platform that Iraq and North Korea have modified to create space launch vehicles (as a cover to extend the range of these missiles, no doubt, but also as legitimate efforts to acquire the ability to enter orbit). (*Source:* photo courtesy of US DoD)

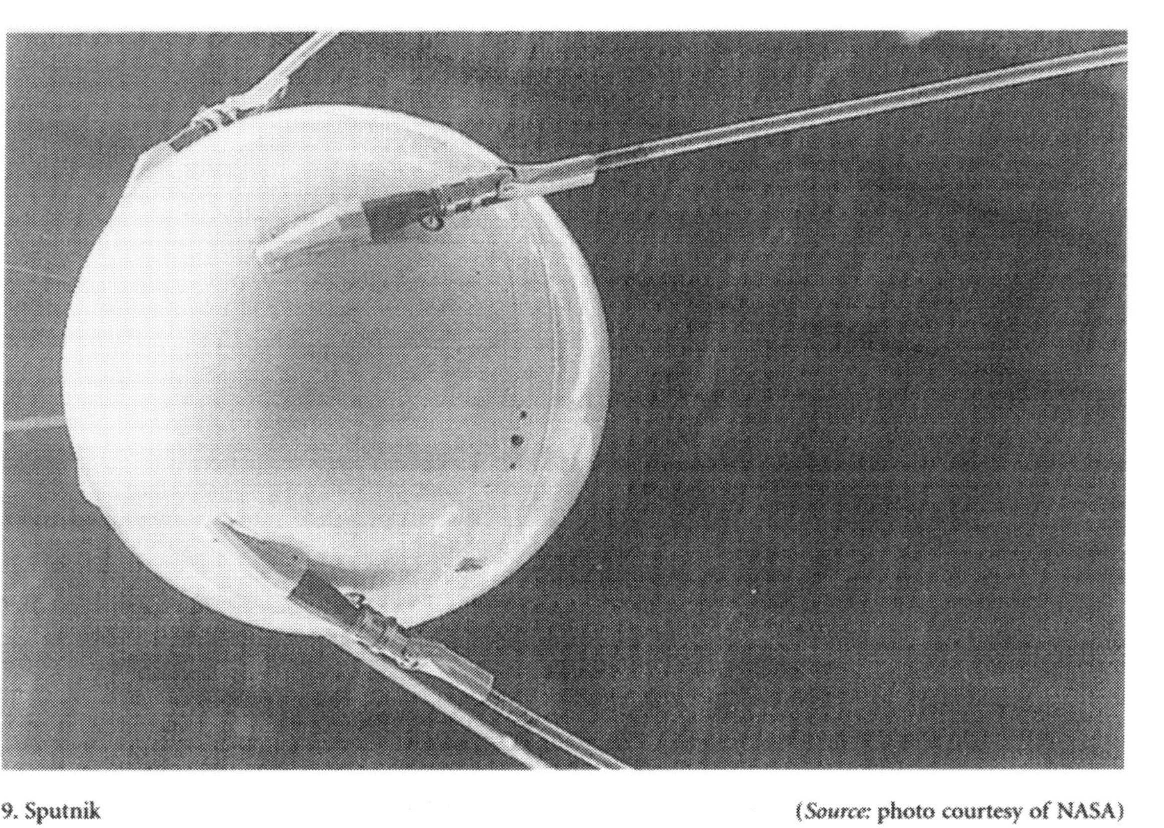

9. Sputnik (*Source*: photo courtesy of NASA)

10. A-Bomb and Sputnik hysteria.

Sputnik brought Cold War hysteria to a peak, as the Soviets demonstrated they could now directly attack the United States. Below is a family fallout shelter in Akron, Michigan.

(*Source*: courtesy of NARA, Records of the Defense Civil Preparedness Agency)

In the photo to the right, American troops march unprotected near an atomic explosion for 'Exercise Desert Rock,' Las Vegas, Nevada, 1 November 1951.

(*Source*: courtesy of NARA, Records of the Office of the Chief Signal Officer)

11. Yuri Gagarin.
Note: Yuri Gagarin became a Soviet and world hero as the first man in space with the launch of Vostok 1. The massive Soviet SLV was frightening.
(*Source:* images courtesy of NASA)

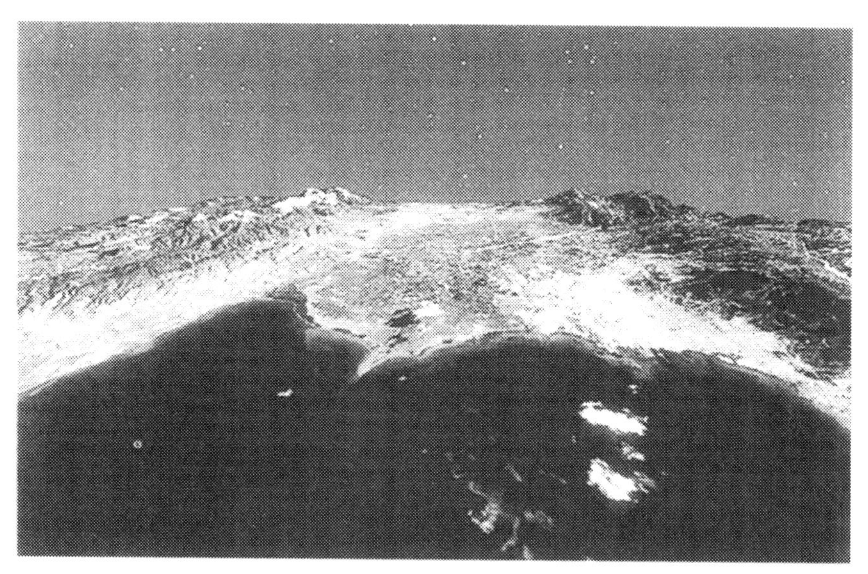

12. Satellite imagery.
Note: This view of Port Au Prince, Haiti, is a multispectral image created by Naval Space Command from a variety of military and commercial Earth resources satellite data.
(*Source:* courtesy of US Space Command)

13. HOPE-X. The HOPE-X (H-II Orbiting Plane – Experimental)

(*Source:* image courtesy of NASDA)

14. Symbolic claiming of the Moon (*Source:* courtesy of NASA)

15. Artist's conception of a future space colony. (*Source:* courtesy of NASA Ames)

16. Inhabiting space.
    Dandridge Cole proposed hollowing out asteroids for human habitats, and provided extensive details on the process. To the left is an artist's conception of a low-Earth space station constructed by robots.
    (*Source:* image courtesy of NASDA)

17. US Space Command Control Center.
    From inside the Cheyenne Mountain Complex, Space Control Center crews keep track of about 8,000 man-made objects orbiting the Earth including spacecraft, satellites, rocket bodies, and debris.
    (*Source:* photos courtesy of US Space Command)

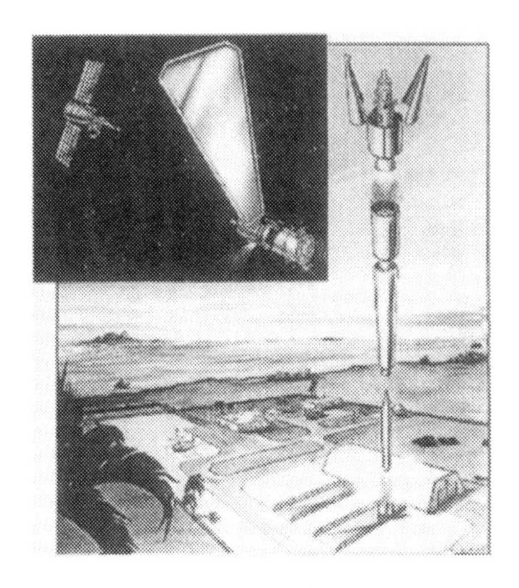

18. US and Russian ASAT programs. The US Army's Kinetic Energy Anti-Satellite (KE ASAT, left) interceptor uses a visible light optical seeker to track and engage a target in space. A multi-engine propulsion system positions the vehicle. A sail-like device unfolds shortly before impact to strike and disable the target satellite while holding space debris to a minimum.
(*Source:* courtesy of US Army Space and Missile Defense Command)

The Russians maintain the old Soviet Coorbital ASAT (right). This satellite assumes an orbit in proximity with its target and then detonates.
(*Source:* courtesy of DoD)

19. Patriot missile battery. (*Source:* image courtesy of US Air War College)

20. Space supremacy challengers: China.
A Chinese 'Long March' CZ-2 on pad and at launch at the Jiuquan space center in the Gobi Desert. The Chinese intend to use a variant of this launch vehicle for their manned space program (*Source:* courtesy of INPE)

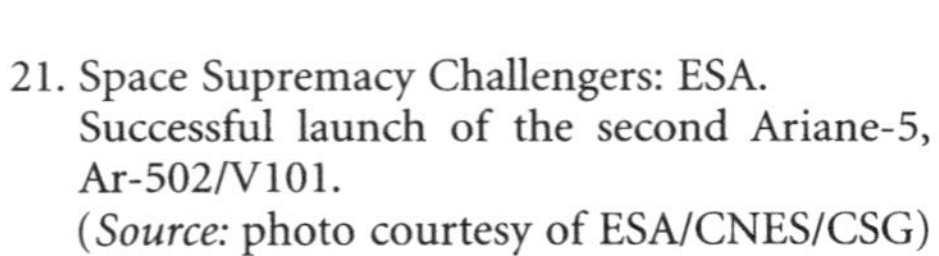

21. Space Supremacy Challengers: ESA. Successful launch of the second Ariane-5, Ar-502/V101. (*Source:* photo courtesy of ESA/CNES/CSG)

22. Space Supremacy Challengers: Japan. Heavy-lift prototype H-IIA Launch Vehicle GTV-1, at Tanegashima Launch Center. (*Source:* photo courtesy of NASDA)

23. Space Supremacy Challengers: Russia. Soviet-made Space Shuttle Buran ('snowstorm') on the Energiya heavy-lift launch vehicle. Baikonur Cosmodrome. (*Source:* photo courtesy of NASA)

German effort is called Horus-Sanger and is expected to be operational in the first part of this century. The Japanese craft, called HOPE, is anticipated for approximately the same time frame. Such planes may need to 'cruise' or glide to a landing from outer space for a distance up to 10,000 miles, crossing numerous national boundaries in the process. The US Space Shuttle already lands in this fashion, and several small satellite launch providers use boosters horizontally launched from the belly or wings of a modified passenger jet. When these vehicles become operational they will require an accepted and precise definition of air and space environments if, for nothing else, determinations of legal responsibility in cases including noise and environmental infringements. Given the inconsistency of international air law as it is applied worldwide (evident in the 1983 Soviet shooting down of Korean Air flight 007 that had wandered into restricted air space over Siberia), a definition of outer-space limits will be necessary to prevent misunderstandings and future catastrophes.

The approaches to delimitation of outer space are myriad, and include geophysical definitions, such as the upper limit of the 'atmosphere' (a difficult definition in itself, as it stretches from 20 to 20,000 miles, depending on the minimum particle-density criteria of atmosphere at different latitudes, times of day and year, and regions); meteorological criteria, including the altitude at which physical phenomena have no effect on the surface of the Earth (generally considered to be 40–50 miles, the limit of the mesosphere – though the ionosphere extends to 300 miles); the demarcation between 'aeronautics' and 'astronautics' (determined by the propulsion system of the transportation medium, already shown to be problematic in aerospacecraft that could conceivably use both); multioperational regional definitions including 'neutral' or 'contiguous zones', low and high-Earth orbit, etc.; any area beyond the 'effective control' of the expanse above terrestrial territory; the point where the gravitational pull of the Earth is no longer measurable; the minimum altitude at which space records ('firsts') can be counted (62 miles, agreed to by the United States and Soviet Union at the 4 October 1960 meeting of the International Aeronautics Federation; the lowest orbital altitude, or perigee, of a satellite; and finally, an arbitrary demarcation established for a fixed period of time or subject to periodic review.[7]

The two most prevalent approaches for defining outer space have been spatial and functional. The spatial approach explains that space begins just below the lowest point at which an object can be maintained in orbit. This has also been called the 'Karman primary jurisdiction line', the point at which aerodynamic flight ends and centrifugal forces take over, about 52 miles (named after Theodore Von Karman, its postulator). This seems to be the most likely candidate for ultimate implementation, as it is currently the most precise. The functional approach is based on the propulsion systems of the air/spacecraft and is legally based in the 1919 and 1944 International Air

Conventions, which defined aircraft as 'any machine that can derive support from reactions of the air'.[8] Under this definition, space begins just beyond the maximum height at which aerodynamic flight is possible. Objections raised by the use of aerospacecraft have already been presented. A combination spatial/functional definition may be possible, but both probably cannot be used simultaneously. To do so would leave a 'no man's land' or undefined region between the lowest satellite orbit and the highest air flight path. Of course, a third option exists. This dark-horse candidate proposes air and space law combine and become indistinguishable – in other words, free overflight by any air or spacecraft – the unlimited right of innocent passage. For this to happen, states would have to retreat from their current stance on sovereignty and place some of their security needs in the hands of some form of global federation of states, perhaps even an expanded-authority United Nations. The idea is neither new nor completely preposterous. In 1963, the eminent political scientist Karl Deutsch, attempting to project possible futures for outer space 25 years hence, suggested 'a possible way out of the dilemma' of ever more deadly space competition based on nationalist tendencies would be 'to explore the possibilities for establishing limitations of sovereignty, including mutual concessions of the right to overflights, inspection, and joint agencies operating by majority rule'.[9] As already mentioned, 'open skies', a policy in which aircraft overflights by any country would be allowed in peacetime (given a minimum advance notice and flight plan), has been a long-standing goal of the United States. In November 1991, Russia for the first time agreed in principle to the idea, and moderate success has been achieved between the two former superpower antagonists. Global implementation, however, remains to be seen. Moreover, as we shall see next, air space remains in place above national boundaries, outer space does not.

Sovereignty

One would tend to think that the precedence for outer space delimitation should be analogous to air law, a simple upward extension. In fact, for this application, air law is virtually useless in the environment of outer space. The farther 'out' one goes, the more difficult it becomes to determine what is above any given point on the earth. The current air regime asserts 'every state has complete and exclusive sovereignty over the air space above its territory'.[10] This right stems from the 1919 Paris Convention, which 'provided that every state had complete and exclusive authority over its superadjacent air space'.[11] The Paris Convention was confirmed during World War II at the 1944 Chicago Convention on International Civil Aviation. At the time, there seemed to be no reason – at least no technical imperative – to establish an upper limit for air space.[12]

In all these early decisions, the right of air space jurisdiction is ultimately based in the Roman legal custom of *cujus est solum, ejus est usque ad coleum*

('Who owns the land owns it up to the sky').[13] This definition of air space is acceptable for aircraft, since, due to gravity and the relatively small altitudes concerned, the air space above the earth can be monitored and controlled. It can be possessed. There is a legally important distinction here: the air is not susceptible to sovereignty, but the air space is. Outer space does not appear to have such legally definable advantages. In the air, 'what goes up must come down'. In space, up and down is relative. Most important, the space in outer space above a territory is not stable. Due to the rotation of the Earth, it is not constant. With one critical exception, claims of sovereignty based in air law are highly problematic.

Unlike air space, which historically has had a starkly enclosed definition, the boundaries of which extend upward from the center of the earth through politically drawn terrestrial boundaries, the sea has traditionally been divided into territorial, contiguous, and open subregions. Prior to 1958, the limit of territorial seas had been generally recognized as between 3 and 12 miles. The International Conventions on the Law of Sea of 1958 and 1960 were unable to formalize a universal legal limit for territorial or contiguous seas, or for high seas, although the characteristics of each of the regions were defined. Article I of the Conventions states 'the high seas are defined as all waters beyond the territorial sea' – even though the limits of the territorial sea could not then be agreed upon. This proved to be an obliquely useful working precedent for the outer-space regime. Legal descriptions and universal agreements were established despite the absence of a working definition of the limits of space. Like the sea, outer space can be divided into subregions, usually defined by their distance from the earth. These distinctions, described in astropolitical terms, include near-Earth and geostationary space, cislunar and translunar space, deep space, etc., and are usually put forward by military or nationalist supporters who wish to derive maximum control of the commons for the benefit of their constituencies. In a stylized modern analogy to the tragedy of the commons illustration, this is comparable to use and possession by the 'rational herdsmen' of commons outer space. A preference for maximum state gain with losses (if any) distributed equally among all states.

Despite the zero-sum nature of negotiations that follow, precedents for the division of space into distinct regions with concise boundaries and definitions of sovereignty have been set by formal treaty. Generally speaking, the working delimitation and legal characteristics of outer space were extracted from a combination of air and sea law precedents. If a single example of direct precedence exists, it is probably in the body of law describing air activities above the open or high seas. In this combined or overlap realm, aircraft of all nations observe a convention of 'joint use rights' or common use provisions detailed in both sea and air conventions.[14]

In astropolitical or *Astropolitik* terms, the only definition of sovereign space that may truly matter is one that incorporates the notion of a region that can be effectively defended. This definition is regularly trotted out for display and then roundly criticized by the civilized communities of scientific researchers and progressive ideologues before being placed back in its pen, and has not been seriously considered. This proposition dates from the seventeenth-century writings of Samuel von Pufendorf, commenting on the Roman principle of *usque ad coloeum*. It continues to the formula of the 1885 Berlin Conference, which set the limit of air space control 'upward into space as far as the scientific programs of any state ... permits such state to control it'.[15] Sovereign territory is defined, under this scheme, as that region within which a state has the power to make its laws effective to the exclusion of all other states.[16] The tradition in this line of reason extended from sea law, in which territorial seas were initially limited to 3 miles, the distance a land-based cannon could effectively fire on hostile fleets, thereby protecting the sovereignty of coastal seas from intrusion. As coastal batteries became more sophisticated, the standard limit was stretched to 6 then to 12 miles. In an age of shore-to-ship missiles, some nations have claimed a territorial ocean limit up to 200 miles, the current limit of a state's Exclusive Economic Zone (EEZ).

The effective-control definition is not so preposterous to modern sensibilities as one might think. Some US policymakers claimed that justification for U-2 reconnaissance aircraft operations over the Soviet Union and other communist states was implicit, because they were beyond the reach of anti-aircraft weaponry. Senator Eugene McCarthy asked Secretary of State Dean Rusk if this very justification had been put forward to the Soviets. Not seriously, was the reply.[17] Of course, when the Soviets shot down Gary Powers with a ground-to-air missile in 1960, this definition lost popularity in the United States.

Registration and liability

The Convention on the Law of the Sea requires that each nation maintain a registry of ships, but allows individual nations to apply their own rules and regulations for registration, safety, and the like.[18] In contrast to sea law, aircraft have the additional requirement of *holding* the nationality of the state in which they are registered.[19] This requirement suggests a stronger link between the state and responsibility, or liability, for the actions of aircraft registered to them. It also allows greater flexibility in preparing, implementing, and enforcing international health and safety standards.

The need to establish responsibility in outer space was apparent by 1960, when debris from a US Transit navigation satellite was deliberately destroyed after an awry launch and subsequently landed in a (fortunately) uninhabited region of eastern Cuba.[20] In that instance, the onus was clearly on the United States. Since Cuban–American relations were at a significant low point, an immediate precedent for cooperation could not be established. Worthy of note, and appropriate to this analysis, the most spectacular instance of international space liability came in 1978, when the Soviet nuclear-powered intelligence collection satellite, Cosmos 954, unintentionally de-orbited, spewing radioactive waste over a significant region of northern Canada. Under the provisions of the outer-space regime then in place, the Soviet Union (under considerable duress) acceded to full responsibility and agreed to pay for all damages.[21] The financial amount of the damages was no doubt the source of that duress, given the USSR's lack of hard currency at the time, but the necessity for maintaining state secrets regarding satellite nuclear propulsion technology forced their hand. They wasted no time in asserting their clean-up responsibilities and dispatching a team to the frozen regions to retrieve potentially sensitive space reactor and guidance technology.

The requirements for registration of objects in space are stricter than those for sea or air, with the justification that such registration is necessary because of the greater potential for global physical and/or environmental damage. A further question on liability rises from the problem of national launch systems carrying foreign payloads into orbit. This issue goes beyond the simple carrying of cargo analogous to air and sea operations. Once the launching platform releases the satellite, the satellite may no longer be under the control of the launching nation. Upper-stage separations and ignitions, and all on-orbit activities are quite routinely handled from control facilities in various international locations. The launch nation may, after satellite separation, have no more legal or moral obligation for subsequent damage by the satellite – though unquestionably for the first and second-stage rocket bodies. The point of liability transfer, or overlap if there is any, must be determined. One can imagine severe legal bickering over whether the satellite-caused damages were the fault of the launching state or the controlling one.

The most compelling reason for registration of spacecraft, according to policymakers, is to enhance national security. In reference to the 1967 Outer Space Treaty ratification, UN Ambassador Arthur Goldberg stated: 'This is a matter of national security. We believe that when there is registration of launchings this gives us an opportunity to, and the world community to, check up on whether the launchings are, indeed, peaceful or whether they are for some other purposes.'[22] The registration issue is thus intrinsically tied to the extant regime's insistence on the use of outer space for 'peaceful purposes' only.

Innocent passage

The definition of innocent passage for sea areas states that passage is innocent so long as it is not prejudicial to the peace, good order, or security of the coastal state. Unlike registration and liability, in which requirements are progressively stricter for sea, then air, then space regimes, the definitions for innocent passage do not adhere to such a historically linear pattern of control. Innocent passage on the seas is far less strict than the air regime, and the space regime is the least constrained of all. Innocent passage on the oceans, for example, allows for photographic and other reconnaissance activities in certain instances, and the former Soviet Union employed a fleet of so-called fishing trawlers equipped with sophisticated radar and electronic surveillance equipment close to US and NATO shores. The lax provisions of sea law also assisted the secretive Soviet space program in its ability to monitor and control spacecraft globally. When land-based territory was either unavailable or militarily unsecure, the Soviets dispatched a fleet of space surveillance and control ships to collect space and other data and information worldwide. The historic establishment of the role of innocent passage in outer space has already been discussed.

Explicitly accounted for in the 1919 Paris Convention and in Article V of the 1944 Chicago Convention, 'a provision is made for the right of innocent passage by aircraft *not engaged* in scheduled international air services' (emphasis added).[23] Since it had wandered off its scheduled international flight path, this curious stipulation gave the Soviet Union the legal (if not moral) right to shoot down Korean Air Liner flight 007 in 1983. In addition, the Chicago Convention includes provisions against overflights by 'pilotless aircraft', the allowance for the establishment of military or safety related prohibited or no-fly zones; and that states 'may prohibit or regulate the use of photographic apparatus in aircraft above its territory'.[24] These limitations had potentially extreme ramifications for the overflight of spacecraft. If air and not sea law conventions had been accepted, the Soviet Union and others would have had a stronger case against the United States' use of intelligence collection spacecraft. Even so, the Soviet Union routinely denounced the US reconnaissance satellite efforts (while denying that their own, more extensive space reconnaissance program even existed[25]), in part because of these existing international air law conventions.

Air and sea law precedents, that seem intuitively to be the proper point of reference for forming space law, are not the only foundations of the current international space regime. Previously established multilateral treaties also became an important source. The reason is simple facility. Where international treaties already exist, diplomats can accept already negotiated and accepted principles as the basis and point of departure for a new agreement. Time and effort are saved, and consistency is more likely.

THE ANTARCTIC TREATY

It may seem odd, if not completely arbitrary, to include the international Antarctic treaty as a formal antecedent of the Outer Space Treaty, but the analogy is really quite keen. Antarctica is a vast and desolate place, inhospitable to human habitation, and at least equivocal in its potential for future economic gain. No one knows the eventual resource potential of this huge continent. It is, in these respects, quite similar to outer space. Yet in direct comparison to outer space, it is a 'veritable Garden of Eden'.[26] The evolution of the Antarctic regime is, like outer space, steeped in the history of the International Geophysical Year (IGY). It is the history of international cooperation spurred by national competition. Of the 12 nations that participated in the Antarctic portion of the IGY, seven had preexisting claims of sovereignty on the continent.[27] These countries were (and remain today) Argentina, Australia, Britain, Chile, France, New Zealand, and Norway. Three of these claimants – Argentina, Chile, and Britain – have overlapping claims. The five additional participating nations that have no *official* claims and do not recognize the claims of the others are Belgium, Japan, South Africa, the United States, and Russia (as the former USSR). Even so, these states have for the most part gone through the necessary and traditional prerequisites of claimant states without formally declaring their intentions. The United States, for example, has some of the strongest legal claims in the region, based on early expeditions of discovery by Wilkes, Byrd, and Ellsworth, but has refrained from taking any formal claims action.

Various traditional justifications for claiming territory on the continent have been cited. The strongest under international law is effective occupation (requiring sustained manning). Should the United States ever decide a formal claim declaration is in its best interests, it may have the strongest case based on just this criterion. Its Amundsen-Scott base at the South Pole has been continuously occupied since 1957.[28] Other strong cases could be made for Britain's primacy claim (based on first discovery and occupation); the contingency (or geographical affinity) claims of Argentina, Chile, and South Africa; the further historical claims of Argentina and Chile based on their position as heirs to the former Spanish Empire; and Pan-American primacy based on the Monroe Doctrine (certain European-claimed regions of Antarctica are, after all, in the Western Hemisphere). The most pervasively recognized method of sovereignty claim has been used by all seven claimant states and several non-claimant states wishing to keep their options open. This is called 'symbolic claiming', the mechanics of which include leaving flags and named plaques, establishing post offices and issuing stamps, assigning civil servant staffs, and other symbolic gestures of the claiming nation on the territory in question.

This discussion of sovereignty claims in Antarctica demonstrates the affinity this continent's history has for outer space. Many of the nations that have entered or are contemplating entering the outer-space environment have already gone through the motions of staking claims to outer-space territory. By 1967, both the Americans and the Soviets had 'planted the flags' on the moon, and in the same manner split claims on Venus (Soviet Union) and Mars (United States).[29] The first Soviet moon shot carried symbolic claiming essentials in its nosecone, numerous objects inscribed with the hammer and sickle and the letters 'CCCP', even though they insisted that they would never assert a territorial claim.[30] This was followed by a photographic expedition to the far side of the Moon. Shortly thereafter, the Soviets released a map in which they invoked the ancient right of discoverers by unilaterally naming the prominent features (in Russian, of course, not Latin), suggesting claimant rights based on discovery. More recently, the Russians have gone to great trouble and expense to permanently man an orbital space station from 1987 to 2000 (the space station *Mir*; excepting financial troubles in 1990 forced a brief hiatus). That effort was clearly made to strengthen their international claim through the symbol of effective occupation.[31] With this political background of territorial position-jockeying in Antarctica and early space flight, it may seem surprising that the nations eventually agreed to establish a treaty for the peaceful and cooperative use of the continent that was the first of its kind in diplomatic history.

Proponents of functionalism and the value of low politics in influencing the policies of nations through bureaucratic and epistemic communities point to the example of the Antarctic Treaty as a triumph for their theories.[32] Maybe so, but the process was fraught with difficulty and dominated by national agendas. Following the perceived cooperative experience of the IGY, the United States proposed the continent be used for peaceful purposes only. The idea was met with skepticism until the 12 nations involved agreed to draft a treaty for common use if and only if existing claims would not have to be renounced – allowing the states to keep them in diplomatic reserve for unanticipated future events – nor would limited symbolic or 'reserved claims' like those of the United States and USSR be set aside or constrained in any way.[33] Under these conditions, arrangements were still amazingly difficult and preliminary negotiations between presumably and publicly cooperating states took over a year.

The Preamble to the Antarctic Treaty states, 'it is in the interest of all mankind that Antarctica shall continue forever to be used for peaceful purposes'.[34] This now politically incorrect (due to gender specificity) statement summarizes the reason for getting together in the first place, and was not contested. The Treaty also stated that the Continent was to be used for peaceful purposes *only* (Article I). The Antarctic had equivocal economic potential, but its military potential (especially as a hiding place for nuclear submarines), as well as its potential as a battlefield between competing claimant states in what could conceivably escalate into a more general conflict, was substantial. The Treaty also includes the provision that all nations will have unlimited access to any other nation's facilities for the purpose of inspection to ensure compliance (Article VII). Further, the exploration and exploitation of the continent is to be carried out with the greatest amount of cooperation (Articles II and III). Nuclear explosions and the dumping of radioactive waste are prohibited (Article V). One of the aspects addressed, but inadequately covered by the Treaty, was the issue of areas of responsibility and liability. Without a determination of sovereignty in an area inhabited by men and women, the issue of responsibility is somewhat clouded. The existing international courts simply had no jurisdiction in these matters, and international agreement on legal liability was left to later negotiators (Article IX). Despite the omissions, the Treaty has held without major incident.

Twelve states signed the Treaty initially, and six more have since been incorporated (Poland in 1977, Germany in 1981, Brazil and India in 1983, China and Uruguay in 1985), bringing the total to 16 signatories with decision-making authority. Fourteen more states have acceded to the terms of the Treaty but have no consultative rights.[35] Several US Congressional Representatives decried the Treaty when it was adopted in December of 1959, and again when it came into force in June of 1961 (after ratification by all 12 original IGY participating states), because they thought the United States had given away the continent to the Soviets – who hadn't even set foot there until the IGY.[35] Still, and despite the fact that it never did settle the outstanding claims issues, the Antarctic Treaty was hailed as an ideal symbol of international cooperation, and was structurally and ideologically the base model for the future regime on outer space.

NEGOTIATION HISTORY OF THE OUTER-SPACE REGIME

The United States has been committed to the notions of international law and individual freedom from the earliest days of its history. Its first foreign war was against the Barbary Pirates of the North African coast over the issue of piracy on the high seas.[36] Though the United States failed to participate, Woodrow Wilson and his 'Fourteen Points' established the United Nations' predecessor, the League of Nations. Franklin Roosevelt's 'Four Freedoms' (freedom of speech and expression, freedom of worship, freedom from want, and freedom from fear) became the basis of the post-war International Bill of Human Rights.[37] It is not surprising, in light of its historical positions, that on 10 January 1957, in his State of the Union Address, President Eisenhower asked 'the international community [to] seriously consider a plan to mutually control outer space missile and satellite development'.[38] This plan was to incorporate the tenets of common heritage and peaceful cooperation. Eisenhower followed words with action by endorsing the Aeronautical and Space Act of 1958, which espoused a peaceful and beneficial aim to carry out the civilian space program of the United States 'for the benefit of all mankind' – a plain ruse according to prominent space historians.[39] McDougall flatly claimed that 'NASA emerged in part as eyewash'.[40] It was US policy to insist on the prohibition on military use of space, 'contingent upon the establishment of effective inspection'.[41] Given Soviet secrecy, the potential fruits of that policy were equivocal. Of interest, it had been and is still the policy of the United States to insist on verification when negotiating arms control treaties. During Senate ratification hearings on the Outer Space Treaty, it seemed plausible that a new precedent might be set in this regard. Since the United States did not anticipate having the means to do so in the *near* future, it seemed reasonable *not* to seek verification by inspection in the case of limiting weapons of mass destruction in orbit. The Space Shuttle now has the capability to conduct inspections in low-Earth orbit, but the treaty is not under review.

The stage was thus set for talks on cooperation to begin, and they did so with the congeniality of a welterweight boxing match. With experts on air and sea law on hand, and a fresh agreement on Antarctica to use as a guide, the two Cold War Blocs were ready. One of the first major obstacles in the negotiations over space applications was in the realm of legitimate space activity as defined by the 'peaceful' uses of outer space. The Soviet Union claimed the difference was clear and should be structured along the lines of military (illegitimate) or non-military (legitimate). Since nearly every conceivable space application had at least some military uses, the United States answered, the distinction should be between peaceful and aggressive uses of space.[42] The Soviets countered that nearly every military space application could be described as peaceful, even the stationing of weapons in space (as a defensive measure, of course). In time the United States buckled under to claims of hair-splitting. The Outer Space Treaty, as it was eventually penned, would prove to be more a modification of the Soviet view than of the US view.[43]

As part of the negotiations, on 12 January 1958, Eisenhower sent a proposal to the Soviet Union that called for the banning of ICBMs in space.[44] This initiative was the first step in a plan to neutralize Soviet rockets. Since ICBMs in their ballistic arc must pass through outer space *en route* to their target, the next logical move would have been to call for the abandonment of the legally useless ICBMs. This was clearly a propaganda effort designed to portray the United States as the peacemaker. Of course, the proposal was unacceptable to the Soviets. In 1958, the Americans had the ability to strike deep into the Soviet Union with nuclear weapons via the bombers of the Strategic Air Command (SAC) based on foreign soil. The Soviets had no such foreign bases from which to launch a counterstrike. Without ICBMs, their nuclear forces held no strategic value. The Soviets, it could be argued from a realistic point of view, might have acceded to these conditions, since ICBMs would only be used in the event of global war, in which case all international treaties would be voided. But that was an impossible position at the time, because the Soviets did not have the prolific armada of missiles publicly attributed to them. To agree to a treaty, even deceitfully, might show the world that their power was not as grand as many believed. That outcome was untenable. Eventually, this power posturing would be Khrushchev's undoing. Having gained office on claims of an intolerable missile gap, once in office and privy to classified data, Kennedy knew the Russians were hopelessly outgunned in nuclear missiles.

This was the information he acted on when he publicly stood down Khrushchev over the placement of missiles in Cuba. Kennedy knew the Russians had not the arsenal to trade nuclear salvos with the United States, and he also knew Khrushchev would never admit it. Khrushchev backed down and lost his power domestically. The next generation of Soviet leaders would not make the same mistake, and embarked on a crash program that brought nuclear parity with the United States by 1968 and superiority by 1970. Lyndon Johnson, speaking to a group of local government officials and educators in Nashville, confirmed the point:

> I wouldn't want to be quoted on this, but we've spent thirty-five or forty billion dollars on the space program. And if nothing else had come out of it except the knowledge we've gained from space photography, it would be worth ten times what the whole program has cost. Because tonight we know how many missiles the enemy has and, it turned out, our guesses were way off. We were doing things we didn't need to do, building things we didn't need to build. We were harboring fears we didn't need to harbor.[45]

For appearance sake, if nothing else, the Russians had to demand the right to use their publicly perceived 'advantage' in ICBMs. But the Soviets quickly turned the tables. They responded to Eisenhower by saying they would agree to eliminate missiles from space if the United States would agree to withdraw nuclear weapons from all foreign bases.[46] This counter-proposal was equally unacceptable to the Americans.[47] Without the nuclear deterrent, it was assumed that the Soviets' preponderance in conventional weapons would allow them to dominate Europe. The swapping of mutually unacceptable proposals did much to foster the image of cooperation.

Although Eisenhower first proposed that space should be free of weapons, it was the Soviets who, on 15 March 1958, proposed that it was truly the purview of the United Nations to establish a program to oversee the international use of space.[48] As in previous proposals, it was coupled with the requirement that the United States eliminate foreign bases. Again, the United States could not accept. Instead, it countered with a proposal that the United Nations establish an *ad hoc* committee to explore the problems and possibilities for international cooperation in space.

The Ad Hoc Committee on the Peaceful Uses of Outer Space (AHCOPUOS) was awkward from the beginning. The original AHCOPUOS, as proposed by the United States, was to have nine members, all with a demonstrated interest in space applications. The Soviet Bloc would have only one representative under this formula, as only the Soviet Union had so far demonstrated a space capability (it may be for this reason that the Soviet Union accelerated its cooperative scientific ventures with all its captive satellite states, in order to gain political leverage in future international organizations). The Soviets argued this arrangement was unconscionable. Since they were the *leading* space power (in their view and the view of most of the world), they should have at least equal representation with the West, and they counter-proposed a representative makeup of three delegates each from the West, the Soviet Bloc, and the unaligned or third world. The United States argued that the committee should not be politicized and that the representation should be based upon a demonstrated interest or ability in space and on an accurate reflection of the demographic composition of the United Nations.[49] The impasse could not be overcome, and so a new compromise proposal, sponsored by the United States, was put forward, above the objections of the Soviets, to the General Assembly. Under this scheme, Soviet representation increased to three (adding Czechoslovakia and Poland), but total membership increased to 18 – with 15 Western and non-aligned representatives.[50] The General Assembly accepted the new alignment and officially created the AHCOPUOS. The Soviet Union, its two satellites, plus intended members India and the United Arab Republic refused to participate. With 13 of the 18 members attending, however, a quorum was declared, and the committee forged ahead.

The major products of the AHCOPUOS were resolutions that the United Nations would not establish an international space agency (partly because of the fear that it would recreate the experience of AHCOPUOS, even though both superpowers had supported the idea of a United Nations space agency just one year earlier);[51] that a small, expert group of space professionals be established within the Secretariat to assist in advising and coordinating assistance in space matters; and that a permanent committee be established to continue the international political and legal discussion of space cooperation established by the AHCOPUOS.[52] The recommendations submitted to the General Assembly in July 1958 were hardly earth-shaking. It seems odd that the United States, with a clear superiority in the committee, did not press for a stronger, more amenable agenda. They surely felt that without the participation of the Soviets and Indians, the resolutions of the Committee would not carry much weight and were therefore a futile exercise. Perhaps for that reason, the only recommendation acted on by the Secretariat and the General Assembly was the establishment of a permanent outer space committee.

The debate over the permanent committee followed along the same lines as the one over the *ad hoc* committee and centered on representation. Once again, the Soviets – because of their dubious preeminence in space – insisted on parity, with one third representation each for the Soviet, Western, and non-aligned blocs. The United States, because of the greater number of countries in the West with legitimate space interests, insisted on superior Western participation. The compromise solution again increased the size of the committee to 24 representatives: 7 from the Soviet Bloc, 12 from the West, and 5 from non-aligned countries.[53] This compromise was accepted by the Soviets because it gave them near parity by bloc (8 representatives would have been, in their view, parity of one-third) and by the West because, with 12 of the 24 representatives, it gave them an effective veto.[54] Equally important from the Soviet view, it gave them a forum to 'fulminate against the illegal' US efforts in espionage from space.[55] Thus the permanent Committee on the Peaceful Uses of Outer Space (COPUOS) was established in December 1959 by unanimous vote in the General Assembly, with a smaller mandate and a more divided representation than its ineffective temporary predecessor. Despite the ringing endorsement of the whole of the United Nations, political rivalries paralyzed the new committee. In its first two years of existence the COPUOS could not even convene, and it accomplished nothing.

A grand turnaround in the fortunes and influence of COPUOS occurred late in 1961. On 25 September of that year, President Kennedy addressed the General Assembly and proposed the United Nations Charter be extended beyond the terrestrial sphere to the entire universe.[56] The new mandate should begin with a space-based, global weather monitoring and communications system. Following this rousing call to action, the first meeting of the COPUOS was held, with each nation striving to out-cooperate the other. In less than a week, the United States and the Soviet Union had agreed upon a draft resolution on the principles of space exploration. The agreement, tagged United Nations Resolution 1721, was passed unanimously by the General Assembly on 20 December 1961.[57] Considering the process by which it was enacted, it was a significant achievement. Resolution 1721 stated that the realm of international law included outer space and the celestial bodies, and that the exploration and use of space was free and open to all nations. Additionally, the Resolution called for a registry of all space launches to be maintained by the Secretariat, the establishment of an international cooperative agreement on space-based weather monitoring and communications, and expansion of the COPUOS to 28 members (two more each for the United States and the Soviet Union).[58] Eventually, the COPUOS would swell to 53 members; reducing the effectiveness of the committee by making any decision process it would undertake a cumbersome trial.[59]

Following acceptance of the Resolution, continuing negotiations for the establishment of a legal regime in outer space were complicated by the Soviet submission of a broad 'Declaration of Basic Principles'. The Declaration was another propaganda effort and was succinctly described and critiqued by then Deputy Assistant Secretary of State Richard Gardner. Within the Declaration, he claimed, were four disputed positions, all of which were challenged by the United States.[60] The first position held that space should not be used for 'propagating war, national hatred, or enmity between nations'. This position was rejected by the United States because of a somewhat dubious claim that, since the Soviet Union argued for and then refused to sign a similar agreement at a Geneva arms reduction conference, the Soviets could not be trusted to carry through with this resolution even though they had initiated it. The second position called for all nations to submit for prior discussion and agreement any space projects that 'might hinder the exploration and use of outer space for peaceful purposes by other countries'. This position was rejected as untenable, as it would give the Soviet Union an effective veto over any space project they might declare as militarily valuable. The third disputed plank in the Soviet draft declared that all space activities be carried out 'solely and exclusively by states'. This provision would rule out private enterprise in space activities and forcibly impose socialist principles on the realm of outer space.[61] It was also clearly an attack on the lucrative and expanding space-based international telecommunications market, dominated to date by the Americans. The last disputed Soviet position denounced the use of intelligence collection satellites as 'incompatible with the objectives of mankind in the conquest of outer space'. Gardner argued that reconnaissance from space, like the high seas, was consistent with international law, and, more importantly, that the use of space in this manner would some day 'prove important in monitoring disarmament agreements'. Also, the United States would no longer be able to continue air reconnaissance flights, and space reconnaissance seemed the most reliable method for monitoring the Soviet Union's military.

Senator Albert Gore made the US response to the Soviet challenge in an address to the UN General Assembly.[62] Gore was representing the US delegation, and his statement was considered a major US policy announcement. He called for the negotiation of an international legal regime in outer space; a treaty banning the testing of nuclear weapons in outer space; the precluding of weapons of mass destruction based in space; the preclusion of scientific experiments in space with potentially harmful ecological effects; and the establishment of a global space-based communications and weather monitoring system. The Soviets agreed to drop their demands for three of the four disputed positions in their Declaration of Basic Principles (the propaganda position, the weakest of the US rebuttals, was not placed in the subsequent UN resolution but was affirmed by the passage of UN Resolution 110, which condemned the use of propaganda designed to provoke or encourage any threat to peace) and accepted the addition of the US principles. The result was the unanimously approved Declaration of Legal Principles Governing the Activities of States in the Exploration and Use of Outer Space in 1963. The principles agreed to in that Declaration eventually became the basis for eight of the first nine articles of the Outer Space Treaty.

The General Assembly, spurred by allegations of partisanship and foot dragging by all sides, passed a resolution on 21 December 1965 (International Cooperation on the Peaceful Uses of Outer Space), that 'urged' the COPUOS to prepare a draft statement on outer space – specifically addressing questions of astronaut safety and return, and international liability. On 7 May 1966, President Johnson announced a desire by the United States to formalize an agreement addressing these problems in the form of a multilateral treaty. On

30 May, Soviet Ambassador Gromyko replied that the Soviet Union was ready to negotiate. Jointly, on 30 June, the Americans and Soviets submitted draft treaty proposals to Secretary-General U Thant for action. The members of COPUOS gathered in Geneva on 12 July 1966 to hammer out an agreement on space principles. The dates are so tediously incorporated because the negotiations were remarkable for their speed. They were finished on 16 September 1966, a scant ten weeks that included a six-week break from 4 August through 12 September.

The purpose of the Treaty was not to address in detail all of the issues of concern, but to create a broad guideline for future negotiation. Under this formula, no party gained all that it wanted, but no party's major interests were unduly injured. A flawed process, to be sure, but widely recognized as a major achievement: 'Any sort of reasonably coherent statement that has been ratified by nearly a hundred countries around the planet, including the superpowers, in an effort to profess a consensus, is important'.[63] A synopsis of the rules and decision-making procedures of the outer-space regime follows.

THE AGREEMENTS OF THE INTERNATIONAL OUTER-SPACE REGIME

The international outer-space regime is composed primarily of four generally recognized treaties and a fifth unratified – though to date unchallenged – treaty on the Moon and celestial bodies. In addition, a developing world initiative on the division of spoils from the 'common heritage' of space is evolving. The first document, the Treaty on the Principles Governing the Activities of States in the Exploration and Use of Outer Space, Including the Moon and Other Celestial Bodies (1967), is referred to throughout the literature as the Outer Space Treaty or OST. It was agreed to by unanimous declaration of the General Assembly of the United Nations on 19 December 1966 and entered into force on 10 October 1967. The OST was concerned only with broad principles and eschewed getting mired down in details – that was to be a requirement of subsequent Treaties. It contains a Preamble and 17 Articles, and its major provisions are:

- The exploration and peaceful use of outer space is in the 'common interest of all mankind'. (Preamble)
- Exploration and use of outer space 'shall be carried out for the benefit and in the interests of all countries, irrespective of their degree of economic or scientific development, and shall be the province of all mankind'. Further, the exploration of space shall be open to 'all States' in accordance with international law and the facilities established for the scientific investigation of

the Moon and other celestial bodies shall be open with 'free access to all'. (Article I)

- Outer space, including the Moon and all celestial bodies, is not subject to national appropriation or claim of sovereignty. (Article II)
- States party to the Treaty agree not to place 'nuclear or any other kinds of weapons of mass destruction' in orbit around the earth nor install such weapons on the Moon or any other celestial body (this is the Article that is generally cited in arguments that the 1980s Strategic Defense Initiative (SDI, or 'Star Wars') was in contravention of existing international agreement). Further, the establishment of 'military bases, installations, and fortifications, the testing of any type of weapons, and the conduct of military maneuvers' on the Moon or any celestial body is prohibited; however, the use of military personnel or 'any equipment or facility necessary for peaceful exploration' shall not be prohibited. (Article IV)
- All astronauts are 'envoys of mankind' and so every effort shall be made to render them assistance in the 'event of accident, distress, and emergency'. Should an astronaut be forced to land on the territory of any signatory, that astronaut shall be 'promptly returned to the State of registry of their space vehicle'. (Article V)
- States shall be responsible for all national activities in outer space, 'whether such activities are carried on by governmental agencies or by non-governmental entities', including terrestrial damage during launch and operation. (Articles VI and VII)
- States regain jurisdiction over any property and personnel placed into outer space and any object or component parts 'found beyond the limits of the State' of ownership shall be returned to said State upon request. (Article VIII)
- States shall endeavor to explore outer space in a spirit of cooperation, allowing observation of space activities where equitable, and with regard for the ecology of the Earth and outer space. (Articles IX through XI)
- 'All stations, installations, equipment, and space vehicles' on the Moon or any celestial body shall be open to representatives of all nations, subject to 'reasonable advance notice'. (Article XII)

Thus the OST provides a working outline for all of the concerns of the two opposing Blocs in negotiations comprising the previous nine years. It also establishes the astropolitical dictum that strategic or potentially militarily significant territory should be denied to a potential enemy if it cannot be directly controlled. Moreover, it is the foundation of the *de jure* and *de facto* subordination of private interests in extra-terrestrial commercial development, and exemplifies the principles and norms of a regime that has no place for *Astropolitik*.

The Agreement on Activities of States on the Moon and Other Celestial Bodies (UN General Assembly Resolution 34/68) is the second basic document of the outer-space regime. It was also unanimously approved by the General Assembly of the United Nations and consists of a Preamble and 21 Articles. Much of the text reaffirms and expands definitions and principles contained in the Outer Space Treaty Articles V and VIII. Major provisions of this agreement are:

- Recognizing the strategic military, economic, and scientific potential of the Moon and other celestial bodies, this Agreement attempts to 'prevent the Moon from becoming an area of international conflict'. (Preamble)
- Any reference to 'the Moon' includes 'any orbits around or other trajectories to or around it'. The term 'other celestial bodies' is limited to those within the solar system, exclusive of the earth, saving potential conflict for the distant future. (Article I)
- The Charter of the United Nations, its declarations and principles, in accordance with international law, extends to the moon and other celestial bodies. (Article II)
- The Moon is to be developed 'exclusively for peaceful purposes', using the preferred US terminology. Therefore, no nuclear or other weapons of mass destruction shall be placed on or in orbit around the Moon. No military facilities or military maneuvers shall be allowed, though military personnel are not barred. (Article III)
- Exploration of the Moon and other celestial bodies 'shall be carried out for the benefit and in the interests of all countries, irrespective of their degree of scientific development'. Not irrespective of their contribution, however. (Articles IV and V)
- The Secretariat of the United Nations shall be informed 'to the greatest extent practicable and feasible' of the activities of states on and about the moon and other celestial bodies. (Article V)
- States shall take appropriate measures to avoid disrupting the natural environment of the Moon and other celestial bodies. (Article VII)
- Declares the 'moon and its resources to be the common heritage of mankind'. (Article XI)
- All vehicles, installations, and property on the Moon and other celestial bodies shall be open to other states in order that 'Each state party may assure itself the activities of other state parties in the exploration and use of the moon are compatible with the provisions of this Agreement.' (Article XV)
- If disputes cannot be resolved by peaceful methods appropriate to the circumstances, a state party may appeal to the Secretary-General, without seeking the consent of any other party concerned, for resolution. (Article XVI)

The foregoing Resolution does little to clarify the OST, and arguably muddles it, leaving open to interpretation all the contentious issues of the negotiations.

The third leg of the regime is the Convention on International Liability for Damage Caused by Space Objects (1973). This Convention was actually begun in 1958, when a need for assignment of liability was evident, but it was also the most contentious and took the longest to ratify, finally entering into force on 9 October 1973. Successfully invoked by Canada against the Soviet Union after the aforementioned de-orbit of Cosmos 954 spewed radioactive material over a significant stretch of arctic tundra, this Convention has had more practical value than the others to date. It consists of a Preamble and 28 Articles. Its major provisions are:

- Recognizes that damage can be caused by space operations despite precautionary measures undertaken by states involved. Therefore, an international legal regime is necessary to mitigate liability and strengthen international cooperation. (Preamble)
- The launching state is absolutely liable for damage caused by its spacecraft on the Earth or to aircraft in flight. In the case of damage occurring above the surface of the Earth, fault must be determined to assign liability. (Articles II–III. Issues of joint liability are discussed in Articles IV and V)[64]
- A Claims Commission shall be established within one year of proper submission of evidence of damage having been received. The Claims Commission will decide the merits of the claim and determine compensation, if any, to include claims expenses. (Articles XIV, XVIII, and XX)

The last ratified leg of the regime is the Convention on Registration of Objects Launched into Outer Space (1976). This Convention basically codifies the customary system of space registration in existence since 1962. It consists of a Preamble and 12 Articles and entered into force on 15 September 1976. It is important in that registration will be the first cause for determining ownership in cases of liability (outlined previously). Major provisions follow:

- Each state shall maintain a registry of objects launched into space and inform the Secretary-General of the existence of that registry. The Secretary-General shall be informed of all launches and shall maintain a separate registry. Full and open access to the latter registry is mandated. (Articles II, III, and V)
- At a minimum, launching states will provide the Secretary-General with the following information: name of launching state or states; an appropriate designator for each object launched; the date and 'territory or location' of launch; basic orbital parameters including period, inclination, apogee, and perigee; and the 'general function' of the space object. Of course, more information is acceptable. (Article IV)

There is a final unratified component of the outer space regime. In 1979, the General Assembly released the Agreement Governing the Activities of States on the Moon and Other Celestial Bodies – The Moon Treaty (1979).

This Treaty has been called the first of the next-generation revised space law because it represents a fundamental change in the definition of *res communis* from the traditional Western view of 'equal access' to the view espoused by the former Soviet Bloc and Less Developed Countries (LDCs) of 'equal benefit'.[65] This Treaty is notable for first use of the term *res communis* in the body of its text, but it has proven unacceptable to the dominant spacefaring nations, the United States in particular, because of its historical misuse of the term. Despite the reticence of any spacefaring nation to ratify the treaty, no state has yet gone against its provisions.

The official documents of the outer-space regime have now been described, but several other treaties and conventions complete the framework. The Anti-Ballistic Missile (ABM) Treaty of 1972 also pertains to the legal framework in space. This bilateral treaty between the United States and the Soviet Union requires that neither state undertake the development, testing, or deployment of ABM systems that are land, air, sea, or space-based. Each nation would further make no effort to interfere with the other side's ability to monitor compliance to the treaty, including the use of deception or deliberate concealment and electromagnetic jamming. Indeed, only two fixed ABM sites, one in defense of the national capital and one at a single testing site, were allowed. Although the Soviet Union created, and the Russian state still maintains, a series of concentric ABM rings around Moscow to protect the national elite, the United States has never deployed such a system. After the Treaty was formalized, and construction begun, Washington lawmakers realized that deployment was a disastrously bad idea in a populist democracy, and quickly halted production. Two reasons dominated the change in view: (1) it seemed immoral for the lawmakers to spend billions on themselves for defense, yet legally proscribe even a dime for defense beyond the Washington Beltway (an argument that would persuade Reagan to go ahead with the Strategic Defense Initiative, despite the treaty specifications above); and (2), would nuclear war truly be less likely if those who made the decision to go to war were effectively protected? The consensus was 'no'. The Soviet Union, a dictatorial and non-democratic state completely without accountability to the electorate, had no such constraints on its actions.

By 1985, the United States was arguing that the language of the ABM Treaty was ambiguous and at the very least, unrealistically restrictive. The treaty was signed without anticipation of technological breakthroughs that gave the Americans a decided edge in the development of Strategic Defense Initiative (SDI) or 'Star Wars' applications. Under a unilaterally declared interpretation that was less binding, the US position became that research for SDI was permissible, but testing and deployment were equivocal. Currently, the United States is advocating the construction and deployment of a ground-based interceptor modeled on the Patriot theater anti-missile system (the combat success of which has been dubious at best) to defend against limited, accidental, or rogue state/terrorist attacks. Russia, and much of the international community, roundly denounces the US plan. Not only is it illegal, they aver, at best it threatens to undermine efforts to reduce nuclear and conventional arms and at worst spark a new arms race.

This ABM example clearly shows the continuance of the geo/astropolitical dictum – if a state cannot guarantee dominance of a vital area or location, then it must deny that dominance to potential enemies. This was the clear motivation of the negotiations described herein. With the demise of the Soviet Union, the likelihood that the Russians will dominate space technology diminishes proportional to the plummeting vitality of their economy. The United States stands as the only nation currently likely to develop space mastery, and so the many international treaties based on Cold War parity are eroding.

The 1963 Limited Test Ban Treaty prohibits all nuclear detonations in space, and set the stage for the more comprehensive Non-Proliferation Treaty (NPT) that followed. Signed only by those states who had nuclear capability at the time, and those who anticipated never having it, the treaty further requires that signatories refrain from so much as encouraging such detonations by any party, to include the distribution of technology, resources, or financial assistance that may go toward the development of such a capacity. Specifically, however, the treaty does not cover/condemn accidental explosions by a nuclear-powered spacecraft. Such is the chance we take.

The 1977 Environmental Modification Convention (ratified by the United States in 1980) prohibits states from modifying the environment in any way in order to damage another state party. This includes the possibility of such fanciful armaments as earthquake and typhoon weapons, one supposes, but also covers the manipulation of resources to change the natural dynamics of Earth development. It specifically adds space to this prohibition. It does not, however, limit the development and testing of environmental modification techniques.

Not all international treaties and conventions have been so committed to the socialized exploration of outer space. Although recognized only by the participating states, at least one of these makes direct sovereignty claims on a portion of legally defined outer space. In December of 1976, the equatorial states of Brazil, Columbia, Ecuador, Indonesia, Kenya, Uganda, and Zaire declared that their national sovereignty extended to the geostationary belt, 22,000 miles above the equator.[66] This so-called Bogata Declaration was 'in strict violation of custom, common sense, and the Outer Space Treaty'.[67] It has never been accepted by the international community, and probably never will be, but it remains important because it is representative of a growing desire in the LDCs to seize a greater share of the common goods. It is historically curious, and ethically unfortunate, that the position it espouses is analogous to the colonial oppression from which all these nations once suffered. Oddly enough, the legal basis for such a claim dates to the Roman *usque ad coleum* doctrine, already discussed, and just as importantly to the Papal Bull of 4 May 1493, in which Pope Alexander VI attempted to divide the New World between Spain and Portugal. Called the 'hinterland principle', it established the process of discovery that he who owned the coast could claim the region inland to an indefinite extent.[68] The Bogata Declaration is justified by the declaring states on the claim that the atmosphere is aptly described as the *coastal region* of outer space, and thus it provides the segue necessary to return to the dictums of *Astropolitik*.

The problem with the Declaration is not one of orbital mechanics, for here the claimants can make a serious case, but in the case they make based on extant international law. The Less Developed Countries of the equatorial belt have modified the old Soviet position that *capitalist* international law is morally invalid, to the proposition *industrialized* or *developed states'* international law is inapplicable. The Declaration stated:

> The Outer Space Treaty cannot be considered as a final answer to the problem of the exploration and use of outer space, even less when the international community is questioning all the terms of international law which were elaborated when the developing countries could not count on adequate scientific advice and thus were not able to observe and evaluate the omissions, contradictions and consequences of the proposals which were prepared with great ability by the industrialized powers for their own benefit.[69]

The immorality of international law, claimed the signatories, stems from the contention that it was incorporated before many of the LDCs either existed or were in a position to make a rational defense of their position. A better argument for this declaration is that geostationary orbit is a physical resource arising from its natural dependency on the planet and is therefore not subject to extant space law. Such an argument is easily rebutted because the phenomenon of the geostationary orbit is dependent upon the earth as a whole (not just that territory directly 'below' it) and, moreover, that it is highly problematic to argue the geostationary orbit is not 'in' space.[70] A more compelling argument followed, that the geostationary orbit is a scarce international resource that is being monopolized by a few space powers that were not sharing their profits in the spirit of 'the common heritage of mankind'. The latter point causes a guilty squirming on the part of the well-endowed industrial states, but space commerce goes on.

The astropolitical view described in this book is that national rivalry and competition have spurred the most spectacular development of space to date, and in the near future there is no change looming. While it is morally desirable to explore space in common with all peoples, even the thought of doing so makes weary those who have the means. The decision not to return to the

Moon was made before the Moon Treaty was established, for example, but its very existence has made the moon a less attractive place for commercial development than ever before. It is simply not reasonable to expect a state to make an extraordinary investment in the exploitation of a region or product from which it can not reap a tangible reward, in this case due to a prior international agreement that drastically limits its ability to operate militarily and would force it to disperse any forthcoming profits.

The preceding survey of the outer-space regime begs a series of important questions. So what if the *de facto* astropolitical outer-space regime was established on conflicting and antagonistic bases? If the result is cooperation, or at least the promise of cooperation, aren't the nationalist means acceptable to the ultimate emplacement of internationalist ends? The *de jure* regime is established in principles of precedence and international law, no matter how contentiously argued. Without a doubt, the establishment of laws, by which we all agree to cooperate and function in society, is a necessary function of peaceful coexistence; but is the current regime, intended to promote beneficial exploration of space, instead acting to stifle space exploration? What kind of regime is necessary to renew national or corporate commitment to space development? Is cooperation in outer space inevitable in the long term, and more importantly, is it even useful in the near term?

Under the current outer space regime, the only frontier in space that has been truly opened is in near-Earth space. A large communication satellite industry has grown up, regular NASA space shuttle missions take place, and the International Space Station is slowly being cobbled together. But the chances for further human exploration and settlement of the Moon, Mars, and beyond, crucial to both the official hype about and popular enthusiasm for space exploration, continues to recede over time. The United States, Russian Federation, and other states with space-launch capability have been content to establish toeholds in LEO. Extrapolating from the current pace of activity in space, manned missions to Mars within the first half of this century are unlikely, regardless of NASA projections.

The failure to open space beyond LEO to human exploration, settlement, and commercial development plainly cannot be attributed to technology shortfalls. The Apollo lunar landings were achieved with computers markedly less advanced than those available in many homes today. Rocket engines once developed for multistaged heavy-lift cargo capacity could be manufactured again. Several types of less expensive single stage to orbit launch vehicles are in development or prototype. Innovative communications and fresh multispectral and electronic imaging techniques, combined with remarkable advances in miniaturization and software applications, provide the potential foundations for a renaissance in space commerce and industry. No, it is not a lack of appropriate technology that has stifled the exploration and exploitation of space. Instead, much of the blame can be found in political motivation, or more precisely, in its absence. The reality is that political decisionmakers in the United States and the other states with space-launch capacity have little or no pressing political or economic interest in the further opening of this frontier.

Neither bureaucratic nor corporate interests are politically mobilized to press for the levels of government spending necessary to push the boundary of human activity in space, even for a return to the Moon. At best, bureaucratic and corporate interests have been mobilized to defend existing programs or struggle for shares of declining government spending for space programs. Even promotion of space commercialization is essentially limited to activities in LEO. The bottom line is that the OST and the existing socialized space regime discouraged productive competition among space capable states. The long-term consequence is that space development is trapped in LEO parochialism:

> The Outer Space Treaty of 1967 was a tragedy because it drained away the energy the remaining twenty years of Cold War could have provided to space exploration. Had this not occurred, had the momentum of Apollo been allowed to continue, the United States would have moved to establish permanent bases on the Moon and Mars by the 1980s, and humanity might well be a multi-planet species today.[71]

This very brief description of an alternative historical trajectory is more than a polemic exercise in denunciation. Space exploration efforts by the United States and the Soviet Union decelerated dramatically after the effective completion of major projects begun *prior to* the adoption of the 1967 Outer Space Treaty. The causal relationship suggested by this sequence of events cannot be dismissed as a mere *post hoc ergo propter hoc* fallacy without ignoring the underlying puzzle. Several new spacefaring states joined the United States and the Soviet Union after 1967, and yet space exploration and development beyond LEO has fallen far short of what was possible given what the then available technology would have permitted. It is not simply that the Americans and Soviets have not established permanent bases on the Moon or Mars. Neither have the Europeans or Japanese. John Hickman[72] has called this a puzzle of collective *in*action, and we offer solutions which contradict much of the conventional wisdom about the development of space as a frontier for human settlement and the international regime which was established to structure that anticipated but unrealized development. Without the intense international rivalry of the Cold War, launching satellites and landing humans on the Moon probably would have occurred decades later than they did. Legitimate complaints about the politicization and militarization of space notwithstanding, Cold War competition was clearly good for the development of space because it forced the pace of activity in ways that scientific research and commerce could not. Ideological and military competition motivated the governments of the United States and Soviet Union to absorb the costs of developing the technology to access space in a comparatively short time period.

COPUOS has been remarkably ineffective since the extraordinary burst of activity that created the OST. Comments made by COPUOS diplomatic representatives of most non-spacefaring states reveal national space policies trapped in a self-defeating effort to redistribute economic benefits from investments in space development made by the spacefaring states. What their remarks suggest is that they have little grasp of the enormous economic promise of space development or the degree to which it has not been realized. COPUOS is not a forum for the discussion of space development policies or actual space projects. Hickman rightly observes that the only things launched at contemporary COPUOS meetings are sterile exchanges of pious internationalist rhetoric.

The core problem in international space law is that the practical effect of collectivizing space has been counter to its intended purpose of encouraging the development of outer space. Indeed, it would seem to have had precisely the opposite effect. The reason is that the treaty solved an entirely *speculative* collective action problem, a 'tragedy of the commons' in outer space, in the belief that common pool resources were wasted in the competitive scramble of states to claim sovereignty over the new frontier. The treaty may actually have resulted in a collective *inaction* problem as states failed to invest in the development of space because an important incentive for its development had been eliminated. The argument here is that in rendering space and all celestial bodies *res communis* rather than *res nullius*, and thus eliminating them as proper objects for which states may compete, the treaty dramatically reduced the impetus for the development of outer space. Some celestial bodies, the Moon, Mars, and larger asteroids in particular, represent potential new national territory for states, and in the realist/*Astropolitik* paradigm, states are hard wired to acquire and hold territory.

According to Hendrik Spruyt, the sovereign nation-state emerged as the dominant state form, first in Europe and then across the planet, because it was superior to the three alternative state forms; the individual city-state (Genoa, Florence, and Venice), the city league (Hansa), and the multinational borderless empire (Holy Roman Empire and Roman Catholic Church).[73] The advantages of the sovereign nation-state in this competition lay not only in the exclusive economic exploitation of a national population and territory but also in its interaction with other sovereign nation-states in the new state system. Control over territory, even territory with little or no population, was then and remains today an essential criterion for statehood. That the modern nation-state continues to be motivated to acquire and hold territory is evident in their willingness to use military force to resist the loss of existing territory to separatist movements and in disputes over territories such as the former Spanish Sahara, West Bank, Spratley Islands, and Aksai-Chin Plateau. The point is driven home by considering the hypothetical permanent loss of all national territory by a state that retains possession of its bureaucratic organizations and non-territorial assets. Would it continue to be deemed a state? Clearly, having lost its *res*, the former nation-state would cease to be a state and become a Non-Governmental Organization (NGO), and in consequence, a creature of lesser status in international affairs.

Having been deprived of the possibility of assuming sovereign possession of new territory discovered and claimable on celestial bodies and in space, states did the same thing that individuals and firms do when domestic law deprives them of the possibility of assuming legal possession of real estate. They rationally choose not to make investments that would lead to its development. In the absence of some immediate political return in the form of new national territory, the attractions of political, economic, and social returns in the near term from investment in or consumption by states are likely to be underwhelming.

The perverse consequence of the OST was the inducement of individually rational behavior by decisionmakers in the few spacefaring states with the technology and fiscal resources to undertake the development of outer space to *not* do so. This deprives all of humanity much less all states of the long-term benefits of the development of outer space. By collectivizing outer space, the OST vested legal rights in all states that they would not or could not exercise. That spacefaring states would not is the result of disincentives. The actual tragedy of the commons is that the effort to achieve collective action resulted in collective inaction.

Application of the Coase theorem makes the insight more explicit.[74] In its most straightforward form, the Coase theorem asserts that if individual property rights exist and transaction costs are low or zero, then resource allocation will be optimal regardless of how property rights were initially assigned. This theory of market exchange is simply an argument that the assignment of property rights will result in the efficient allocation of resources because individuals with the ability to use property more efficiently will purchase it from the existing owners. One important implication is that distributive justice is irrelevant to the efficient allocation of resources. Thus any assignment of property rights is preferable to no assignment of property rights. If the recognition of national sovereignty over territory under international law is substituted for protection of individual property rights under domestic law, and the motivation of states to acquire territory is substituted for the motivation of individuals to acquire wealth, then the logic of the Coase theorem would dictate that any assignment of sovereignty over territory would be preferable to no assignment. Therefore, if the policy goal is to encourage the development of outer space, then any assignment of sovereignty over territory in space and on celestial bodies would be preferable to the existing structure of vesting collective rights in all states. If the assignment of sovereignty achieves some measure of distributive justice, then so much the better. The preferred solution is to let market-style forces determine relative values of assigned sovereignty for all states (see below, p. 178). Without doubt, however, without the investment in space development by the spacefaring states and/or their national firms, the non-spacefaring states cannot possibly receive any economic benefits from the collective ownership of space. With investment in space development by the spacefaring states and/or their national firms, non-spacefaring states *could* reap some economic benefit from space.

Is the collectivization of all of outer space under international law a permanent disability? Fortunately, the answer is 'no'. Under international law, state parties to a treaty may withdraw from its obligations through negotiation, novation, substitution, cancellation, or, *rebus sic stantibus*, when events overcome the intent of the original treaty. Moreover, Article 17 of the OST articulates a straightforward mechanism for withdrawal: 'Any state party to this treaty may give notice of its withdrawal from the treaty one year after its entry into force by written notification to the Depositary Governments. Such withdrawal shall take effect one year from the date of receipt of this notification.' Thus, a state party need merely announce its intention to withdraw and then wait one year. Withdrawal of a single state party to the treaty would not necessarily terminate the treaty between the other state parties. Yet the decision of an important spacefaring state not to be bound by the treaty obviously endangers the entire regime. The decision of the United States or China to withdraw from the OST would have far greater implications for the survival of the international space regime than the same decision by Bangladesh, Burkina Faso, or Papua New Guinea. The equality of states under international law remains nothing more than a useful fiction. Great power, in the tradition of *Realpolitik*, still matters. For the OST to remain good international law, it must be accepted as such by the major spacefaring states of the twenty-first century: the United States, Russia, the European Union States, Japan, and China. One defection from the regime by a member of this group would no doubt lead to its effective collapse, as the remaining spacefaring states are unlikely to use the kind of coercion necessary to enforce the regime. A more likely response to such a defection is a scramble to make competing claims to extraterrestrial sovereignty, based on historical precedent and effective occupation.

What would be the immediate effect of a new emphasis on territorial claims on the non-spacefaring majority of states? The harsh reality is that following a hypothetical 'scramble for the Moon' or any other land-grab scenario, Bangladesh, Burkina Faso, and Uruguay would own no less of the Moon than they now do. That a claimed right to ownership has no economic value unless the property can be used or the legal right to ownership sold or bartered is crucial to understanding the interests involved. Although scrambles for territory by spacefaring states would probably increase the public and private investment necessary to develop resources in outer space, and would include the emergence of some new and determined spacefaring states, left alone it would also exacerbate international inequality.

An alternative and superior solution to the collective inaction problem created by the OST could be the result of new international treaty making. It is probably preferable to replace the old regime with a new one rather than simply drop the existing flawed regime. A new treaty could continue to designate genuine common pool resources as *res communis* while permitting spacefaring states to claim sovereign ownership of territory on celestial bodies and other geo/astrographic positions while affording non-spacefaring states some opportunity to benefit from the exploitation of those same celestial bodies. The proposal could achieve these objectives through a more nuanced application of Coase theorem principles. A new norm that would permit states to claim sovereignty over territory on the larger celestial bodies such as the Moon and Mars according to a simple proportional allocation rule should be established. For example, a state would be permitted to claim sovereignty over territory in proportion to its share of the Earth's land surface. Which specific territory a state could claim would depend upon the priority of arrival by its human representatives with the stipulation that all territorial claims must be contiguous and reasonably compact. This would prevent the mischief of a state claiming a 1 kilometer strip of Martian territory spiraling from pole to pole. Priority of arrival would have the added benefit of spurring manned exploration. Another acceptable option would be pre-arrival assignation of territory in an analogy to privatizing the commons for its most efficient use. By assigning parcels of celestial bodies and other territories by lot, non-spacefaring states could seek rent for their property from states able to exploit the territory. The latter option may be more amenable to the non-spacefaring states, and would still encourage space exploration and exploitation. Non-spacefaring states might even realize an economic bonanza if a particularly valuable resource is found on their parcel, and spacefaring states bid fairly for mining or other use rights.

That the extant regime has stifled space exploration seems obvious. A new regime that harnesses national imperative and market incentives to re-ignite the Space Age is needed, but it will not be enough if states do not explore and embrace effective strategies for space control and exploitation. Whether it occurs in the next few decades or in the twenty-second century, the focus of space activities will inevitably move from the space immediately surrounding Earth to the rest of the solar system. In the short term, satellite communications and surveillance (both civilian and military) should continue to be the primary focus of development. Although far from inevitable, space mining and human settlement should follow.

NOTES

1. I. White, *Decision-Making for Space: Law and Politics in Air, Sea, and Outer Space* (West LaFayette, IN: Purdue University Press, 1971).
2. Ibid., p. 25; see also A. A. Coca, 'Vitoria and the International Law of Outer Space', *IISL*, No. 27 (1984), p. 25.
3. Statement by Ambassador Goldberg, 'Hearings Before the Committee on Foreign Relations, United States Senate', 90th Congress, 1st Session, 7 March 1967 (Washington, DC: US Government Printing Office, 1967), p. 55.
4. Ibid., 15.
5. M. Allehurst, *A Modern Introduction to International Law*, 5th edn (London: George, Allen & Unwin, 1984), p. 289.
6. A. Wilson, (ed.), *Interavia Spaceflight Directory* (Geneva: Interavia SA, 1989), p. 402.
7. All examples from D. Wadegoankar, *The Orbit of Space Law* (London: Stevens & Sons, 1984), pp. 39–40, and L. Bloomfield, 'The Prospects for Law and Order', in J.E.S. Fawcett (ed.), *Outer Space: New Challenge to Law and Policy* (Oxford: Clarendon Press, 1984), pp. 155–6.
8. Bloomfield, 'Prospects for Law and Order', p. 156.
9. K. Deutsch, 'Outer Space and International Prospects: A Look to 1988', in J. Golden (ed.), *Outer Space and World Politics* (New York: Praeger, 1963), p. 159.
10. International Civil Aviation Organization (ICAO) Treaty of 1947, Article II, cited in Fawcett, *Outer Space*, p. 16.
11. Paris Convention on Air Law, Article I., cited in N. Goldman, *American Space Law International and Domestic Issues* (Ames, IA: Iowa State University Press, 1988) p. 103.
12. S. Latchford, 'The Bearing of International Air Navigation Conventions on the Use of Outer Space', United States Senate, Committee on Aeronautical Sciences, 'Legal Problems of Space Exploration' (87th Congress, 1st Session, 1961), p. 495.
13. Bloomfield, 'Prospects for Law and Order', p. 153.
14. Goldman, *American Space Law*, p. 102. The common use provisions for aircraft above the high seas are detailed in both sea and air conventions.
15. W. McDougall, *...the Heavens and the Earth: A Political History of the Space Age* (New York: Basic Books, 1958), p. 186.
16. Bloomfield, 'Prospects for Law and Order', p. 153.
17. Goldberg, 'Hearings before the Committee on Foreign Relations', 7 March 1967, p. 17.
18. White, *Decision-Making for Space*, p. 82.
19. Ibid., p. 108. White cites the 1947 Chicago Convention on Civil Aviation, Chapter III, Article 17.
20. Bloomfield, 'Prospects for Law and Order', p. 151.
21. See J. Oberg, *Uncovering Soviet Disasters: Exploring the Limits of Glasnost* (New York: Random House, 1988), pp. 198–210.
22. Goldberg, 'Hearings before the Committee on Foreign Relations', 13 March 1967, p. 60.
23. White, *Decision-Making for Space*, p. 109.
24. Ibid., p. 107.
25. See *Soviet Military Power: An Assessment of the Threat*, 1988 (Washington, DC: US Government Printing Office, April 1988), pp. 62–7.
26. H. Odishaw, 'International Cooperation in Space Science', in Fawcett (ed.), *Outer Space*, pp. 116–17; and P. Quigg, 'Antarctica: The Continuing Experiment', *Foreign Policy Association Headline Series*, No. 273 (March–April 1985), pp. 3–7.
27. Quigg, 'Antarctica', pp. 14–15.
28. Ibid., p. 17.

29. Goldman, *American Space Law*, p. 70.
30. Bloomfield, 'Prospects for Law and Order', p. 157.
31. A. Wilson (ed.), *Interavia Spaceflight Directory* (Geneva: Interavia SA, 1989), pp. 182–93.
32. On functionalism the basic text is D. Mitrany, A Working Peace System (London: Royal Institute of International Affairs, 1943). Neofunctionalists are still best represented by R. Keohane and J. Nye, *Power and Interdependence: World Politics in Transition* (Boston, MA: Little, Brown, and Company, 1977).
33. Quigg, 'Antarctica', p. 19.
34. *The Conference on Antarctica: Conference, Documents, the Antarctic Treaty, and Related Papers* (Washington, DC: Department of State Publication, 1960), p. 61.
35. Quigg, 'Antarctica', p. 62.
35. Ibid., p. 22.
36. G. Robinson and H. White, *Envoys of Mankind: A Declaration of the First Principles for the Governance of Space Societies* (Washington, DC: Smithsonian Institution Press, 1985), p. 176.
37. Ibid.
38. Quoted in D. Kash, *The Politics of Space Cooperation* (Englewood Cliffs, NJ: Prentice-Hall, 1967), p. 96.
39. Robinson and White, *Envoys of Mankind*, p. 168.
40. W. McDougall, *...the Heavens and the Earth*, p. 228.
41. Ibid., p. 181.
42. Ibid., p. 182.
43. Ibid., p. 260. See also Kash, *Space Cooperation*, p. 96.
44. 'Letter from Eisenhower to Premier Bulganin' Department of State Bulletin (10 March 1958), p. 373.
45. Quoted in W. Burrows, *Deep Black: Space Espionage and National Security* (New York: Random House, 1986), p. vii.
46. 'Soviet Memorandum of May 5, 1958', *Department of State Bulletin* (7 July 1958), p. 19. Also cited in Kash, *Space Cooperation*, p. 98.
47. See S. Shaffer, and L. Shaffer, *The Politics of International Cooperation: A Comparison of US Experience in Space and in Security* (Denver, CO: University of Denver Press, 1980), p. 16.
48. Kash, *Space Cooperation*, p. 99.
49. Bloomfield, 'Prospects for Law and Order', p. 164.
50. White, *Decision-Making for Space*, p. 179.
51. Kash, *Space Cooperation*, pp. 104–5.
52. Bloomfield, 'Prospects for Law and Order', p. 165.
53. McDougall, *...the Heavens and the Earth*, p. 258.
54. Kash, *Space Cooperation*, p. 106.
55. McDougall, *...the Heavens and the Earth*, pp. 258–9.
56. Bloomfield, 'Prospects for Law and Order', p. 167.
57. Kash, *Space Cooperation*, p. 109.
58. Ibid., p. 112; and McDougall, *...the Heavens and the Earth*, p. 260.
59. White, *Decision-Making for Space*, p. 180.
60. Gardner, R. 'Cooperation in Outer Space', *Foreign Affairs*, January (1963), p. 7.
61. See also Robinson and White, *Envoys of Mankind*, pp. 167–8, for a fuller discussion of Soviet attempts to establish socialism in space.
62. A. Gore, 'Statement to the United Nations General Assembly', 3 December 1963. Cited in Kash, *Space Cooperation*, pp. 117–18.
63. Robinson and White, *Envoys of Mankind*, p. 183.

64. Ibid. 'The Liability Convention is having significant effects. NASA is requiring indemnification from its passengers and payloads on the Shuttle for the absolute liability that the government bears.'
65. N. Goldman, 'Transition and Confusion in the Law', in D. Papp and J. McIntyre (eds), *International Space Policy: Legal, Economic, and Strategic Options for the Twentieth Century and Beyond* (New York: Quorum Books, 1987), p. 154.
66. Wadegoankar, *The Orbit of Space Law*, pp. 43–5. See also B. Cheng, 'The Legal Regime of Aerospace and Outer Space: The Boundary Problem', *Annals of Air and Space Law*, Vol. 5 (1980), p. 323.
67. Robinson and White, *Envoys of Mankind*, p. 170.
68. Bloomfield, 'The Prospects for Law and Order', p. 157.
69. Ibid., p. 170.
70. Wadegoankar, *The Orbit of Space Law*, p. 43.
71. J. Hickman and E. Dolman, 'Resurrecting the Space Age: A State-centered Commentary on the Outer Space Regime', unpublished manuscript.
72. R. Zubrin, *Entering Space: Creating a Spacefaring Civilization* (New York: Jeremy P. Tarcher and Putnam, 1999), p. 14. I am indebted to John Hickman for providing me with this citation and for the many hours of discussion to refine these notions.
73. H. Spruyt, *The Sovereign State and its Competitors: Analysis of Systems Change* (Princeton, NJ: Princeton University Press, 1994).
74. R. Coase, 'The Problem of Social Cost', *Journal of Law and Economics*, Vol. 3 (1960), pp. 1–44.

6

Astrostrategy: Power, Policy, and Applications

> War is not a mere act of policy, but a true political instrument, a continuation of political activity by other means.
>
> Carl von Clausewitz[1]

That the world is undergoing fundamental change in the aftermath of the Cold War has become almost axiomatic. Policymakers search for a new paradigm that will guide them through the tumult of the new era. They are inundated with possible courses of action from academics with piles of fresh data and pundits with the gift of perfect hindsight. The result has been a loss of initiative by all the remaining great powers, and the one remaining superpower. They choose inaction not because there is too little information available, but because there is too much. The world system is in turmoil, and there appears to be no authoritative solution on the horizon. Conferences are held and committees are formed. More data are generated, and still there is no scheme to gather it all in. There is no formula to make sense of it. In space, the void of policy and strategy is as desolate as the cosmos.

When indecision and inaction result from such a jumbled mass of conflicting opinions, Michael Doyle avers, the most fruitful means of making sense of the cacophony is to 'reexamine the time-tested classics of ways of war and peace'.[2] He professes the continuing relevance of the three dominant world views of the twentieth century – realism, liberalism, and socialism – and argues persuasively that they maintain their validity in the twenty-first. Colin Gray is more adamant in his insistence that 'there are elements common to war and strategy in all periods, in all geographies, and with all technologies'.[3] Gray cautions, however, that just because strategy has consistent and universal historical patterns, it does not make the application of policy in new terrain and with new technologies simple or easy. Space policy and strategy is a case in point, with many attempting to codify a vision and few, if any, achieving a semblance of authority. That a return to the classics is warranted in such situations, and a return to the enduring concepts of strategy and doctrine desirable when attempting to clear a path through the rubble of broken conjectures, is ardently accepted here. To be sure, this text has endeavored to describe and clarify the place of foundational geopolitical and realist theories that inform and guide its model, and to make a case that space power and strategy are logical heirs to a consistent line of political thought.

Strategy, grand strategy in particular, is not simply the efficient military application of force. Since grand strategy is ultimately political in nature, that is to say the ends of national strategy are inextricably political, yet the means or dimensions of strategy are not limited. Edward Luttwak describes grand strategy as the 'highest level of final results',[4] and includes not just the outcome of tactical and operational battles (the 'interactions of the lower, military levels'), but the 'formal exchanges of diplomacy, the public communications of propaganda, secret operations, [intelligence], and all economic transactions of more than private significance'.[5] Here the military dimension is but one to consider, and within the military dimension, subdimensions cannot be neglected. Clausewitz posited five elements of military strategy: moral, physical, mathematical, geographical, and statistical.[6] Gray provides us with no fewer than 17 elements of strategy, grouped into three broad categories; People and Politics, Preparation for War, and War Proper.[7] Astropolitics requires that at least six dimensions are considered and accounted for when forming and applying policy:

(1) *Society and culture*: The astropolitical society must be farsighted and enthusiastic for space exploration and conquest. It must be prepared to forgo expenditures on social programs and various personal commodities to channel maximum funds into the national space program. It must be imbued with national esprit. It must be industrious to use Mahan's concept, and fascinated with new technologies and the acquisition thereof. It must revere science and the study of technology. It must be tolerant, not only to accept the potentially paradigm-shifting revelations of scientific exploration at this magnitude of effort, but to be able to accept competing alternatives to scientific standards so that an academic marketplace of ideas can flourish. It must have a sense of adventure, or at least have a sector of society willing to undertake the tremendous risk involved in space exploration and to make heroes of those who do. The society must consider space conquest a moral imperative, necessary to the survival of the human race, and must also perceive themselves as best equipped to dominate in this arena so as to bring the best ethical and moral values of the Earth into new realms. If the society does not already incorporate these sentiments and attributes, it is up to the government to inculcate and nurture them.

(2) *Political environment*: The astropolitical state must be efficiently organized for massive public technology projects (e.g., self-sustaining space station). Perhaps counterintuitively, this means liberal democratic and capitalist in character. The centrally planned economies of the twentieth century showed

a fearsome ability to marshal resources and to coerce their populations into the sacrifices necessary to construct national space programs, but they were unable to sustain them at the highest levels. Related to the first dimension, and now part of the strong state/weak state literature, governments that rely on force or perceptions of efficiency for governing legitimacy (essentially authoritarian models) must expend tremendous amounts of political and monetary resources in maintaining social order (police power) or economic competence (planned production through micro-management). In the former instance, the authoritarian state gains its legitimacy by its ability to project force, that is, to protect its citizens from both internal (criminal activity) and external (foreign militaries) harm. If it cannot monitor and control its population, or cannot protect that population from foreign adventurism, it cannot justify outward expansion. In the latter case, the centrally planned economy must outperform the decentralized counterexample of the free market. Neither requirement is likely to be met in the astropolitical future. The liberal democratic state, on the contrary, receives its legitimacy from the will of the people. It should not need to expend excessive funds on social control. If its people are imbued with an astropolitical vision, they will support tremendous space program expenses without the need for the state to waste resources in forcing compliance. As to the economy, Marx recognized that free-market capitalism is the most efficient producer of wealth, and the historical record shows the folly of attempting to compete with it using other means and models. A free people committed to space exploration will generate the wealth necessary to sustain a long-term vision for space dominance.

(3) *Physical environment*: The terrain of space and the terrestrial basing requirements of space support operations have already been discussed in Chapter 3, and need no further elaboration here. The physical requirements of the spacefaring state itself are also of interest, however. The state should be large enough in physical terms to incorporate a broad natural and industrial resource base and have the sites needed for terrestrial space support. It should also be large enough in terms of population so as to support the extreme expense, through taxes, of space domination efforts, and to continually renew the large number of inventive and high-technology positions required in support of space operations.

(4) *Military and technology*: Because of the risk involved, military personnel have always been at the forefront of space exploration. The military should be organized and trained in such a way that personnel have maximum initiative to deal with a multitude of contingencies and unanticipated events, within the framework of a state-determined strategy and policy. The vast distance and communications lag inherent in space travel will require brazen ingenuity and formidable courage. In order to maximize efficiency, the potential space-dominant state must integrate all its armed forces, and use the advantages of space control to maximum effect. The state must be preoccupied with

technology innovation. It must be the world leader in new applications and technologies. Included in this dimension is the requirement for centers of higher learning (for technological innovation) and military science (for strategy and tactics). The state must be prepared to fund massive scientific projects (of the order of the Manhattan Project, e.g. super-conducting super collider).

(5) *Economic base*: The industry of the state must be robust, high-tech, and adaptive to ongoing innovation. New applications for space resources and space explorations products are imperative. Government assistance in research and technology, and the free distribution of those results to civilian industry, is vital. Civilianized or commercial space industry is paramount. When the government acts as a discriminating monopolist, allocating resources by deciding authoritatively which companies shall produce what goods, it can marshal extraordinary financial clout in the effort but the market can better determine the most cost-effective and highest quality providers of space products through the mechanism of free and decentralized entrepreneurship. Logistics and supply lines must be identified, monitored, secured and controlled where vulnerable. Anticipation to future needs, given the lag in innovation and production, is paramount. The state should be prepared to reinforce areas of successful strategic production with subsidies and the release of classified technology, if needs be, but within the free-market paradigm should loathe interceding unless market failure is evident. Entrepreneurship is as vital to the state wishing to dominate space as it was to the early domination of the seas by Britain.

(6) *Theory and doctrine*: Strategy is more than just military maneuver and tactics. Theory and doctrine are more than just operational plans. They are the means for organizing knowledge, the lens through which we perceive the world around us, through which we evaluate and make sense of the infinite database of reality. Space theory and doctrine must encompass and coordinate all of the dimensions just listed. The number of categories or dimensions is not as important as the concept that all relevant variables are accounted for. Gray finds 17 dimensions, a number likely to be revised and changed, but his effort to integrate all pertinent concepts is impressive. A plan of coordinated advance is necessary along all dimensions of the spectra in order for strategy to succeed. A force of the highest trained and best-equipped soldiers will be trapped and decimated if their logistics chain is ignored. The most fervent space power proponent as head of state is unlikely to succeed in the liberal democratic state if she/he cannot shape a complementary consensus among the population. Yet theory and doctrine do more than just coordinate and illuminate. The difference between theory or doctrine-driven strategy and, say, technology-driven strategy is profound. The first integrates new technology into a coherent vision; the latter abandons foresight and follows the apparatus wherever it leads. One is proactive, the other reactive. One wins, the other

loses. When one accepts the authority of technology (or economics, or any other dimension) over strategy, the analogy is to the child who receives a hammer for a gift. Suddenly, a world of nails appears, and they all need pounding.

STRATEGIES FOR OUTER SPACE

The paucity of coherent space strategies, under this definition, is surprising. An interest in space domination is evident from at least 1946 with the first government-sponsored RAND Corporation Study concerning a *Preliminary Design for an Experimental World Circling Spaceship*.[8] To date, only James Oberg's *Space Power Theory*, a comprehensive effort commissioned by the United States Space Command, approaches the requirements laid out above.[9] In between and now beyond, only a few fragmentary expositions of reasoned space strategy are to be found.

In 1961, Dandridge Cole undertook a poll of 423 leaders of the astronautic community, asking their opinion of his 'Panama Hypothesis[:] that there are strategic areas in space which may someday be as important to space transportation as the Panama Canal is to ocean transportation.'[10] According to Cole, roughly 80 percent answered in the affirmative. Cole advocated human colonization of asteroids, or planetoids, those 'three-dimensional islands of the new three-dimensional sea', as stepping stones to outer space conquest.[11] At least six factors influenced his focus on these celestial bodies: (1) as a source of new knowledge about the origin of the solar system and possibly life itself; (2) as a potential threat, asteroids or meteors could be deflected from a collision course with Earth; (3) as way stations for fueling interplanetary expeditions; (4) as raw materials for Earth industry; (5) if hollowed out, as desirable protected locations for colonies; and (6) again if hollowed out and then propeled, as massive space ships capable of sending sustainable human colonies to populate the planets of other stars.[12] His vision was remarkable, but targeted to younger audiences of space enthusiasts. It did not make significant strategic inroads. At the same time, Cole's exhortations were falling on the wrong ears, the United States and Soviet Union were in the midst of declaring all of space unpossessable, making his primary arguments moot. The general sentiment led to the first of the two primary schools of space power theory: space as strategic *sanctuary* and space as the ultimate *high ground*.

Compatible with the view that space is the province of all humankind, and that its riches belong to all the peoples of Earth, is the notion that space is a sanctuary from the evils of this planet. Why spread the disease of war and violence to the cosmos? Indeed, from this perspective space may be the only hope for the future of humanity. As we destroy our planet through nuclear or political abuse and environmental misuse, space as a pristine frontier looms ever more valuable as the last, best refuge of humanity. And it could work. Antarctica has been collectively held as an international common for over 40 years (though its resource potential has barely been tapped). The same model could and should apply to space, say the space sanctuary proponents. The argument is an old one. Alton Frye wrote in 1963:

> There is a strong American consensus in support of the basic elements of national space policy. The world will be a much safer place if we can succeed in maintaining space as a sanctuary for purely peaceful activities. [But] how do we keep the arms race from spreading to this new arena? Presently the United States hopes to accomplish this noble purpose by a declared policy of abstaining from developing space weapons. While pressing for international agreement on the peaceful use of space, we promise the Soviets that we will refrain from orbiting weapons of mass destruction so long as they do not station such devices in space.[13]

Yet even Frye recognized that despite the noble intentions of his argument, space had been militarized already, and weaponization of the realm was moving apace. David Zeigler provides a subtler and more powerful argument.[14] His space as strategic sanctuary thesis argues that the militarization of space actually detracts from the security of states that pursue it. Whereas a space militarization policy may have been consistent with Cold War strategies, it may not be at all appropriate in a post-Cold War world. Although the sanctuary argument, 'in the strictest sense, [claims] space is a sanctuary when it is completely unthreatened by terrestrial or space-based weapons', Zeigler, too, admits this is problematic.[15] Space is already militarized, and there seems to be little or no chance it could be demilitarized perfectly in the near future. So Zeigler suggests a more flexible and useful claim is that space is a sanctuary 'so long as nations truly intended never to use space weapons', a condition he claims exists precariously today.[16] Initially, the United States and the world embraced the space as sanctuary policy because of the extraordinary vulnerability of their fragile but immensely useful on-orbit assets. Blatant arming of space or the creation of new and effective anti-satellite (ASAT) capabilities would only serve to induce other states to match or surpass US capability, and would threaten its most expensive and vital military support link. Additionally, the deterrent logic of MAD might be abrogated in the deployment of space-to-ground weapons in the future. The 30–35 minute warning of an ICBM attack, and at least several-minute warning of Medium- and Short-Range Ballistic Missile (MRBM; SRBM) attack were deemed necessary for calculated national responses. Nuclear bombardment from space-based platforms would bypass satellite and ground radar monitoring systems thus providing no effective warning time, and the potential for surprise attack would have been increased. In practice, however, Zeigler must conclude the fragile basis for his point. The world's spacefaring nations *had* been publicly employing the sanctuary argument even as they cautiously and covertly developed space weaponization policies. The intent to use weapons was always publicly denied, but privately reserved as a viable option.

Still, in the current post-Cold War environment, Zeigler maintains that the need for space sanctuary is greater than ever before. First, states increasingly deploy and rely on space systems for battlefield support, so just the threat of losing those systems makes states less secure overall. If states were monitoring terrestrial crises with satellites, any attempt to deprive them of that information (through jamming, laser 'blinding', or direct ASAT attack) could be interpreted as preparation for imminent hostilities. States so deprived might feel compelled to launch a first strike. Second, it is unwise and premature to invest heavily in space weapons when so many pressing battlefield hardware and personnel requirements go unfilled. All of the services have seen cuts in budgets that affect readiness and morale. Space weapons are costly and, in Zeigler's view, grossly overrated. In addition, space weapons are simply not as cost-effective as passive countermeasures against enemy space capabilities. Third, the United States' 'physical security, economic well-being, and democratic expansion depend on the quality of American international relations', and any attempt to weaponize space would be 'unacceptably provocative', leading to 'global instability'.[17] Ultimately, Zeigler's argument rests on the conviction that military space power has been overstated, and that existing US conventional capabilities are more than adequate for its security needs (if properly funded) even with the loss of space-based support. The claim is not convincing.

Space as the ultimate high ground is the more prevalent view, and as a counter to the space sanctuary argument it stems from the notion that the weaponization of space is inevitable. So long as the fight is surely coming, one ought to stake out and maintain the best defensive positions and be prepared for any contingency. In 1997, then Commander-in-Chief of US Space Command General Joseph Ashy declared that the United States was becoming so dependent on space systems for its armed forces that it had (perhaps unwittingly) created an enormous incentive for future enemies to target them. The United States, Ashy said, 'must be prepared to defend these systems':[18]

> It's politically sensitive, but it's going to happen ... we're going to fight in space. We're going to fight *from* space and we're going to fight *into* space ... That's why the US has development programs in directed energy and hit-to-kill mechanisms. We'll expand into these two missions – space control and space force application – because they will become increasingly important. We will engage terrestrial targets someday – ships, airplanes, land targets – from space. We will engage targets in space, from space.[19]

Given the situation described by General Ashy, and the linked realities that Russia's massive co-orbital ASAT facilities are still operational and that the US has tended to concentrate its capabilities into a few multi-mission satellites (as opposed to the old Soviet model of relying on multiply redundant single-mission ones), it is conceivable that even a limited functional ASAT capability could do extraordinary damage to US military preparedness. The high-ground perspective is not just a counter to the sanctuary argument, however. It has an independent history based on the tactical imperative of seizing the dominant terrain of the battlefield. The high ground offers the side that holds it commanding overviews, fields of fire, and defensive position. In this view, space is the 'ultimate high-ground' for the terrestrial battlefield.[20]

The 1991 Gulf War served as the coming-out party for space support. No less an authority than Arthur C. Clarke dubbed it 'the world's first satellite war'.[21] Without question, the now-critical functions of outer space assets were featured throughout that conflict. From early warning and detection of missile and force movements to target planning and battle damage assessment, space-based intelligence gathering assets proved themselves legitimate combat force multipliers. In Kosovo and Serbia, as the century gave way to a new millennium, space assets were even more effective. The most surprising and enduring contributions evident in the expanded military role of outer-space technology, however, may have come from the previously underappreciated value of navigation, communications, and commercial imaging and weather prediction satellites.[22] With these performances, space warfare has emerged from its embryonic stage and is now fully in its infancy. In the post-Cold War era, downsizing of traditional military forces continues, access to customary forward basing is increasingly withdrawn, high-technology Command, Control, Communications and Intelligence (C^3I), and mission support is integrated into routine operating procedures, and reliance on intelligence forecasting for optimal troop deployments is emphasized. In this transitional environment, employment of space systems for all levels of inter-state conflict is likely to increase significantly. The merit of space capability was so apparent that despite substantial reductions in US Department of Defense (DoD) procurement budgets following the Gulf War, investments in space-based capabilities significantly increased:

> The result is that investment in space systems is taking an increasingly larger share of a shrinking total DoD investment budget; in fiscal year 1993, space investment will exceed fifteen percent of total investment, a doubling of the share since fiscal year 1986. For comparison purposes, the space investment budget now exceeds total investment in the Army by 20 percent, whereas in fiscal year 1986 it was less than half.[23]

At the same time, counter-pressures for limiting or reducing military and military-support activities in space remain viable. The end of the Cold War has dampened the various services' enthusiasm for pressing for expensive new space theater of operations, as new funding made available for space will likely be drawn from existing conventional force structure. With a new era of extended peace potentially at hand, at least in the realm of superpower rivalry, popular support for the militarization of outer space is equivocal. Long-standing efforts at confirming space as the common heritage of mankind and a sanctuary have been renewed. Calls to abandon space expenditures and instead demands for increased domestic spending on terrestrial infrastructure and quality of life are made, as critics of national space programs incorrectly view money spent on military and civilian space projects to be worse than wasted. In this milieu, where does the national strategy of the United States now stand?

ASSESSING CURRENT US SPACE STRATEGY

The United States is the dominant power in space, and so its policies will impact on all other spacefaring states. Given the mutual incompatibility of a common heritage perspective and a space control agenda, it is unlikely that the policy will remain coherent. A review is warranted to verify the dictums of astropolitics are in place and to evaluate the efficacy, or lack thereof, of its guidelines.

After summarily dismissing, then abolishing, the previous administration's National Space Council (coordinator of the commercial, civilian, and military space programs of the United States), and allowing the space enterprise to languish for over two years, President Clinton belatedly attempted to articulate a wide-ranging national position. His 1995 declaration of space policy identified five overarching goals.[24] In order, they are to: (a) enhance knowledge of the Earth, the solar system and the universe through human and robotic exploration; (b) strengthen and maintain the national security of the United States; (c) enhance the economic competitiveness, and scientific and technical capabilities of the United States; (d) encourage state, local and private-sector investment in, and use of, space technologies; and (e) promote international cooperation to further US domestic, national security, and foreign policies. The dimensions of this policy appear at first to conform to a notion of grand strategy as defined above, but closer examination shows the policy has little value for guidance. It appears to be no more than a somewhat organized collection of existing *ad hoc* national space policy declarations of the previous decade. Not surprisingly, curious and patently paradoxical statements abound, for example: 'The United States rejects any claims to sovereignty by any nation over outer space or celestial bodies, or any portion thereof, [yet p]urposeful interference with space systems shall be viewed as an infringement on sovereign rights.'[25] Within this and the following mandate, the various military services have attempted to carve out a mission for space:

> Improving our ability to support military operations worldwide, monitor and respond to strategic military threats, and monitor arms control and non-proliferation agreements and activities are key priorities for national security space activities. [N]ational security space activities shall contribute to US national security by: (a) providing support for the United States' inherent right of self-defense and our defense commitments to allies and friends; (b) deterring, warning, and if necessary, defending against enemy attack; (c) assuring that hostile forces cannot prevent our own use of space; (d) countering, if necessary, space systems and services used for hostile purposes; (e) enhancing operations of U.S. and allied forces; (f) ensuring our ability to conduct military and intelligence space-related activities; (g) satisfying military and intelligence requirements during peace and crisis as well as through all levels of conflict; (h) supporting the activities of national policymakers, the intelligence community, the National Command Authorities, combatant commanders and the military services, other federal officials, and continuity of government operations.

Of course, any imaginable policy or strategy could be knit together from these woolly parameters. The armed services have all cautiously advanced proposals to further their parochial interests while complying with what they perceive to be the general sentiments of the White House. The Joint Chiefs of Staff have provided a general and complementary guideline for near-term policy called 'Joint Vision 2020'.[26] As in previous incarnations, the focus remains on warfighting, with four operational concepts; dominant maneuver, precision engagement, focused logistics, and 'full spectrum' dominance. What purports to be new is a jargon- and acronym-laced list of fuzzy catch phrases like 'focus on multinational and interagency interoperability', and 'MOOTW' (Military Operations Other Than War). Where the text is intelligible, 'Joint Vision 2020' reads like a recruiting pamphlet ('The US military today is a force of superbly trained men and women who are ready to deliver victory for our Nation') or an acceptance speech ('The overall goal of the transformation described in this document is the creation of a force that is dominant across the full spectrum of military operations – persuasive in peace, decisive in war, preeminent in any form of conflict').[27] It uses patriotic rhetoric to bring acceptance of its subdued but primary goals, including the willingness to fight for and in space.

For its part, the United States Space Command released its 1998 'Long Range Plan'. In keeping with the President's mandate and in compliance with Joint Vision 2020 expectations, the plan is based on the primary assumption that the protection of military and civilian/commercial space assets is in the vital national interest. Space power is currently a force multiplier on the battlefield, aver the authors; commercial space expenditures and revenues will increase at 20 percent or more annually; rivals including commercial and military adversaries will emerge to challenge US space superiority. To prevent the increasing US reliance on space assets becoming a future liability, Space Command is the logical focal point to coordinate military space operations. Within that self-described mandate, 'Our Long Range Plan identifies required capabilities, Concepts of Operation, new organizations and partnerships to achieve these operational concepts.' These operational concepts include the notion of: (1) Space Control, that is, guaranteed access to space and the ability to deny enemies' access to; (2) Global Engagement, which requires worldwide satellite indications and warning monitoring (intelligence) and ballistic and cruise missile defense; (3) Full Force Integration, the conceptual and operational integration of conventional and space forces to the point that 'air, land, and sea [c]ommanders exploit space assets as intuitively as their more traditional assets'; and (4) Global Partnership, the strengthening of military space capabilities through incorporating or 'leveraging' commercial, other US agency, and allied national assets to the fullest.[28] The vision is a critical link on the path to a complete strategy for space, but Space Command is still not sure of its footing. That Oberg's *Space Power Theory* – paid for, published and officially released by Space Command – has the front-page caveat that the 'opinions, conclusions and recommendations expressed or implied are those solely of the author' and 'do not necessarily represent the views of US Space Command, the Department of Defense, or any other US Government Agency', is a not too clever way of hedging its bets with the Executive Office.

The US Air Force, attempting to become the leader in space force applications, identifies its plans to meet future requirements with the paired 'Global Engagement' and 'New World Vistas' policy statements. The latter is a technology-driven attempt to maximize cost-utility in a shrinking budget ('Affordability restrictions demand caution at this point'[29]), and therefore has dubious utility for grand strategy and useful policy planning. One point that is vigorously asserted, however, is that the 'future force will include a mix of weapons, both space- and groundbased, able to shoot photon- and kinetic-energy munitions against enemy space and ground assets'.[30] The Army and Navy, too, have jumped on the bandwagon. The Army is leading efforts for ground-based, aerospace defenses. As an extension of traditional air defense capabilities, the MIRACL laser and planned ground-based anti-missile interceptor are undergoing testing for anti-satellite operations.

Clearly, current US space strategy is focused on technological capabilities, and to a lesser extent on developing military and commercial capabilities. Given ambiguous and weak leadership from the top, strategy is perhaps naturally timid, hedging, elusive, evasive, and contradictory. When vision is not provided, followers will focus on the concrete: current and future technology and systems applications.[31] What space power can and could do becomes the essence of thinking about strategy, when it should be limited to operations and tactics. These elements are not to be panned, they are critical to fighting and winning war, but they are not the equivalent of strategy. To turn the analysis around, what one can say about the current US space strategy is that it most certainly is not decisive, guiding, or illuminating. In a word, it is not *strategic.*

AN *ASTROPOLITIK* POLICY FOR THE UNITED STATES

Astropolitik gets its moniker from the old, now completely discredited German school of *Geopolitik.* It is meant to be a constant reminder of the inherent flaws of letting the cultural dimension (specifically hypernationalism) drive grand strategy. One should also be struck by the affinity with the doctrine of *Realpolitik.* This most extreme of the political realist theories makes no attempt to hide its ruthless concentration on the national interest and the cold, calculating central role of raw power in politics. It is widely criticized by those who do not have power, widely employed by those who do. Such is the case today that in space, at the very least, the United States can adopt any policy it wishes and the attitudes and reactions of the domestic public and of other states can do little to challenge it. So powerful is the United States that should it accept the harsh *Realpolitik* doctrine in space that the military services appear to be proposing, and given a proper explanation for employing it, there may in fact be little if any opposition to a *fait accompli* of total US domination in space.

What follows is the framework of the *Astropolitik* grand strategy. It is not the only strategy available to the United States, nor is there any effort to deny the existence of a superior strategy. It is simply the logical output of an *Astropolitik* analysis. No attempt will be made to create an unconvincing argument that the United States has a right to domination in space, or that other states through their enmity are forcing their hand. Such simply would not be true. Only a brief attempt will be made to argue that, in this case, might does make right. The persuasiveness of the case will be based on the self-interest of the state, and stability of the system. It is a policy and a case lifted directly from words of the Athenians in Thucydides' infamous 'Melian Dialogue', perhaps the most precise and enduring statement of *Realpolitik* ever made.[32]

Just as the Athenians could argue that Melian neutrality was more damaging to their interests than outright hostility, *Astropolitik* declares that the lack of a hostile space power at the present is more damaging to US space interests than having aggressive, competing military space programs with which to cope (an argument specifically constructed in Chapter 4). In a parallel line of reasoning, the Athenians believed the toleration of a weak neutral close to the borders of its empire was a sign of weakness in themselves. It could induce current allies to switch to neutrality, depriving them of needed revenues (via tribute). The lack of an enemy in space is most assuredly causing complacency in the United States, stunting the expansion of its space capabilities, and further causing our allies (in Europe and Japan specifically, but in Israel most notoriously) to develop their own potentially conflicting military space capacities because they cannot be sure of US commitments in the future. The United States does have one significant edge over the Athenians in that it can advance a broad moral argument for space domination. Athens was fashioning a coercive empire of dependent states, the United States is not. The US form of liberal democracy, unlike Athenian mob democracy, is conducted within the rule of law. It is admirable and socially encompassing. If any one state should dominate space, it ought be one with a constitutive political principle that government should be responsible and responsive to its people, tolerant and accepting of their views, and willing to extend legal and political equality to all. In other words, the United States should seize control of outer space and become the shepherd (or perhaps watchdog) for all who would venture there, for if any one state must do so, it is the most likely to establish a benign hegemony.

The *Astropolitik* plan could be emplaced quickly and easily, with just three critical steps. First, the United States should declare that it is withdrawing from the current space regime and announce that it is establishing a principle of free-market sovereignty in space (along the guidelines articulated in Chapter 5). Propaganda touting the prospects of a new golden age of space exploration should be crafted and released, and the economic advantages and spin-off technology from space efforts highlighted, to build popular support for the plan.

Second, by using its current and near-term capacities, the United States should endeavor at once to seize military control of low-Earth orbit. From that high ground vantage, near the top of the Earth's gravity well, space-based laser or kinetic energy weapons could prevent any other state from deploying assets there, and could most effectively engage and destroy terrestrial enemy ASAT facilities. Other states should still be able to enter space relatively freely for the purpose of engaging in commerce, in keeping with the principles of the new regime. Just as in the sea dominance eras of the Athenians and British before them, the military space forces of the United States would have to create and maintain a safe operating environment (from pirates and other interlopers, perhaps from debris) to enhance trade and exploration. Only those spacecraft that provide advance notice of their mission and flight plan would be permitted in space, however. The military control of low-Earth orbit would be for all practical purposes a police blockade of all current spaceports, monitoring and controlling all traffic both in and out.

Third, a national space coordination agency should be established to define, separate, and coordinate the efforts of commercial, civilian, and military space projects. This agency would also define critical needs and deficiencies, eliminate non-productive overlap, take over the propaganda functions iterated in step one above, and merge the various armed services space programs and policies where practical. It may be determined that in this environment a separate space force, coequal with army, navy and air forces, be established, but it is not deemed vital at this time. As part of the propaganda effort, manned space efforts will need to be accelerated. This is the one counter to the efficiency argument of the new agency, but it is necessary. Humans in space fire the imagination, cull extraordinary popular support, and, while expensive, Oberg makes the subtle argument that humans 'have and will continue to possess a keener ability to sense, evaluate, and adapt to unexpected phenomena than machinery'.[33] A complementary commercial space technology agency could be subordinated or separated from the coordination agency, to assist in the development of space exploitation programs at national universities and colleges, fund and guide commercial technology research, and generate wealth maximization and other economic strategies for space resources and manufacturing.

That is all it should take. These three steps would be enough to begin the conceptual transition to an *Astropolitik* regime and ensure that the United States remains at the forefront of space power for the foreseeable future. The details would be sorted out in time, but the strategy clearly meets the elementary requirements previously articulated, from social and cultural to theory and doctrine. It places as guardian of space the most benign state that has ever attempted hegemony over the greater part of the world. It harnesses the natural impulses of states and society to seek out and find the vast riches of space as yet unidentified but universally surmised to be out there while providing a revenue-generating reserve for states unable to venture out. It is bold, decisive, guiding, and, at least from the hegemon's point of view, morally just.

The moral argument has many levels, and stems from both the high-ground and the modified-sanctuary theses (accepted here) that the weaponization of space is inevitable. The operational level contradiction is quite simply that it is unconscionable to assign to the military services the task of controlling space, and then deny them the best means with which to do it. To the military, it is the equivalent of sending a soldier into combat without a rifle. At the strategic level it thwarts the gloomier predictions of the awful result of space weaponization by preempting the process. Most theorists who lament the coming inevitability of space militarization do so on some variation of the notion that once one state puts weapons into space, other states will rush to do the same, creating a space-weapons race that has no productive purpose and only a violent end. Other assumptions are generally along the line that conflict and bloody war must eventually reach the cosmos, and delaying or holding off that eventuality is the best we can hope for. By seizing the initiative and securing low-Earth orbit now, while the United States is unchallenged in space, both those assumptions are revealed as faulty. The ability to shoot down from space any attempt by another nation to place military assets in space, or to readily engage and destroy terrestrial ASAT capacity, makes the possibility of large-scale space war and or military space races less likely, not more. Why would a state expend the effort to compete in space with a power that has the extraordinary advantage of holding securely the highest ground at the top of the gravity well? So long as the controlling state demonstrates a capacity *and a will* to use force to defend its position, in effect expending a small amount of violence as needed to prevent a greater conflagration in the future, the likelihood of either scenario seems remote. To be sure, if the United States were willing to deploy and use a military space force that maintained effective control of space, and did so in a way that was perceived as tough, non-arbitrary, and efficient, other states would quickly realize that they had no need to develop space military forces. It would serve to discourage competing states from fielding opposing systems much 'in the same fashion that the Global Positioning System (GPS) succeeded in forestalling the fielding of rival navigation and timing systems'.[34] In time, US control of low-Earth orbit could be viewed as a global asset and a public good.

To make the last point clearer, a brief excursus on one of the more contentious policy debates of the day – ballistic missile defense or BMD – is offered for consideration. The 'most likely' area in which the United States might 'act unilaterally' to put a space-based weapons system in place is in the area of BMD.[35] The debate over *where* the next generation BMD system is best placed is certainly not over, and a space-based system at this time is not the front runner for deployment. But the advantages of a system that could eliminate the threat of accidental, rogue state, or terrorist launches of nuclear missiles is so compelling that it is highly likely to be attempted regardless of opposition efforts.

The widely held belief that the Reagan military build-up of the 1980s (in truth begun by President Carter in the last year of his administration), and in particular the energy and monies spent on the Strategic Defense Initiative (SDI or 'Star Wars') was at least partially, if not primarily responsible for the breakup of the Soviet Union and the end of the Cold War, is a popular tenet of the US right in justifying military expenditures. If you want peace, prepare for war, goes the old adage. Partisans of the American left vigorously denounce the notion that Reagan in general and SDI in particular had anything at all to do with the end of the Cold War. Frances Fitzgerald's response is typical.[36] Reagan, she claims, was simply not capable of formulating such a far-reaching policy. His belief in a laser-based protective shield around the US was pure fantasy. While the *Astropolitik* perspective is highly sympathetic to the claim that military confrontation, particularly the threat of SDI, was indeed the straw that broke the Soviet camel's back, it is not necessary to dwell on that contentious issue to make the moral case for a new space-based missile defense system, but the legacy of such a system must be briefly described.

The 1972 Anti-Ballistic Missile (ABM) Treaty placed strict constraints on the ability of the two superpowers to defend themselves from missile attack. The logic was simple, if morally perverse. The deployment of an effective ABM defense would eliminate the threat of guaranteed retaliation, the vaunted 'second strike' capability that would deter any state from attempting a crippling 'first strike'. The necessity of *mutual and assured* destruction was the dominant principle in the precarious balance of terror that would supposedly ensure world peace. Still, neither side wished to eliminate completely their ability to research and test ABM capability. By treaty then, two ABM sites were allowed each side. One surrounding and protecting the national capital composed of no more than 100 missiles, and another smaller site for research and development.

The fact that the Soviet Union (and now Russia) deployed and maintained, into at least three generations, an ABM screen around Moscow, while the Americans quickly abandoned efforts to protect Washington, highlights the moral nature of the two governments. Congress and the President quickly realized that releasing massive funds for the protection of lawmakers in Washington, while spending not a dime or an iota of effort to defend any other city, was a reelection nightmare. Moreover, it did nothing to detract from the prospects of nuclear war. If the leaders of the state are (at least partially) protected from nuclear attack, would they be more or less willing to initiate actions or employ diplomatic tactics that could lead to war? The answer clearly appeared to be toward the more precarious side of the equation. For these two reasons, that the government was not more deserving of protection than the people, and that such protection increased (*vice* decreased) the likelihood of nuclear war, the Americans never deployed an operational, Treaty-allowed ABM system. The official US argument was that it was just not cost-effective to deploy a system of no more than 100 protecting anti-missiles, since all the Soviets had to do was overwhelm that defensive capacity with 101 missiles. The Soviet leadership, by contrast, had no qualms about protecting themselves from limited nuclear attack, regardless of the expense.

At some point, the student of nuclear war politics will ask, what of today? If a missile were launched, accidentally or on purpose, what would be the result? The answer, bluntly stated, is that it would hit and destroy its target. There remains today no means to protect the citizens of this or any country (excepting the city of Moscow) from nuclear devastation. From this perspective, on 23 March 1983, President Reagan offered to the nation a plan:

> If the Soviet Union will join with us in our effort to achieve major arms reduction, we will have succeeded in stabilizing the nuclear balance. Nevertheless, it will still be necessary to rely on the specter of mutual retaliation, on mutual threat. And that's a sad commentary on the human condition. Wouldn't it be better to save lives than to avenge

> them? Are we not capable of demonstrating our peaceful intentions by applying all our abilities and our ingenuity to achieving a truly lasting stability? I think we are. Indeed, we must.[37]

Immediately opposition was apparent. The core of negative views centered on two general arguments: the United States *cannot* deploy SDI, and it *should not* deploy SDI. The first argument is technical, the second normative. It is extraordinarily interesting to note that the bulk of the published technical opposition came from journalists and non-scientists, while the scientists tended to argue publicly that SDI was morally flawed. At any rate, the pared down technology argument was that the President's ambitions were too complex. The possibility of a perfect nuclear shield could never be realized, regardless of the amount of research effort and expense applied. As with the previous example of the ABM Treaty, the Soviets could simply overwhelm whatever capacity the United States could deploy. The normative or moral arguments were more dispersed. The most compelling at the time was that if the United States could develop a nuclear shield capacity, the Soviets would have to attack before the shield could be deployed, or lose forever their ability to wage nuclear war on the United States. The other prominent moral argument was that the vast amounts of money being spent on space defense could be better used on domestic programs like public education, highway and transportation upgrades, and the like. Besides, the protesters argued, the mutual deterrence of the balance of terror was apparently working, why fix something that wasn't broken.

The first argument, that the technology to deploy a missile defense shield will never be developed, is defeated by analogy. History is replete with scientific advances over the popular howlings that a thing can't be done ('man will never fly', comes to mind). The ingenuity of the scientific community accepts such dares willingly. The real technical question is not can the task be done, but can the task be done for the amount of money available? Thirty-five to three hundred billion dollars, the original cost estimates, are in retrospect far too low. Three to five trillion dollars, however, might just turn the trick.

The second, which contains two primary embedded contentions, argument is also flawed. The first contention, that fielding SDI would *compel* the Soviets to attack the United States in advance of operational deployment is astonishing. It presupposes that the United States, once safe from the Soviet nuclear threat, would be ready and willing, indeed anxious to devastate the Soviet state with a rain of nuclear bombardment. No other assumption could cause the Soviets to attack the United States prior to the deployment of SDI but still at a time the United States could launch a devastating retaliatory strike. Put bluntly, in order to believe the Soviets would be forced to attack peremptorily, one must assume that mutual assured destruction of both sides was preferable to the *inevitable* destruction of just the Soviet side by the Americans.

In the manner of a backhanded compliment, the preceding logic supports the notion that the only reason World War III did not occur is because of the massive nuclear retaliation threat maintained by the two superpowers. It suggests that both sides (or in this case, the US side only) were so obsessed with destroying the other forever that without the risk of mutual extinction they surely would have done so. If one side showed the tiniest weakness, had either ever been vulnerable, the other was ready and willing to use its nuclear arsenal. This notion of course belies the historical record. From 1945 to 1951, the United States had atomic then nuclear monopoly, and until at least 1963 it had a large advantage in nuclear weaponry, yet chose not to use it.

The latter of the embedded contentions is also problematic. It presupposes that spending on space weapons and technology will take away from the quality of life on Earth. Aside from the banal statement that the quality of life is minimized by death, forgoing a defensive system to put increased funds into infrastructure also assumes that the funds for SDI research would have been made available instead for expenditures preferred by the opponents of the program. This is unlikely, as the state would simply shift the appropriations to more conventional areas of the military budget. Even if the death of a program gave an unexpected windfall of public funds, again unlikely since most of the proposed money was for future budgets, there is no guarantee that monies saved would not go back to the public in the form of lower taxes. It also assumes there is no productive benefit to the state from research and development in space weapons applications. To the contrary, the US and world economies have already benefited greatly in the miniaturization and computing technologies developed for the SDI/BMD programs. Military space programs, not the least of which is a robust space launch capacity, are the backbone of many civilian space operations, and the resultant economic advantages of telecommunications, navigation, earth-sensing, and weather satellites are obvious. The spin-off technology and follow-on economic effects of space research and development are abundant, and must be factored into the cost calculations of the state.

Nonetheless, the complaints of the nay-sayers were heard. The United States was unwilling to spend the massive amounts of money necessary to develop an imperfect shield for missile defense. With the end of the Cold War, the old deterrence arguments fell apart, but so did the impetus for deployment. By the second half of the Bush presidency, however, new threats emerged to challenge BMD planners. The prospect of having to deal with a limited or accidental missile launch increased in relative importance. In the wake of rapid Russian military devolution especially, the security of ballistic missiles was threatened, and even the locations of nuclear missiles and materials were sometimes in doubt. Would the Russians, hard pressed for convertible currency, sell technology, warheads, and missiles to other states or perhaps terrorist organizations? 'Rogue' states like Iraq and North Korea were known to be working on limited ballistic missile and nuclear warhead programs. The primary threat to the world in this new environment was less global conflagration from massive strikes, but localized devastation from limited ones. SDI no longer had to protect the United States and its allies from thousands of nuclear missiles, but now from just dozens. The technical arguments against SDI with this new mission vanished.

The pro-deployment moral argument, that there ought be some protection against limited strikes, carried the day. The SDI's prototype Brilliant Pebbles/ Brilliant Eyes ABM architecture was downgraded from a nuclear shield to a partial, global defense mechanism. The scheme would place a network of independent sensors and kinetic kill batteries in space. If an unannounced or unplanned launch occurred anywhere in the world, it would be detected and evaluated (by the specific characteristics of its heat signature). If a threat, targeting data would be passed to the orbiting launch platform, and a tiny aerospace projectile would be sent down the Earth's gravity well to engage the missile. With this design, from 24 to 100 simultaneous launches of missile weapons anywhere in the world could be detected, engaged, and destroyed.

By 1990, the plan was changed to a simpler, single-shot hit-to-kill kinetic engagement interceptor, with on-board sensors. Advances in miniaturization and computer speed meant that these autonomous weapons could be mass-produced and would weigh less than 20 kgs each. These Brilliant Pebbles would be scattered about low-Earth orbit and could function independently. The expenses of the modified Brilliant Pebbles remained high, possibly up to $300 billion. With the 1992 changeover to the Clinton administration, the plan was scrapped. Clinton, a vigorous opponent of SDI before claiming office, was won over by proponents of the need to maintain at least research and development funding for BMD, and quietly submitted budgets that would allow minimal research requirements to be met. By 1996 Congress was passing authorization bills for new defense systems over the objections of President Clinton. With North Korea and Israel demonstrating medium-range ballistic missile (MRBM) potential, and Iraq, Iran, and Libya (among others) thought to be developing similar capacities, and Pakistan detonating a nuclear device, Clinton and Congress in 1999 authorized the development of a light, mobile, ground-based BMD system to thwart very limited nuclear attacks against specific targets. The concept is generally known as Theater Missile Defense (TMD).

A ground based anti-missile system to defeat incoming ballistic missiles is much less expensive than a space-based one, but vastly inferior. First because of the limited range of the interceptor, it must be assigned to a point target or area to be effective. A TMD battery in New York could not defend an attack on Los Angeles. A space-based system would have global presence. Wherever the threat occurred, the system would be ready to intercept. Surprise missile attack would be impossible. Second, because the TMD engages the incoming missile, collateral damage will occur in or near the defense point. As an illustration, the Patriot missile (model for the current TMD light BMD system) defense of US positions in Saudi Arabia during Desert Storm engaged Iraqi SCUDs in the unpowered, down side of the ballistic arc. In one instance, a Patriot missile successfully engaged a SCUD missile, knocking it off course. The rocket body landed on a barracks causing heavy casualties; perhaps more than if the rocket with its warhead had hit its intended target. In a nuclear warhead scenario, even if the warhead is rendered inoperable, radioactive material could be spread over a significant region in the defending state's territory. Damage from chemical or biological weapons could also be severe, even with a successful engagement. A space-based system would engage the target in the boost phase of flight; meaning that whatever state launched the missile would likely suffer the collateral damage of its destruction. Another advantage to boost phase targeting is that missiles with multiple warheads will not have separated, maximizing the defensive effect and minimizing the defensive problem of multiple independent re-entry vehicles (MIRVs). Third, and tied in closely with the second factor, TMD systems will engage targets that are spiraling down the gravity well while they must propel themselves up the well. Space-based systems will do so traveling down, the energy and maneuver advantages of which have already been described, to attack slower-moving and hence more vulnerable targets.

Without question, from military applications and strategic perspectives, space-based BMD systems are superior to terrestrial (ground, sea, or air) based ones. They also have exceptional political advantages. *Any* BMD system will receive criticism from potential adversaries, as is evident with the routine vocal opposition that comes from Russia and China to any proposed US TMD system. Because of criticism and retaliatory threats made by the opposing states, domestic and allied support has been hesitant and unsure. If the state is willing to deploy BMD anyway, by using a space-based system instead of a ground-based one it should be able to gradually regain widespread popular support. One of the advantages of the mobile TMD system, say its advocates, is that it could be dispatched to threatened areas as needed. True enough, but imagine the problems associated with some possible deployments – to Israel, say, or to Taiwan. As much as the United States would insist that the deployment was for defensive purposes only, it would be a clear and possibly inflammatory sign of preference for one side over the other. A space-based system would forever be on alert, and would avoid the political problems of terrestrial basing altogether. The United States would not have to deploy physically to the threatened territory to be able to intercept and destroy hostile missile activity – regardless of the side that launched first. US impartiality could be asserted and maintained. Retaliations, too, could be controlled. While a US TMD battery in Israel could conceivably shoot down an incoming ballistic missile from Iraq, what would prevent the Israelis from shooting back in anger? The

United States would need to deploy the system in both states. Eventually, they would have to be deployed in all states, and any hope of countering the space-based system with a fiscal restraint argument would be lost. Moreover, the human operators of the TMD battery would be at risk. Their capture or casualties in their ranks could force the United States to get directly involved in the conflict. Knowing this, they could be particularly desirable targets for either side. In other instances, the United States might not have the time to deploy a TMD battery to a hostile theater, or may be politically unable to do so. The case of an Indian–Pakistan or an Iraq–Iran exchange comes readily to mind.

In all these described circumstances, with a space-based BMD system the United States could effectively uphold the principle that aggression is wrong in international politics, as first stated in George Bush's post-Gulf War declaration of a New World Order. The United States could stop the launching of missiles at any state from any state or substate actor, without taking sides or further inflaming the issue. If it were willing to do so, and would act decisively and non-arbitrarily to prevent any hostile aggression from crossing national borders, the US-owned and operated space-based BMD system could be seen as a global asset. The world would be free of the fear of missile-based nuclear war. As a critical element of an overall *Astropolitik* strategy, it has tremendous political advantage and virtually no political liability.

The moral superiority of the realist argument is revealed in this context. By following the three-part *Astropolitik* strategy – immediately renouncing the OST and acting to structure a property-based free-market regime in its place; deploying a space-based BMD system which would eliminate missile-borne threats and guarantee domination of space; and establishing a proper, cabinet or ministry level space coordination agency to encourage space efforts and promote popular support for space exploration – a dominant liberal democracy like the United States can usher in a new era of peace and prosperity.

NOTES

1. C. von Clauswitz, *On War*, ed. and trans. M. Howard and P. Paret (Princeton, NJ: Princeton University Press, 1976), p. 87.
2. M. Doyle, *Ways of War and Peace* (New York: Norton, 1997), p. 17.
3. C. Gray, *Modern Strategy* (London: Oxford, 2000), p. 1.
4. E. Luttwak, *Strategy: The Logic of War and Peace* (Cambridge, MA: Belknap Press, 1987), p. 177.
5. Ibid., p. 179.
6. Clausewitz, *On War*, p. 183.
7. Gray, *Modern Strategy*, p. 24.
8. Rand Corporation, *Preliminary Design for an Experimental World Circling Spaceship*, 5/2/46.
9. J. Oberg, *Space Power Theory* (Colorado Springs: US Space Command, 2000). D. Lupton,

On Space Warfare: A Space Power Doctrine (Maxwell AFB, AL: Air University Press, 1998) and R. Newberry, *Space Doctrine for the Twenty-First Century* (Maxwell AFB, AL: Air University Press, 1998), are notable contributions from the perspective of the American Air Force.

10. Cited in D. Cole and D. Cox, *The Challenge of the Planetoids* (Philadelphia, PA: Chilton Press, 1964), p. xiii.
11. Ibid., p. 5.
12. Ibid., pp. 5–6.
13. A. Frye, 'Our Gamble In Space: The Military Danger', *The Atlantic Monthly*, Vol. 212, No. 2 (August, 1963), p. 48–9.
14. D. Zeigler, 'Safe Havens: Military Strategy and Space Sanctuary', in M. DeBlois (ed.), *Beyond the Paths of Heaven: The Emergence of Space Power Thought* (Maxwell AFB, AL: Air University Press, 1999), pp. 185–245; see also M. Deblois, 'Space Sanctuary: A Viable National Strategy', *AirPower Journal*, Vol. 12, No. 4 (Winter 1998), pp. 41–57.
15. Zeigler, 'Safe Havens', p. 191.
16. Ibid., p. 192.
17. Ibid., p. 223.
18. J. Heronema, 'A.F. Space Chief Calls War in Space Inevitable', *Space News*, 12–18 Aug 1996, p. 4.
19. K. Grossman, and J. Long, 'Waging War in Space', *The Nation*, 27 December 1999.
20. T. Karras, *The New High Ground: Strategies and Weapons of Space Age Wars* (New York: Simon and Schuster, 1983).
21. Cited in J. Burgess, 'Satellites' Gaze Provides New Look at War', *Washington Post*, 19 February 1991, p. A13.
22. Especially the Global Positioning Satellite, or GPS. See M. Ripp, 'How Navstar Became Indispensable', *Air Force Magazine* (November 1993), pp. 46–9; M. Jennison, 'The 'Civil'-ization and Internationalization of Satellite Navigation', a paper presented at the *Sixth Biennial Conference on the Law Relating to National Security Activities in Outer Space*, Colorado Springs (March 1994); and I. Lachow, 'The GPS Dilemma: Balancing Military Risks and Economic Benefits', *International Security*, Vol. 20, No. 1 (Summer 1995), pp. 126–47. On the increasing interconnectivity of civilian and military applications of commercial imaging systems, see V. Guta, 'New Satellite Images for Sale', *International Security*, Vol. 20, No. 1 (Summer 1995), pp. 94–125.
23. US Senate, Committee on Armed Services, *National Defense Authorization Act for Fiscal Year 1993 Report* (102nd Congress, second session), Report 103–352 (Washington, DC: GPO, 1992), p. 85.
24. National Science and Technology Council, 'National Space Policy', http://www.whitehouse.gov/WH/EOP/OSTP/NSTC/html/fs/fs-5.html, 19 September 1996.
25. Ibid.
26. *Joint Vision 2020* (Washington, DC: US Government Printing Office), June 2000.
27. Ibid.
28. USSPACECOM, 'Long Range Plan', http://www.fas.org/news/usa/1998/04/lrp-fs.htm; see full text at http://www.peterson.af.mil/usspace.
29. *New World Vistas: Air and Space Power for the 21st Century*, Summary Volume, http://afosr.sciencewise.com/afr/sab/any/text/any/vistas.htm#app2, p. 11; 'Global Engagement: A Vision for the 21st Century Air Force', http://www-cgsc.army.mil/usaf/Pubs/GlobalEngagement.htm, revised July 1999.
30. P. Grier, 'New World Vistas', *Air Force Magazine*, Vol. 79, No. 3 (March 1996), p. 3.
31. David Lupton's excellent operational work, *On Space Warfare: A Space Power Doctrine* (Maxwell AFB, AL: Air University Press, 1988), is still a standard for analyzing space capabilities.

32. Thucydides, 'The Melian Dialogue', in *History of the Peloponnesian War*, transl. S. Lattimore (Cambridge: Hackett, 1998), pp. 295–301.
33. Oberg, *Space Power Theory*, p. 129.
34. Ibid., p. 150.
35. Ibid.
36. F. Fitzgerald, *Way Out There in the Blue: Reagan, Star Wars, and the End of the Cold War* (New York: Simon and Schuster, 2000).
37. R. Reagan, 'The Conclusion of President Reagan's 23 March 1983 Speech on Defense Spending and Defense Technology', Appendix A, in S. Miller and S. Van Evera (eds), *The Star Wars Controversy* (Princeton, NJ: Princeton University Press, 1986), p. 257.

7

Conclusion

In 1968, Stanley Kubrick adapted Arthur Clarke's short story 'The Sentinel' into one of the signature films of the space age. The script for *2001: A Space Odyssey* was co-written by Clarke and Kubrick (Clarke wrote the novel of the same name when the movie was already in production). Clarke prided himself on technical accuracy, and Kubrick was rigorous, almost fanatical, in his devotion to realism and detail. This was no Buck Rogers death-ray farce. No faster-than-light engines, personnel transport beams, or unexplained gravity fields were conjured to advance the plot. This was not Hollywood audacity; the audience was not expected to suspend its disbelief to accept the premise of the story. Everything we saw was presumed to be within our sure grasp. In 30 years, we would have a permanent presence on the Moon, a fully functional giant wheel space station in low-Earth orbit, and regular passenger services to both. This was not the lunatic prophecy of an amateur yarn spinner, making up technical marvels to fill gaps in the story. This was real; it was what NASA and the Soviet space programs would accomplish – easily – before the end of the century.

The new millennium is here. Where did the future go?

COOPERATION AND COMPETITION

Through the course of this book, descriptions of the contentious situation from which the current space regime emerged have been offered. Attempts have been made to show how the regime, purposefully designed to limit confrontation, unintentionally stifled positive competition and fruitful exploration. The impetus for this has been a poorly understood application of geo/astropolitical dictums, wherein the necessity of denying potential enemies has triumphed over the importance of establishing effective control. One of the primary purposes of this work is to advance a more nuanced application of the geopolitical theories that historically informed diplomatic strategy and shaped national space policies. The academic taboos against geopolitical study after World War II are fading away, and the revival of neogeopolitical theory is now ready to mature and transform into a coherent body of astropolitical theory. Astropolitics and *Astropolitik* can and should be used to chart current and future development of national space strategy and policy, and a working framework is provided here. The potential social and political pitfalls of *Astropolitik* must be fully understood, monitored, and aggressively culled, however, through constant vigilance and blunt awareness of the dark record of past expressions of *Geopolitik*.

The setting and history of the political development of the outer space Regime clearly shows the intrigue, political maneuvering, and strife that characterized the era. The curious fact that the apparently cooperative outer space regime arose from Cold War competition is undeniable, and in the serious space literature it goes unchallenged. Donald Brennan, for example, has argued: 'It is worth stressing at the outset that the competition in space technology generally, and in its military applications specifically, is one of the aspects of the Cold War and cannot be divorced from that setting.'[1] The fundamental question, amidst all this discord, is why did cooperation, even if only the appearance of cooperation, become so prevalent an obsession?

Possibly because in its developmental stage, as a result of space flight's direct association with ballistic missile and nuclear weapon development, a chord of universal terror was struck in our communal consciousness. Our collective anxieties overcame our rationality. It quickly became politically incorrect to suggest anything but cooperation and peaceful exploitation when speaking of outer space, for fear of the stark alternatives. Cooperation, in reference to space development, became unassailable. Without a doubt, it was thought by space policymakers and enthusiasts that cooperation in space would become the very salvation of humanity, rescuing us from our precipitous descent into oblivion. Even if the world's states were not truly cooperative today, in time they surely would be. As soon as all people came to realize that humankind's destiny was a shared one, then peace and cooperation would be inexorable, and inevitable. In astrodeterminist parlance, the image of a united future in space would generate a social model of tranquility from which terrestrial security and prosperity *must* flow.

Almost universally, then, world opinion leaned heavily toward the notion that outer space should be non-appropriable by the terrestrial nation-states, who would bring the great corruption of the Age of Man – war – to the pristine heavens. The petty squabbles of Earth should be contained here, on the planet, and ultimately overcome by the greater communal destiny of the future. Much of the impetus for that view, it has been argued repeatedly, comes from the images of Earth transmitted from manned space missions. The Earth is envisaged as a solitary, delicate sphere, hovering vulnerably in the empty vastness of space.[2] The image was a powerful and sobering one. Civilization may have been preconditioned to accept it, however. The image of humanity clinging to a sliver of habitable space in the hinterlands of the galaxy had been taking shape for decades thanks to the efforts of social critics and scientists. The popular early astronomer Harlan True Stetson remarked, long before the advent of space flight but certainly in anticipation of it: 'Thus man's view of the cosmos changed from his little homocentric picture of creation to a scheme so vast that were it not for his own self-consciousness he might well regard himself as out of the picture.'[3]

Not only were we suddenly packed together, and in our biological niche quite separated from the rest of the cosmos, we were extremely fragile and precariously exposed. All people, if not exactly brothers and sisters, were in this view at least reluctant castaways trapped in the same ecologic 'lifeboat'. This analogy has spurred a litany of environmental polemics and soliloquies on the rational and normative ramifications of lifeboat survival and 'lifeboat ethics'.[4] One view is that we must all pull together, put aside our petty jealousies and parochial needs and strive for the common good. On the other hand, lifeboat ethics demand tough choices. Who gets to survive? Who must be tossed overboard? In both instances, the individual must eschew self-interest and must now work to salvage and perfect the species. The human condition can be viewed as a condition of communal ethics from this vantage, referring to the minimally acceptable behavior for group survival in such a craft, with the universe as an unfathomable cosmic ocean. What lifeboat ethics denies, however, is the possibility of finding an island shore with abundant food, water, and resources for the necessities of life. *Astropolitik* demands a search for that cosmic island and the life-sustaining resources it can provide.

What happens to the Earth from the perspicacity of an outer-space vantage happens to all people, therefore the exploration and exploitation of outer space is the direct business and concern of all its inhabitants. We are all united in our struggle; we are all one species. Whether we opt for rationed equality for all to survive, or rational expulsions of the sick and weak so that the strong can thrive, our destiny is recognized as indivisible. This is the exemplary argument put forward by the new breed of international idealists in the neo-liberal standard. The power of international agreement and the growing importance of institutionalized UN patronage are highlighted. Cooperation is good and right. Cooperation is a desirable end in itself. From the realist school, which dominated the politics of the day, came a different vision.

For the statesmen steeped in the tradition of balance-of-power politics and political intrigue, the practical value of declaring space a human commons was clear. The riches of space and the full advantages of space control were unknown. Since neither superpower could be sure of the coming capabilities of the other, it seemed prudent to do everything possible to hinder the dominance of the other – specifically, to declare space the unilateral province of all peoples while working feverishly to acquire the technological means and legal justifications to gain dominant control of it. The rhetoric of space cooperation became a cover to buy time. For the non-superpower states harboring future ambitions in space, it was equally important to keep the playing field open until they were ready and able to seize an advantageous position of their own.

For power-optimizing realists, cooperation is an important tool. It allows time to regroup, reevaluate, and reorganize. According to a 1959 Congressional Report, maintenance of free-world confidence in the strength and leadership of the United States was paramount. At the time, with the almost daily announcements of a new scientific breakthrough from the Soviets, confidence in US leadership was reeling. Our allies needed reassurance of our capacities and of our resolve:

> The best way to solidify this confidence [in the scientific leadership of the US] is by a program of general and genuine free world cooperation. Future misfirings there will be. And free world reactions to them will be far different, morally and psychologically speaking, if other nations have a direct stake in at least some of the project. A program which allows foreign participation in the design and building of future satellites could benefit this country in two ways: (1) by providing new ideas for improved techniques; and (2) by cementing popular alliances which lie at the heart of the stable world order.[5]

Henry L. Roberts, writing for the influential Council on Foreign Relations in 1956, made a similar statement:

> To resist further Communist advance the United States must maintain its overseas commitments and develop them to the best advantage. The value of alliances, however, is not confined to bolstering overseas areas which are threatened; alliances can also be an important source of military, political, and economic strength ... We must promote, so far as it is in our power, cooperation and mutual confidence among our allies in Europe and Asia. In a period in which diplomatic maneuver may be of decisive importance in determining the course of events, it is necessary to check the Soviet effort to split alliances and isolate the United States.[6]

Thus cooperation had more than a socially calming role, it had political value as well in the competition for allies and for advanced technology. Along with the dubious missile gap that would soon emerge in campaign rhetoric, the popular press touted a Western 'engineer gap' with the Soviets. It was believed that the communist colossus was churning out so many technicians and scientists that the United States could not hope to catch up in the near term. The solution was to tap into the scientific reservoirs of allied nations. In the new age of technology, information, innovation, and scientific prowess directly translate into battlefield supremacy. The loser of the space race, it was thought, was doomed to lose the Cold War. Cooperation, at least with Western allies, was essential as part of a global power strategy.

Stephen and Lisa Shaffer assert that US interest in international space cooperation stemmed from a wide variety of political goals, including: (1) creating an image of openness *vis-à-vis* the negative image of Soviet secrecy; (2) increasing US prestige by giving maximum visibility to US accomplishments; (3) providing access to foreign scientists to supplement US scientific capabilities; (4) pressuring the Soviet Union to open its programs to the scientific community; and (5) enlisting support of the international community for the prohibition of military activities in space and promoting the peaceful uses of outer space by providing opportunities for participation. Principal economic and technological goals are: (1) to obtain access to other countries for tracking stations, launch sites, and ground receive stations; (2) to increase 'brainpower' working on space projects; (3) to improve the balance of trade through creating new markets for US aerospace industries; (4) to save money through cost-sharing on Research and Development; and (5) to expand research opportunities through the expansion of the knowledge base.[7] International cooperation, we see here, is inherently competition-driven. Besides, it just might work. Functionalists have long averred that cooperation becomes endemic through use. The gradual accretion of cooperative venues and treaties, even if initially disheartening, would build an eventual foundation of accord. In this view it does not matter if cooperation was a ruse or simply a stalling tactic to buy time. Cooperation breeds cooperation, and however it is achieved, it is valuable. This was what then Senator Lyndon Johnson meant when he said in 1959:

> If we proceed along the orderly course of full cooperation, we shall by that very fact of cooperation make the most substantial contribution toward perfecting peace. Men who have worked together to reach the stars are not likely to descend together into the depths of war and desolation.[8]

It was believed that nations could get into the 'habit' of cooperation. Continuing efforts in space cooperation would then have a spillover effect into other realms. It would become infectious. For the functionalists, cooperation was a logical outgrowth of space exploration. By its very nature, they believed, space exploration required a united human effort. It would be so demanding – not to mention expensive – that humanity simply would not have the will, time, or resources left over to get themselves mired in major conflicts on earth. This cooperation would lead to other benefits. It would be the end of the Iron Curtain, as scientists and explorers would learn to share data, the concept spilling over and spreading to the political realm. Technology (especially communications and data transmission) would become so cheap and pervasive as to be uncontrollable, limiting governments' ability to be confrontational (a popular line of reasoning in the Digital Age of the Internet). It would lead to an increasingly important role for the United Nations, the natural arbiter of international projects. The omnipresent United Nations would finally establish true global government, and at long last eliminate interstate war. The realist tradition discounts this outcome as a likely possibility, but doesn't burn any bridges.

From the perspective of Cold War propaganda, the most common (and arguably inane) reason for cooperation revolves around the mushy notion that it is somehow just 'better' than conflict. Especially at a time when the world has developed the capacity to destroy itself, isn't cooperation, no matter how unlikely or unsuccessful, morally superior to any attempt to establish supremacy and possibly trigger a nuclear conflagration? In a fine leap of faith, during the Outer Space Treaty ratification hearings, this conversation occurred between Senator Church of Idaho, who was attempting to get ratification of the OST, and his witness, the chief negotiator of that treaty. Somewhat rhetorically, and for the benefit of the press and everyone else in the room, Church asked: 'So far as our national security is concerned, are we not better off with a treaty [than] we would be without [a] treaty?' 'Yes', replied his witness, 'yes, we are.'[9]

AN ASTROPOLITICAL FUTURE

An intriguing dilemma is now presented by the paradox of political cooperation born of competition and rivalry. Could legal and diplomatic cooperation have come about in the absence of military competition? We may never know for sure, but it seems quite possible that cooperation and competition are members of that nebulous set of Great Social Dichotomies; paired concepts that are indefinable and practically impossible without the negative example of their inextricable counterpart. In the realm of outer space, it is difficult to isolate a single case of cooperation in space without finding a basis in competition and conflict. Although he is not as sweeping, Daniel Deudney concurs that '[p]restige and national rivalry have fueled most of the civilian [as well as military] space efforts of both the US and Soviet Union'.[10] The Shaffers insist, 'the extent and character of international cooperation in both space and defense have been shaped by two factors: (1) international competition between the United States and the Soviet Union in the Cold War; and (2) the distribution of relevant capabilities among the cooperating nation-states', a purely neorealist view that echoes the academic arguments of Kenneth Waltz.[11]

Competition is the very measure by which success in space is judged. The prospect of real cooperation brings hails of protest and threats of budget cuts from Congress. Paying lip service to cooperation while being pressured for space spectaculars and intelligence windfalls is difficult at best and hypocritical at worst, but it has been the pattern. Don Kash maintains: 'The most striking finding from what has preceded is the obvious inconsistency between the language and the goals used to justify our program of international competition and the nature of the program as it has been organized both bilaterally and in the United Nations.'[12] Even the process of cooperation has become perversely competitive, as scientists, bureaucrats, and politicians bustle to demonstrate that they are the more accommodating.

But the world's actors change, even if the metaphysical perception of the Earth and humankind remains static. When the outer space regime became codified (prior to 1976), most analysts could foresee only two approaches toward the exploration and exploitation of space; via attempts at military domination by a single state or alliance of states in the larger violent context of Cold War rivalry, or legal military exclusion – the denial of all military activity in space.[13] The first was a nationalist expression and the latter was possible only if guided by the United Nations. In political-science parlance, the schools of realism and internationalism, cold warriors and utopianists represented them. Neither a combination nor compromise approach was ever seriously considered. The gradual cooperation that would emerge from the much studied complex web of interdependence, built by non-governmental agencies with political and scientific organizations, was not believed by realists to hold significant sway over national space policy. Cooperation was merely another tactic, to be used with a military strategist's skill.

Certainly a relatively non-hostile terrestrial situation without Cold War superpower bipolarity was not a significant scenario in anyone's projection – or if it was, it was with the Soviet Union as the clear winner. To be sure, the latter outcome was widely anticipated. In his otherwise incisive and popular book *War and Change in World Politics*, Robert Gilpin wrote that the United States was clearly on the wane, a popular if misguided conception at the time.[14] In an epilogue written for the 1985 edition and reprinted in 1990, he stated that 'the Soviet Union, of course, is the rising challenger, and it appears to be the one power that in years to come could supplant the American dominance over the international system'.[15] Paul Kennedy concurred in his 1987 best-seller, *The Rise and Fall of the Great Powers.*[16] Though he didn't necessarily see the USSR as the inevitable winner, the United States was obviously in the midst of an undeniable demise. Michael Harrington can be excused for his views in *The Twilight of Capitalism*, in which he writes 'we live in the twilight of an epoch, one that has lasted more than four centuries … the successor to capitalism will be collectivist, of course'.[17]

Amidst all this nattering negativism, it seems capitalism has triumphed. In his widely read and criticized article and follow-on text, Francis Fukuyama has declared 'The End of History'.[18] This was an acerbic swipe at the declarations of Hegel and Marx before him, without a whit of apology or uncertainty for whoever might make a similar declaration in years hence. Western liberal democracy, he declared, inextricably bound to capitalism, is the unheralded champion of ideological history. Just wait, say the neo-Marxists, the contradictions inherent in capitalism will come to the fore, and communism will yet triumph. Lenin's noble but ill-advised attempt to accelerate history failed because it tried to establish the communist utopia before capitalism had run its course. Now, with the United States clearly on top, it is only a matter of time. Other detractors of Fukuyama's may agree that communism has been swept aside into the dustbin of history, but just as Hegel could not foresee the rise of communism, and Marx the rise of fascism, whatever will challenge capitalism and liberal democracy in the future has not yet been invented (or if it has, it is not yet popular). As capitalists spread over the globe and suck all of the resources from the Earth, eventually they must concentrate all wealth in the hands of a few, and revolution – even if not communist revolution – is inevitable. For those who see merit in the latter argument, and clearly there is some, *Astropolitik* provides liberal-democratic capitalists with an out. By drawing on the infinite resources of space, liberal democracy and capitalism will never reach wealth saturation.

The popular conception that the Soviet Union was ahead of the United States in space application had been a fashionable subject for the nation's popular media as well. From the near hysteria of *LIFE* magazine following the launch of Sputnik in 1957 to the provocative cover story of *National Geographic* almost 30 years later in 1986, the fear of the communist colossus sold well in doom and gloom United States. In the latter article, Thomas Canby gushed at the progressive accomplishments of the Soviets, just three years before their total collapse: 'Colonist in space, cosmonaut Col. Leanard D. Kizim, has spent more than a year in Soviet space stations. He embodies his nation's unflagging pursuit of a space program in some ways more successful than that of the United States.'[19] The internal contradictions of the Soviet state were covered quite effectively by its apparently successful space program, which in retrospect only served to drain the energy and life of the USSR's weak and fragile economy.

In the absence of Cold War competition, what future in space is already, if slowly, being revealed? Jack Williamson writes:

> No longer is the focus of competition centered exclusively on the Soviet Union. Now feats of the Europeans and Japanese receive a prominence in the media that are often linked with the gap between the expectation and the reality of US technology. These countries have made a conscious effort to become more independent of the United States for access to and utilization of outer space.[20]

Indeed, there seems to be a bevy of potential contenders for space dominance. The Japanese, who are fashionably bashed for their presumably unfair competitive edge leading to an enormous trade deficit with the rest of the world, could be on their way to the status of worthy space competitor. The Europeans, whose Space Agency (ESA) easily ranks third worldwide in space expenditures, has a booming telecommunications industry and holds contracts for over half the world's commercial space launches through 2005. It is even remotely possible that the Russians themselves will realize that their spacecraft assembly lines and existing stock of space hardware could become a lucrative capitalist enterprise. Certainly the infrastructure is in place to allow for a Russian resurgence in space, should their new market economy take off to allow for such expenditure. In an even more exotic scenario, if the Russians combine their infrastructure with the Europeans, as associate or full members of the European Space Agency, the resulting coalition space giant would have ominous potential.

But of those potential competitors, the Japanese and Europeans are long-time allies who share the United States' basic values. A capitalism-driven Russia should also be more of a partner than a competitor. Hence, the greatest current outcries are from those who see the Chinese stealing their way to the Moon, via priceless US technology. In 1999, the People's Republic launched a test version of a future manned space vehicle that could allow them to win the race to be third in indigenous manned space capability, and possibly the second to the Moon. Certainly the United States has shown little interest in going back to the Moon, not since we thought we were desperately racing the Soviets for that crowning honor. Perhaps with another set of socialist rivals we may yet rededicate ourselves, but it seems unlikely. The latter peril still does not raise our collective anxiety to that of the Sputnik challenge, at least enough to rouse us from our apathy and demand a Kennedyesque return to the stars.

No, the likely spur to competition-induced reinvigoration of the space race is not national military advantage, despite its extraordinarily important role on the modern battlefield, but national economic advantage. Athens, Britain, and the United States were powerful trading states before they became world military powers. The opening of the seas accomplished for these states what the true opening of space will in the future – but only if the current regime in outer space is abandoned and replaced with one that inspires exploration and exploitation of the vast riches there.

Ty Twibell has effectively described the legal restraints that have crippled the commercial development of outer space: 'Despite high profit margins [from] technical breakthroughs, the space industry has merely scratched the surface of what it can achieve. However, reaching beyond these current achievements proves near impossible under the current body of space law.'[21] The vast wealth of space is undetermined, and the cost of going there is high. The ambiguous cost-utility calculation alone is enough to make space exploration daunting, though certainly not disqualifying. But no state, much less any corporation, has an incentive to exploit the wealth of space if there are no guarantees that the potential profits gained there can be appropriated.

It is an old principle in international law that a treaty rendered obsolete by time, technology, or events, is no longer binding. *Rebus sic stantibus*, literally 'in these circumstances', the parties cannot be held to the terms agreed upon under bygone conditions.[22] So it may be with the outer-space regime. The Cold

War is over. The great ideological battles waged with the Soviet Union, whose entire existence was encompassed within the twentieth century, have now been forever relegated to the probing domain of political historians. There need be no fretting over the demise of the 1967 Outer Space Treaty, just as there is none for the end of Cold War confrontation.

But a legal vacuum is no substitute for law, even inappropriate law that guides the expectations of actors. The OST should be replaced, not simply abolished. The new regime must rest on principles and norms consistent with capitalism and liberal democracy, and at the same time must recognize the obligation the richer states have to assist the poorer ones in a domain in which they cannot compete. This will provide the dynamism necessary for future space development. All states have a right to pursue happiness as they themselves define it (for a capitalist, that is to gain wealth), and capitalist-based liberal democracy is the most efficient and effective means to guarantee the maximum prosperity for all individuals. Adam Smith's venerable 'hidden hand', which raises the wealth of society when individuals pursue self-benefit, is dominant in a world of abundance. The admonitions of Hardin and Lloyd are valid only in a world of scarcity. The norms encompassed in this new regime are that all states have the right to make claims and to engage in space development so long as they do not break the constructive conventions of the free market. These are, quite simply (1) that no economic competitor shall be prohibited from attempting to gain access to the market (in this case to the commercial possibilities of space), and (2) that no competitor is so wealthy or large that it can dictate the terms of exchange (no economic monopolies or monopsonies). What is too little understood by advocates of the free market, is that while economic monopolies destroy the market, a monopoly of power is essential to its success. Without an effective space regime championed by the lone remaining superpower, violations – or 'market failures' – of the principle and norms are bound to occur. In domestic free market economies, when market failure becomes apparent, the state must intervene to return it to competition. As the example given in Chapter 5 shows, such a regime for outer space is not only easily conceivable, it is simple in its construct. Should the United States or any other liberal democratic state gain military dominance in space, it can and should act as the 'discriminating monopolist' of power to re-center the free market and permit unfettered, productive economic competition.

The rules and decision-making procedures must be based in the capitalist solution to the tragedy of the commons, in other words, privatization where possible and stringent regulation where resources cannot (or should not) be privatized. Advocacy of a first-come first-served approach, as was done in the destructive period of global colonization, is not deemed advisable, though some might find particular merit in a system akin to the American Homestead Act that opened up the West to colonization by offering 160-acre tracts of land to any who could get to them and improve them within five years. The suggestion already offered for parceling out the commons of space is more like that offered for the model depiction of dividing the common pastures of old England. Take the known divisible regions of space and divide them up among the national entities of Earth. The formula can be determined in the future, based on population, GDP (Gross Domestic Product), or statehood – or a combination of all three. The key is that it must be perceived as equitable (in the old pasture commons, roughly equal lots were devised in terms of carrying capacity and then distributed to families by lot). Once the commons is privatized, it should reach its maximum sustainable profitability in short order. This option has the advantage of being immediately profitable to states that do not have access to space (which is why the homestead model is not preferred). These remote landlords could rent or sell their legal claims to the highest bidder. They could enhance exploration by taking rent on contingency, asking for a percentage of gains made off their territory, and use the monies generated to enhance the lives of their citizens. All manner of possibilities will come to bear fruit, but only under a scheme of capitalist privatization.

The astrographically determined divisible areas should be separately charted, subdivided, and distributed. For example, the geostationary belt could be divided into 360 slots (as is done currently) and each slot given to UN recognized states by lot or some other equitable method (as opposed to having states make up fictitious satellite programs to 'reserve' slots as is done now). Owners of existing national satellites in suddenly foreign territory would have to negotiate a suitable fee in order to stay. The Moon could be sectioned into several thousand tracts, each to be dispersed by an equitable, negotiated method. Once privatized, exploitation and speculation will begin at once. Of course, we know that not all curators of privatized commons will do what is in the best interest of their property. Some will be inefficient in managing it, and they will lose out to better profit-maximizers. This is the harsh mechanism of the market that 'weeds out' inefficient users, and to some extent it has a moral justification. Those who ill-use their lands will lose them. Those efficient in exploiting their lands will gain more. But this is not a guarantee, as strip mining and clear-cutting show. Some territory should therefore be set aside, as international commons, much as national parks are in this country. But to maximize space exploration, these must be limited. Despite the pitfalls, the parceling of space commons and distribution of it based on some criteria of useful exploitation makes sense.

The new regime should also serve to limit (though probably can not eliminate) the potential for violence, as competition under these conditions is based on profit and not national honor. But not all violence will stop, and without an effective police force and legal system to adjudicate disputes between land-holders and profiteers, the regime will collapse. An international peacekeeping force could be established, also consonant with the communal goals of the current regime, but this will serve only to perpetuate the extant suboptimal regime. Just as the major trading states of history had to establish strong military forces to patrol the seas, providing a safe operating environment for trade and commerce to prosper, the top spacefaring states would see it in their own best interests to establish a space force capable of dominating the major space trade routes, point locations of commercial and military value, and decisive regions of strategic control necessary to maximize space power. Hegemony has its costs, but the benefits are well established.

The largest state in terms of GDP in a free-trade system has the most to gain. Let us assume that the largest GDP in the system (say, Britain) has an arbitrary value (for comparison) of 100 units (see Figure 7.1). Relative to that value a subsidiary state (say, Prussia) has a GDP of 40 units, or 40 percent of the GDP base of Britain. Liberal capitalism does not maintain that all states always gain equally in free trade, but over time, given a powerful discriminating monopolist (government) to ensure market failures are immediately corrected, all states should see essentially equivalent gains. Here is the dilemma for the realist. Absolute gains are not as important as relative ones. In the example depicted, let us say that over a five-year period, both Britain and Prussia realize 10 percent growth in their GDPs. This appears to be a good and equitable gain from the perspective of the larger state. The smaller state sees that even though both have had the same rate of growth, in absolute terms Britain has increased its GDP by ten units while Prussia has increased its GDP by only four. What was once a difference between them of 60 units, is now an expanded difference of 66 units. To be sure, the rich are getting richer and the poor are getting richer – but the gap is growing!

The larger state obviously sees the advantage, too. It is morally justified that the larger state bear the burden of maintaining the system that works so greatly to its advantage. Militarizing space for the purpose of maintaining and enhancing exploration and free trade (and maintaining a global business climate free from the threat of nuclear or other large-scale war) is a cost the United States, with approximately 20 percent of the world's GDP, should gladly accept.

A new space regime is needed, modeled not on the cooperative regimes of Antarctica and the Deep Oceans (which have not realized a fraction of their enormous resource potential), but on the regimes of free trade embodied in the post-World War II economic system based on the 1944 Bretton Woods Agreement. Just as the WTO and World Bank needed a hegemon to establish them, the success or failure of the new space regime is dependent on astropolitical military imperatives. But not all states that are trying to overturn the current regime see a capitalist model as a useful one. Calls for even more communal sharing agreements are persistent. At the Third UNISPACE Nations Conference on the Exploration and Peaceful Uses of Outer Space, held in July 1999, most members urged the body to create a new set of legal norms

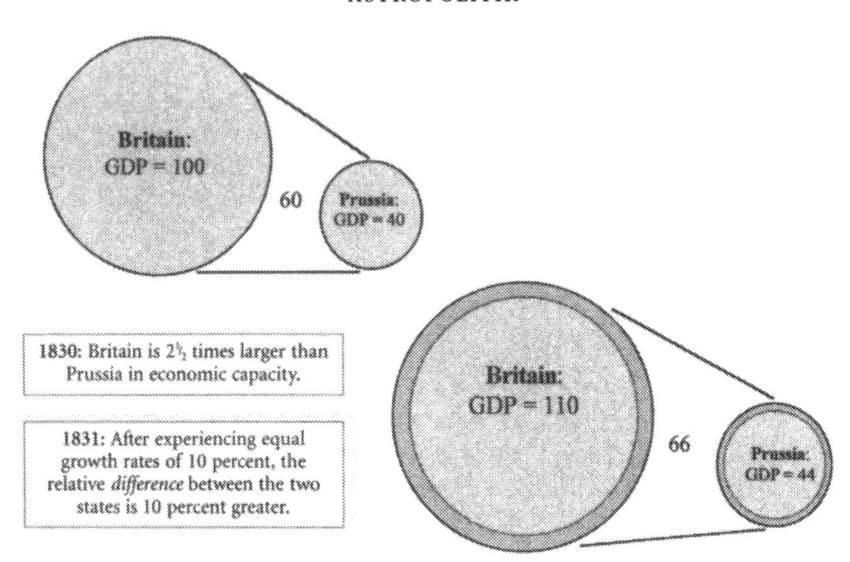

Figure 7.1: Absolute growth rate vs relative growth

that would funnel a *greater* percentage of space technology and wealth to the LDCs. While the conference attendees praised the cooperative advances since the last UNISPACE Conference in 1982, several expressed critical admonition for the continuing pace of the 'militarization' of space – preferring to have all military activities in space stopped – and the disturbing growing interest of private corporations to exploit space should a legal regime change allow for it. On the one hand, members want a greater share of space resources to go to the LDCs, while at the same time seem appear to be doing everything possible to ensure that access to space is severely limited.

The many countries who continually demand a piece of the economic pie which is 'the common heritage of mankind' could stifle the desire of the space capable states to develop the as yet unknown promise of outer space. The potential for economic stagnation that would result if a legally mandated right to an unearned share of the spoils of space were observed is alarming. If there is no incentive to attempt the great risks involved in space exploitation, it may never develop. Thus the greatest challenge to space exploration could become a bizarre form of apathy. Karl Deutsch, writing in 1963, attempted to project the future of space policy 25 years hence. He said the United States 'may well continue the role of critic of national sovereignty, champion of free coastal navigation and free overflights, and of stringent international controls managed by majority voting', but by the 1980s, 'we may find ourselves defending the principles of sovereignty and reciprocity in the face ... [of] large intractable non-Western majorities in the United Nations and other International bodies'.[23]

With an expired Soviet Union and a dilapidated successor in Russia, the

United States is awash with power after its impressive victories in the 1991 Gulf War and 1999 Kosovo campaign, and stands at the forefront of history capable of presiding over the birth of a bold New World Order. As the new millennium unfolds, however, the New World Order seems no longer the apex of liberal Western aspirations, for the United States has been unable to grasp the moment and lead the world toward its new vision. To be sure, the United States has entered a time of great decision. Policymakers can choose to remain wary, and gingerly move along the façade of cooperation predicated upon preventing any one state gaining an unexpected advantage. Or they can choose space domination, secure in the knowledge that no single nation can challenge its front-runner position, in the hope that space exploitation can inject the raw materials necessary to maintain hegemony in an otherwise constricting world of increasing scarcity. In this way, they can choose *real* cooperation, in a new regime, based on a vision of mutual gain and common benefit – not the pseudo-cooperation of the past, motivated by fear. This latter outcome, to be successful, requires a thorough knowledge of the dictates of astrography, astrodeterminism, astrostrategy, and *Astropolitik.*

The challenge of 'Mr Khrushchev's Boomerang' is now history. The realist position, that the United States should seize the current opportunity and forge ahead as the dominant, and possibly exclusive, force in space is justified if one accepts the assertion that it was the moral, military, and economic superiority of the United States that won the Cold War. Continue to push forward, seize the day, argues the realist school. From Sun Tzu to Clausewitz, the great military strategists will advocate pressing the advantage and carrying on the pursuit. James Oberg persuasively argues that of all the criteria identified to be a space power, only one may be truly necessary: the *will* to do so. The United States can take the initiative in space, and it should.

As the great liberal democracy of its time, the United States is preferentially endowed to guide the whole of humanity into space, to police any misuse of that realm, and to ensure an equitable division of its spoils. But if the United States were to abandon its egalitarian values, corrupted by its own power, and follow a path of aggressive expansion into the cosmos using the riches gained to dominate the peoples of the Earth, what then? Does the benign era of *Pax Americana* end? Perhaps, but the likelihood of that outcome depends on one's current view of the benevolence of US hegemony and the future role of ongoing globalism. The argument here is that the checks and balances of liberal democracy make it the least likely of all potential candidates to misuse its power, and history for the most part backs the assertion. If one state *is* to seize control of space, as the astropolitical model suggests, there seems to be little evidence that any other nation is more suitable. If no state does, as is the current situation, then exploration and commerce will remain moribund. The argument – better no ruler of space than even an enlightened one – is fallacious. If no wealth comes from space then it matters little how it is divided.

The dynamic, self-interested pursuit of wealth will maximize space exploration and exploitation, and ultimately all Earth's people will gain. The astropolitical model shows how competition and cooperation can be maximized.

The foregoing is not meant to be an endorsement of continued and permanent nationalist exploitation of space. Once all of humanity is invigorated by space exploration, nationalist rivalry should diminish as we begin to see ourselves as citizens of Earth, separate perhaps from spacefarers (as the astrodeterminist model implies) but united in the source of our common planet heritage. The more diversity we discover in space, the more in common we will feel with every thing and with everyone of Earth. Should life be discovered in the cosmos, especially intelligent life, then on that day we will see the petty differences that divide us into nationalities for the fine points that they are. In the vast ocean of space, we have more in common with each other – no matter how culturally or socially apart – than with any conceivable species from light years away. It seems further obvious that the maximum long-term benefit to be gained from the riches of space will ultimately come as the result of a globally cooperative effort. In this view, it will be necessary to raise the wealth of all people in all states so that the poorest of them can contribute to the fullest extent (the image of Athenian rowers is renewed). All humans have a right to support, and defend if need be, the next great era of our species. The sooner the better, and if that means a nationalist foray into near-Earth space to stimulate exploration and speed the process, then so be it. The current pace is excruciatingly slow, and shows little value returned.

FINAL THOUGHTS

That the space race is over and the Space Age is in decay seems dismally obvious. That it will some day revive seems nonetheless assured. Humanity's future is in the stars. Our indomitable will requires ever-greater challenges. Our insatiable appetites require vast new resources. Eventually we *will* fill this niche that is Earth and spill out into the cosmos. But when and how this inevitable migration takes place is not at all known.

Astropolitics and *Astropolitik* provide a military strategy and a legal-institutional blueprint that should ignite a new space race almost at once. It is not the only possibility, but it follows long-established political traditions and taps into the most dynamic capacities of people and states. The changes promoted are simple, inexpensive, and should prove remarkably effective. There will be complaints, numerous no doubt, that it advocates dooming the future of humanity to a state-centric model that has produced an historically abysmal war record on Earth. Why spread this paradigm out to infect everything we touch in space? The objections are valid, but generally at odds with the wishes of those who would make them. The ultimate goal of astropolitics and *Astropolitik* is not the militarization of space. Rather, the militarization of space is a means to an end, part of a longer-term strategy. The goal is to reverse the current international malaise in regard to space exploration, and to do so in a way that is efficient and that harnesses the positive motivations of individuals and states striving to better their conditions. It is a neoclassical, market-driven approach intended to maximize efficiency and wealth.

Mahan argued that in his age naval power was the clear route to national wealth and international preeminence. More than just natural and man-made endowments were necessary to secure this condition. In addition to a vibrant shipbuilding industry, a protected position astride the sea lanes of commerce, and advantageous coastlines with multiple harbors, Mahan insisted that the people of a seafaring state must have a certain fortitude and industry. In other words, the population must be engaged in and wholly supportive of the national effort to achieve international prosperity. In an age that has gone beyond sail and steam to one that is predicated on technology, communications, and innovation, exploitation of outer space is one modern route to prosperity and affluence. No attempt to reinvigorate the Space Age will succeed if the populations of the states capable of voyaging into and beyond LEO are not fully behind the efforts of their governments and corporations. Before the languishing space exploration efforts of the world fully stagnate and become prohibitively expensive to restart, some effort needs to be made to energize the visionary sections of the global populace.

So powerful is the lure of astropolitics that the relative gains anticipated for the state that successfully dominates space continues to provide a compelling incentive to act unilaterally. This incentive could provide dramatic short-term impetus to space-based expansion that seems to be missing since the most confrontational years of the Cold War period, and within the framework of the *Astropolitik* strategy should provide globally beneficial results. The analysis here is offered as an examination of optimal strategies and likely outcomes given an assumption of near-term continued nationalist military and economic competition (the assumption is made to set the geostrategic model in motion), it is not a prediction or a portend of probable outcomes. Within these analytic limitations, however, many classical geopolitical theories are fully compatible with, and prove remarkably applicable to, this vibrant realm of outer space.

NOTES

1. D. Brennan, 'Arms and Arms Control in Outer Space' in J. Fawcett (ed.), *Outer Space: New Challenge to Law and Policy* (Oxford: Clarendon Press, 1984), p. 124.
2. D. Deudney, *Whole Earth Security: A Geopolitics of Peace* (Washington, DC: Worldwatch Institute, 1983), p. 5.

3. H. Stetson, *Man and the Stars* (New York: McGraw-Hill, 1930), p. 9.
4. A term used by Deudney, *Whole Earth Security*, p. 5.
5. D. Kash, *The Politics of Space Cooperation* (Englewood Cliffs, NJ: Prentice-Hill, 1967), p. 17.
6. H. Stinson, *Russia and America: Dangers and Prospects* (New York: Council on Foreign Relations, 1956), p. 243.
7. S. Shaffer and L. Shaffer, *The Politics of International Cooperation: A Comparison of US Experience in Space and in Security* (Denver, CO: University of Denver Press, 1980), p. 17.
8. Cited in Kash, *Politics of Space Cooperation*, p. 10.
9. Hearings before the Committee on Foreign Relations, United States Senate, 90th Congress, 1st Session, 7 March 1967, p. 18.
10. D. Deudney, *Space: The High Frontier in Perspective* (Washington, DC: Worldwatch, 1982), p. 9.
11. Shaffer and Shaffer, *Politics of International Cooperation*, p. 51; K. Waltz, *Theory of International Relations* (New York: McGraw-Hill, 1979).
12. Kash, *Space Cooperation*, p. 126.
13. L. Bloomfield, 'The Prospects for Law and Order', in J. Fawcett (ed.), *Outer Space: New Challenge to Law and Policy* (Oxford: Clarendon Press, 1984), pp. 163–4.
14. R. Gilpin, *War and Change in World Politics* (Cambridge: Cambridge University Press, 1981).
15. Ibid., 2nd edn, 1985, p. 240.
16. P. Kennedy, *The Rise and Fall of the Great Powers* (New York: Random House, 1987).
17. M. Harrington, *The Twilight of Capitalism* (New York: Simon & Schuster, 1976), pp. 320–1.
18. F. Fukuyama, 'The End of History?', *The National Interest*, No. 16 (Summer) 1989, pp. 3–18; and *The End of History and The Last Man* (New York: Free Press, 1992).
19. T. Canby, 'A Generation after Sputnik: Are the Soviets Ahead in Space?', *National Geographic* Vol. 170, No. 4 (October 1986), pp. 420ff.
20. R. Williamson, 'International Cooperation and Competition in Space', in D. Papp and J. McIntyre (eds), *International Space Policy: Legal, Economics, and Strategic Options for the Twentieth Century and Beyond* (New York: Quorum Books, 1985) p. 105.
21. T. Twibel, 'Space Law: Legal Restraints on Commercialization and Development of Outer Space', *University of Missouri at Kansas City Law Review* 65 (Spring 1997), p. 589.
22. N. Goldman, *American Space Law: International and Domestic Issues* (Ames, IA: Iowa State University Press, 1981), p. 17.
23. K. Deutsch, 'Outer Space and International Politics: A Look to 1988', in J. Golden (ed.), *Outer Space and World Politics* (New York: Praeger, 1963), p. 159.

Bibliography

Air Force Manual 6–1, *Military Space Doctrine* (Washington, DC: Department of the Air Force, 15 Oct. 1982).

Allehurst, M., *A Modern Introduction to International Law* 5th edition (London: George, Allen & Urwin, 1984).

Almond, H., 'Arms Control, International Law, and Outer Space', in U. Ra'anan and R. Pfaltzgraff (eds), *International Security Dimensions of Space* (Hamden, CT: Archon Books, 1984), pp. 221–52.

Anderson, J.K., *Military Theory and Practice in the Age of Xenophon* (Berkeley, CA: University of California Press, 1970).

Andreski, S., *Military Organization and Society* (London: Routledge & Kegan Paul, 1954).

Apter, D., *The Politics of Modernization* (Chicago, IL: University of Chicago Press, 1965).

Ball, D., *Can Nuclear War Be Controlled?* (London: Adelphi Papers, 1981).

Beason, D., 'What Are these Lagrange Points Anyway?', in J. Pournelle (ed.), *Cities in Space: The Endless Frontier*, Vol. III (New York: Ace, 1991), pp. 58–65.

Betts, R., *Surprise Attack* (Washington, DC: Brookings, 1982).

Blainey, G., *The Causes of War* (New York: Free Press, 1973).

Blair, B., *Strategic Command and Control: Redefining the Nuclear Threat* (Washington DC: Brookings, 1985).

Bloomfield, L., 'The Prospects for Law and Order', in J. Fawcett (ed.), *Outer Space: New Challenge to Law and Policy* (Oxford: Clarendon Press, 1984), pp. 155–66.

Blouet, B., *Halford Mackinder: A Biography* (College Station: Texas A&M University Press, 1987).

——, *Geostrategic Thought*, Unpublished Reader (August 1994).

Bluhm, W., *Theories of the Political System* (Englewood Cliffs, NJ: Prentice-Hall, 1971).

Boulding, K., *Human Betterment* (London: John Murray, 1985).

Bracken, P., *The Command and Control of Nuclear Forces* (New Haven, CT: Yale University Press, 1983).

Bremer, D., 'Dangerous Dyads: Interstate War, 1816–1965', *Journal of Conflict Resolution*, Vol. 36, No. 2 (June 1992), pp. 309–41.

——, 'Democracy and Militarized Interstate Conflict', *International Interactions*, Vol. 18, No. 3 (Fall 1993), pp. 231–49.

Brennan, D., 'Arms and Arms Control in Outer Space', in J. Fawcett (ed.), *Outer Space: New Challenge to Law and Policy* (Oxford: Clarendon Press, 1984), pp. 120–34.

Brunn, S., and Yanarella, E., 'Towards a Humanistic Political Geography', *Studies in Comparative International Development*, Vol. 22, No. 2 (1987), pp. 223–38.

Bull, H., *The Control of the Arms Race* (New York: Praeger, 1961).

Burgess, J., 'Satellites' Gaze Provides New Look at War', *Washington Post*, 19 February 1991, p. A13.

Burrows, W., *Deep Black: Space Espionage and National Security* (New York: Random House, 1986).

Canby, T., 'A Generation after Sputnik: Are the Soviets Ahead in Space?', *National Geographic*, Vol. 170, No. 4 (October 1986), pp. 420ff.

Chaisson, E., *Hubble Wars: Astrophysics Meets Astropolitics in the Two-Billion-Dollar Struggle Over The Hubble Space Telescope* (Cambridge, MA: Harvard University Press, 1998).

Chan, S., 'Mirror, Mirror on the Wall ... Are Freer Countries More Pacific?', *Journal of Conflict Resolution*, Vol. 28, No. 4 (December 1984), pp. 616–48.

Cheng, B., 'The Legal Regime of Aerospace and Outer Space: The Boundary Problem', *Annals of Air and Space Law 5* (1980), pp. 323–36.

Cimbala, S., *Uncertainty and Control: Future Soviet and American Strategy* (New York: St Martin's Press, 1990).

Cioc, M., *Pax Atomica: The Nuclear Defense Debate in West Germany During the Adenauer Era* (New York: Columbia University Press, 1988).

von Clausewitz, C., *On War*, ed. and trans. M. Howard and P. Paret (Princeton, NJ: Princeton University Press, 1976).

Coakley, T. (ed.), *C3I: Issues of Command and Control* (Washington, DC: National Defense University, 1991).

Coase, R., 'The Problem of Social Cost', *Journal of Law and Economics*, Vol. 3 (1960), pp. 1–44.

Coca, A., 'Vitoria and the International Law of Outer Space', *International Institute of Space Law* No. 27 (1984), pp. 25–9.

Cohen, S., 'The World Geopolitical System in Retrospect and Prospect', *Journal of Geography* Vol. 89, No. 1 (1990), pp. 2–10.

Cole, D., *Beyond Tomorrow: The Next 50 Years in Space* (Amherst, WI: Amherst Press, 1965).

Cole, D., and Cox, D., *The Challenge of the Planetoids* (Philadelphia, PA: Chilton Press, 1963).

Cole, D., and Levitt, I.M. *Exploring the Secrets of Space: Astronautics for the Layman* (Englewood Cliffs, NJ: Prentice-Hall International, 1963).

'Common Sense and Sputnik', *LIFE*, 21 October 1957, p. 2.

The Conference on Antarctica: Conference, Documents, the Antarctic Treaty, and Related Papers (Washington, DC: Department of State Publication, 1960).

Cox, D., *The Space Race: from Sputnik to Apollo, and Beyond* (New York: Chilton Books, 1962).

Crowe, B., 'The Tragedy of the Commons Revisited', *Science* (28 November 1969), pp. 1103–07.

Damon, T., *Introduction to Space: The Science of Spaceflight* (Malabar, FL: Orbit, 1989).

Deblois, B., 'Space Sanctuary: A Viable National Strategy', *AirPower Journal*, Vol. 12, No. 4 (Winter 1998), pp. 41–57.

Delbrück, *History of the Art of War: Within the Framework of Political History*, Vol. I, transl. W. Renfroe (Westport, CT: Greenwood, 1975).

De Seversky, A., 'The Twilight of Seapower', *American Mercury*, Vol. 52 (1941), pp. 647–58.

——, *Victory Through Air Power* (New York: Simon & Schuster, 1942).

——, *Air Power: Key to Survival* (New York: McGraw-Hill, 1951).

Deudney, D., *Space: The High Frontier in Perspective* (Washington, DC: Worldwatch Institute, 1982).

——, *Whole Earth Security: A Geopolitics of Peace* (Washington, DC: Worldwatch Institute, 1983).

——, 'Forging Missiles Into Spaceships', *World Policy Journal*, Vol. 2, No. 2 (1983), 270–95.

——, 'Geopolitics and Change', in M. Doyle, and G.J. Ikenberry (eds), *New Thinking in International Relations Theory* (Boulder, CO: Westview Press, 1997), pp. 91–123.

Deutsch, K., 'Outer Space and International Prospects: A Look to 1988', in J. Golden (ed.), *Outer Space and World Politics* (New York: Praeger, 1963), pp. 159–75.

Dixon, W., 'Democracy and the Peaceful Settlement of International Conflict', *American Political Science Review*, Vol. 88, No. 1 (March 1994), pp. 14–32.

Dolman, E., 'Geopolitics in the Space Age', *Journal of Strategic Studies*, Vol. 22 (Fall 1999), pp. 83–106.

——, 'US Military Intelligence and the Problem of Legitimacy', *Journal of Small Wars and Insurgencies*, Vol. 11 (2000), pp. 26–43.

——, 'War and (the Democratic) Peace', *Citizenship Studies*, Vol. 4 (2000), pp. 117–48.

Dorpalen, A., *The World of General Haushofer* (New York: Holt Rhinehart, 1942).

Dougherty, J., and Pfaltzgraf, R., *Contending Theories of International Relations: A Comprehensive Survey*, 4th edn (New York, Longman, 1996).

Douhet, G., *The Command of the Air*, trans. D. Ferrari ([1921] New York: Coward, McCann, 1942).

Doyle, M., 'Kant, Liberal Legacies, and Foreign Affairs', Parts 1 and 2 in *Philosophy and Public Affairs*, Vol. 12, Nos 3 and 4 (Summer and Fall 1983), pp. 206–35 and 323–53.
——, 'Liberalism and World Politics', *American Political Science Review*, Vol. 80, No. 4 (December 1986), pp. 1151–69.
——, *Ways of War and Peace* (New York: Norton, 1997).
Dupuy, R.E., and Dupuy, T., *The Encyclopedia of Military History: From 3500 BC to the Present* (New York: Harper & Row, 1970).
Durão Barroso, J., 'The Transatlantic Partnership in the New European Security Context', *NATO Review* 9505-1 (Web Edition) Vol. 43, No. 5 (September 1995), pp. 3–6.
Earle, E.M., 'Adam Smith, Alexander Hamilton, Friedrich List: The Economic Foundations of Military Power', in P. Paret (ed.), *The Makers of Modern Strategy: From Machiavelli to the Nuclear Age* (Princeton, NJ: University Press, 1986), pp. 217–61.
Edwards, C., *Hugo Grotius, the Miracle of Holland: A Study in Political Thought* (Chicago, IL: Nelson-Hall, 1981).
Ehrlich, P., *The Population Bomb* (New York: Ballantine Books, 1968).
Elster, J., *Political Psychology* (Cambridge: Cambridge University Press, 1993).
Farber, H., and Gowa, J., 'Polities and Peace', *International Organization*, Vol. 20, No. 2 (Fall 1995), pp. 123–46.
Fawcett, J.E.S. (ed.), *Outer Space: New Challenge to Law and Policy* (Oxford: Clarendon Press, 1984).
'The Feat That Shook the World', *LIFE*, 21 October 1957, p. 21.
Ferrill, A., *The Origins of War: From the Stone Age to Alexander the Great* (London: Thames & Hudson, 1985).
Fitzgerald, F., *Way Out There in the Blue: Reagan, Star Wars, and the End of the Cold War* (New York: Simon & Schuster, 2000).
Ford, D., *The Button: The Pentagon's Strategic Command and Control System* (New York: Simon & Schuster, 1985).
Forrest, W.G., *A History of Sparta: 950–192 BC* (London: Hutchinson, 1968).
Freedman, L., *The Evolution of Nuclear Strategy* (New York: St Martin's, 1981).
——, 'The First Two Generations of Nuclear Strategists', in P. Paret (ed.), *Makers of Modern Strategy: Machiavelli to the Nuclear Age* (Princeton, NJ: Princeton University Press, 1986), pp. 735–78.
Fruitkin, A., *International Cooperation in Space* (Englewood Cliffs, NJ: Prentice-Hall, 1965).
Frye, A., 'Our Gamble In Space: The Military Danger', *The Atlantic Monthly*, Vol. 212, No. 2 (August, 1963), pp. 46–50.
Fukuyama, F., 'The End of History?', *The National Interest*, No. 16 (Summer 1989), pp. 3–18.
——, *The End of History and The Last Man* (New York: Free Press, 1992).

Gaddis, J., *The Long Peace: Inquiries into the History of the Cold War* (New York: Oxford University Press, 1987).

Gardner, R., 'Cooperation in Outer Space', *Foreign Affairs* (January 1963), pp. 7–35.

Garthoff, R., *Deterrence and the Revolution in Soviet Military Doctrine* (Washington, DC: Brookings Institution, 1990).

Gilpin, R., *War and Change in World Politics* (Cambridge: Cambridge University Press, 1981).

Glassner, M., *Political Geography* (New York: J. Wiley, 1993).

'Global Engagement: A Vision for the 21st Century Air Force', http://www.cgsc.army.mil/usaf/Pubs/GlobalEngagement.htm, revised July 1999.

Goldman, N., *American Space Law: International and Domestic Issues* (Ames, IA: Iowa State University Press, 1988).

——, 'Transition and Confusion in the Law', in D. Papp and J. McIntyre (eds) *International Space Policy: Legal, Economic, and Strategic Options for the Twentieth Century and Beyond* (New York: Quorum Books, 1987), pp. 162–85.

Gottfried, K., and Blair, B. (eds), *Crisis Stability and Nuclear War* (New York: Oxford University Press, 1988).

Gottman, J., *Centre and Periphery* (Beverly Hills, CA: Sage, 1980).

Gray, C., *The Geopolitics of the Nuclear Era: Heartland, Rimlands, and the Technological Revolution* (New York: National Strategy Information Center, 1977).

——, *Maritime Strategy, Geopolitics, and the Defense of the West* (New York: National Strategy Information Center, 1986).

——, *The Geopolitics of Superpower* (Lexington, KY: University of Kentucky Press, 1987).

——, 'Strategy in the Nuclear Age', in W. Murray, M. Knox, and A. Bernstein (eds), *The Making of Modern Strategy: Rulers, States, and War* (Cambridge: Cambridge University Press, 1994), pp. 579–613.

——, 'The Influence of Space Power upon History', *Comparative Strategy*, Vol. 15, No. 4 (1996), pp. 293–308.

——, *Modern Strategy* (London: Oxford University Press, 2000).

Gray, C., and Sloan, G. (eds), *Geopolitics: Geography and Strategy* (London: Frank Cass, 1999).

Grier, P., 'New World Vistas', *Air Force Magazine*, Vol. 79, No. 3 (March 1996), pp. 2–5.

Grossman, K., and Long., J., 'Waging War in Space', *The Nation*, 27 December 1999, p. 3.

Guta, V., 'New Satellite Images for Sale', *International Security*, Vol. 20, No. 1 (Summer 1995), pp. 94–125.

Haley, A., and X, Malcolm, *The Autobiography of Malcolm X* (New York: Ballantine Booth, 1964).

Hardin, G., 'The Tragedy of the Commons', *Science* (13 December 1968), pp. 1243–48.

Harrington, M., *The Twilight of Capitalism* (New York: Simon & Schuster, 1976).

Hawkins, M., *Social Darwinism in European and American Thought, 1860–1945: Nature as Model and Nature as Threat* (Cambridge: Cambridge University Press, 1997).

Heronema, J., 'A.F. Space Chief Calls War in Space Inevitable', *Space News*, 12–18 August 1996, p. 4.

Herres, R., 'Space-Based Support', *Defense '88* (November–December 1988), p. 8.

Herwig, H., '*Geopolitik:* Haushofer, Hitler, and Lebensraum', in C. Gray and G. Sloan (eds), *Geopolitics: Geography and Strategy* (London: Frank Cass, 1999), pp. 218–41.

Herz, J., 'The Rise and Demise of the Territorial State', *World Politics*, Vol. 9 (1957), pp. 473–93.

Hickman, J., and Dolman, E., 'Resurrecting the Space Age: A State-Centered Commentary on the Outer Space Regime', unpublished manuscript.

Hintze, O., *The Historical Essays of Otto Hintze*, ed. trans. F. Gilbert (New York: Oxford University Press, 1975).

Hitler, A., *Mein Kampf*, transl. R. Mannheim (Boston, MA: Houghton Mifflin, 1943).

Hurley, A., *Billy Mitchell: Crusader for Air Power* (Bloomington, IN: University of Indiana Press, 1964).

Jennison, M., 'The "Civil"-ization and Internationalization of Satellite Navigation', paper presented at the Sixth Biennial Conference on the Law Relating to National Security Activities in Outer Space, in Colorado Springs (March 1994).

'Joint Vision 2020', (Washington, DC: US Government Printing Office), June 2000.

Jomini, H., *The Art of War*, translated by G.H. Mendell and W.P. Craighill (Westport, CT: Greenwood Press, 1972).

Karras, T., *The New High Ground: Strategies and Weapons of Space Age Wars* (New York: Simon & Schuster, 1983).

Kash, D., *The Politics of Space Cooperation* (Englewood Cliffs, NJ: Prentice-Hall, 1967).

Keegan, J., *The Price of Admiralty: The Evolution of Naval Warfare* (New York: Viking, 1989).

Kennedy, P., *The Rise and Fall of the Great Powers* (New York: Random House, 1987).

Keohane, R., and Nye, J., *Power and Interdependence: World Politics in Transition* (Boston, MA: Little, Brown, 1977).

Khaldûn, I., *The Muqaddimah: An Introduction to History*, trans. F. Rosenthal (Princeton, NJ: Princeton University Press, 1989).

Klass, P., *Secret Sentries in Space* (New York: Random House, 1971).
Kranzberg, M., 'The Top Line: Space as Man's New Frontier', in D. Papp and J. McIntyre (eds), *International Space Policy: Legal, Economic, and Strategic Options for the Twentieth Century and Beyond* (New York: Quorum Books, 1985), pp. 13–30.
Krasner, S., 'Structural Causes and Regime Consequences', in S. Krasner (ed), *International Regimes* (Ithaca, NY: Cornell University Press, 1983).
Kratochwil, F., *Rules, Norm, and Decisions* (Cambridge: Cambridge University Press, 1989).
Lachow, I., 'The GPS Dilemma: Balancing Military Risks and Economic Benefits', *International Security*, Vol. 20, No. 1 (Summer 1995), pp. 126–47.
Lake, D., 'Powerful Pacifists: Democratic States and War', *American Political Science Review*, Vol. 86, No. 1 (March 1992), pp. 24–37.
Latchford, S., 'The Bearing of International Air Navigation Conventions on the Use of Outer Space', United States Senate, Committee on Aeronautical Sciences, 'Legal Problems of Space Exploration' (87th Congress, 1st Session, 1961).
Layne, C., 'Kant or Cant: The Myth of the Democratic Peace', *International Security*, Vol. 19, No. 2 (Fall 1994), pp. 5–49.
'Legal Principles Relevant to Military Activities in Outer Space', *Department of the Air Force* Office of the General Council, Memo dated 28 February 1994.
'Letter from Eisenhower to Premier Bulganin', *Department of State Bulletin* (10 March 1958), p. 373.
Levitt, I.M. and Cole, D., *Exploring the Secrets of Space: Astronautics for the Layman* (London: Prentice-Hall International, 1963).
'Long Range Plan', USSPACECOM, http://www.peterson.af.mil/usspace.
Linklater, A.,'Citizenship and Sovereignty in the Post-Westphalian State', *European Journal of International Relations* Vol. 2 (1996), 77–103.
Lupton, D., *On Space Warfare: A Space Power Doctrine* (Maxwell AFB, AL: Air University Press, 1998).
Luttwak, E., *Strategy: The Logic of War and Peace* (Cambridge, MA: Belknap Press, 1987).
Machiavelli, N., *The Art of War*, trans. E. Farneworth (New York: Da Capo Press, 1990).
Mackinder, H., 'The Geographical Pivot of History', *Geographical Journal*, Vol. 23, No. 4 (1904), pp. 421–44.
——, *Democratic Ideals and Reality: A Study in the Politics of Reconstruction* (New York: Henry Holt, 1919).
Mansfield, E., *Power, Trade, and War* (Princeton, NJ: Princeton University Press, 1994).
Mansfield, E., and Snyder, G., 'Democratization and War', *International Security*, Vol. 20, No. 1 (Summer 1995), pp. 5–38.

Mahan, A., *The Influence of Seapower Upon History: 1660–1783* (Boston, MA: Little, Brown, 1890).
——, *The Influence of Seapower Upon History: The French Revolution and Empire, 1793–1812* (Boston, MA: Little, Brown, 1892).
——, *The Interest of America in Seapower, Present and Future* (Boston, MA: Little, Brown, 1898).
——, *The Problem of Asia and its Effect Upon International Politics* (Boston, MA: Little, Brown, 1900).
Malthus, T., *An Essay on the Principles of Population*, 6th edn ([1798] London: John Murray, 1826).
Maoz, Z., and Abdolai, N., 'Regime Types and International Conflict', *Journal of Conflict Resolution*, Vol. 33, No. 1 (March 1989), pp. 3–35.
McDougall, W., *...the Heavens and the Earth: A Political History of the Space Age* (New York: Basic Books, 1958).
McLean, A., and Lovie, F., *Europe's Final Frontier: The Search for Security Through Space* (Commack, NY: Nova, 1997).
Mearsheimer, J., *Conventional Deterrence* (Ithaca, NY: Cornell University Press, 1983).
——, 'Back to the Future: Instability in Europe After the Cold War', *International Security*, Vol. 15, No. 1 (Summer 1990), pp. 5–56.
Meilinger, P., 'Giulio Douhet and the Origins of Airpower Theory', in P. Meilinger (ed.), *The Paths of Heaven: The Evolution of Airpower Theory* (Maxwell AFB, AL: Air University Press, 1997), pp. 1–40.
——, 'Alexander P. de Severskey and American Airpower', in P. Meilinger (ed.), *The Paths of Heaven: The Evolution of Airpower Theory* (Maxwell AFB, AL: Air University Press, 1997), pp. 239–78.
Mellor, R., *Nation, State, and Territory: A Political Geography* (New York: Routledge, 1989).
Meyers, T.K., *Understanding Weapons and Arms Control: A Guide to the Issues* (Washington, DC: Brassey's, 1991).
Mitchell, W., *Winged Defense: The Development and Possibilities of Modern Air Power – Economic and Military* (New York: Putnam, 1925).
Mitrany, D., *A Working Peace System* (London: Royal Institute of International Affairs, 1943).
Morgenthau, H., *Politics Among Nations*, 5th edn (New York: Knopf, 1978).
Morrison, J.S., and Coates, J.F., *The Athenian Trireme: The History and Reconstruction of an Ancient Greek Warship* (Cambridge: Cambridge University Press, 1986).
NASA Web Site, 'Two Kinds of Separation in Space: Metric Distance vs. Total Velocity Change (Δv)', *Space Settlements: A Design Study* (http://www.sci.nas.nasa.gov/Services/Education/SpaceSettlement/75SummerStudy/Table of Contents1.html).
National Defense Authorization Act for Fiscal Year 1993 Report, US Senate,

Committee on Armed Services (102nd Congress, second session), Report 103–352 (Washington, DC: GPO, 1992).
National Science and Technology Council, 'National Space Policy', http://www.whitehouse.gov/WH/EOP/OSTP/NSTC/html/fs/fs-5.html, 19 September 1996.
Newberry, R., *Space Doctrine for the Twenty-First Century* (Maxwell AFB, AL: Air University Press, 1998).
New World Vistas: Air and Space Power for the 21st Century, Summary Volume, http://afosr.sciencewise.com/afr/sab/any/text/any/vistas.htm#app2.
Oberg, J., *Uncovering Soviet Disasters: Exploring the Limits of Glasnost* (New York: Random House, 1988).
——, *Space Power Theory* (Colorado Springs, CO: US Space Command, 2000).
Oberg, J., and Oberg, A., *Pioneering Space: Living on the Next Frontier* (New York: McGraw-Hill, 1986).
O'Connell, R., *Of Arms and Men: A History of War, Weapons, and Aggression* (Oxford: Oxford University Press, 1989).
O'Connor, H., *World Crisis in Oil* (New York: Monthly Review Press, 1962).
O'Dell, P., and Rosing, K., *The Future of Oil: A Simulation of the Inter-Relationships of Resources, Reserves, and Use*, 1980–2080 (New York: Archon, 1980).
Odishaw, H., *The Challenges of Space* (Chicago, IL: Chicago University Press, 1962).
Olson, M., *The Logic of Collective Action: Public Goods and the Theory of Groups* (Cambridge, MA: Harvard University Press, 1965).
O'Neal, J., O'Neal, F., Moaz, Z., and Russett, B., 'The Liberal Peace, Interdependence, Democracy, and International Conflict, 1950–1985', *Journal of Peace Research*, Vol. 33, No. 1 (Winter 1996), pp. 11–28.
Organski, A., and Kugler, J., *The War Ledger* (Chicago, IL: University of Chicago Press, 1980).
O'Sullivan, P., *Geopolitics* (New York: St Martin's Press, 1986).
Owen, J., 'How Liberalism Produces Democratic Peace', *International Security*, Vol. 19, No. 2 (Fall 1994), pp. 87–125.
Parker, G., *Western Geopolitical Thought in the Twentieth Century* (New York: St Martin's Press, 1986).
Peterson, S., 'How Democracies Differ: Public Opinion, State Structure, and the Lessons of the Fashoda Crisis', *Security Studies*, Vol. 5, No. 1 (Autumn 1995), pp. 3–37.
Powell, R., 'Stability and the Balance of Power', *World Politics*, Vol. 48, No. 1 (January 1996), pp. 239–67
Quigg, P., 'Antarctica: The Continuing Experiment', *Foreign Policy Association Headline Series*, No. 273 (March–April 1985), pp. 3–7.
Quigley, C., *Weapons Systems and Political Stability: A History* (Washington, DC: University Press of America, 1983).

Ra'anan, U., and Pfaltzgraf, R. (eds), *International Security Dimensions of Space* (Medfors, MA: Archon, 1984).
Rand Corporation, *Preliminary Design for an Experimental World Circling Spaceship*, 5/2/46.
von Ratzel, F., *Politische Geographie: oder, Die Geographie der Staaten, des Verkehres und des Krieges* (Munich, Berlin: R. Oldenbourg, 1903).
Reagan, R., 'The Conclusion of President Reagan's March 23, 1983, Speech on Defense Spending and Defense Technology', Appendix A, in S. Miller and S. Van Evera (eds), *The Star Wars Controversy* (Princeton, NJ: Princeton University Press, 1986), pp. 257–8.
Rhodes, E.J., *Power and MADness: The Logic of Nuclear Coercion* (New York: Columbia University Press, 1989).
Ripp, M., 'How Navstar Became Indispensable', *Air Force Magazine* (November 1993), pp. 46–9.
Robinson, G., and White, H., *Envoys of Mankind: A Declaration of the First Principles for the Governance of Space Societies* (Washington, DC: Smithsonian Institution Press, 1985)
Russet, B., *Grasping the Democratic Peace: Principles for a Post-Cold War World* (Princeton, NJ: Princeton University Press, 1993).
Sabine, G., *A History of Political Theory*, revised edn ([1937] New York: Henry Holt, 1950).
Salkeld, R., *War in Space* (Englewood Cliffs, NJ: Prentice-Hall, 1970).
Schell, J., *The Fate of the Earth* (New York: Alfred A. Knopf, 1982).
Schichtle, C., *The National Space Program: From the Fifties into the Eighties* (Washington, DC: National Defense University Press, 1983).
Schumann, F., *International Politics*, 5th edn (New York: McGraw-Hill, 1953).
Schweller, R., 'Domestic Structure and Preventative War: Are Democracies More Pacific?', *World Politics*, Vol. 44, No. 2 (January 1992), pp. 235–69.
Shaffer, S., and Shaffer, L., *The Politics of International Cooperation: A Comparison of US Experience in Space and in Security* (Denver, CO: University of Denver Press, 1980).
Shirer, W., *The Rise and Fall of the Third Reich* (New York: Simon & Schuster, 1960).
Singer, D., and Small, M., 'The War-Proneness of Democratic Regimes', *Jerusalem Journal of International Relations*, Vol. 1, No. 4 (Summer 1976), pp. 50–69.
Smith, W., *The Ideological Origins of Nazi Imperialism* (New York: Oxford University Press, 1986).
Snodgrass, A., 'The Hoplite Reform and History', *Journal of Hellenic Studies*, Vol. 97 (1977), pp. 84–101.
Snyder, G., 'The Balance of Power and the Balance of Terror', in P. Seabury (ed), *The Balance of Terror* (San Francisco, CA: Chandler, 1965), pp. 184–201.

'Soviet Memorandum of May 5, 1958', *Department of State Bulletin* (7 July 1958), p. 19.

Soviet Military Power: An Assessment of the Threat, 1988 (Washington, DC: US Government Printing Office, April 1988).

'Soviet Satellite Sends US Into a Tizzy', *LIFE*, 14 October 1957, pp. 34–5.

Sprout, H., 'Geopolitical Hypotheses in Technological Perspective', *World Politics*, Vol. 15 (1963), pp. 187–212.

Sprout, H., and Sprout, M., *The Ecological Perspective on Human Affairs: With Special Reference to International Politics* (Westport, CT: Greenwood Press, 1979).

Spruyt, H., *The Sovereign State and its Competitors: Analysis of Systems Change* (Princeton, NJ: Princeton University Press, 1994).

Spykman, N., *The Geography of Peace* (New York: Alfred Knopf, 1944), p. 43.

Spykman, N., 'Geography and Foreign Policy', *American Political Science Review*, Vol. 32, No. 1 (1938), pp. 28–50 and Vol. 32, No. 2 (1938), pp. 213–36.

——, *America's Strategy in World Politics* ([1942] Hamden, CT: Archon, 1970).

Stanley, V., and Noggle, P., 'Command and Control Warfare: Seizing the Initiative', *Signal*, Vol. 38, No. 8 (Apr 1984), p. 23–8.

Stares, P., *The Militarization of Space: US Policy, 1954–1984* (Ithaca, NY: Cornell University Press, 1985).

——, *Space and National Security* (Washington, DC: Brookings Institution, 1987).

——, *Command Performance: The Neglected Dimension of European Security* (Washington DC: Brookings Institution, 1991).

'Statement by Ambassador Goldberg', *Hearings Before the Committee on Foreign Relations*, United States Senate, 90th Congress, 1st Session, 7 March 1967 (Washington, DC: US Government Printing Office, 1967).

Stein, P., and Feaver, P., *Assuring Control of Nuclear Weapons: The Evolution of Permissive Action Links* (Lanham, MD: University Press of America, 1987).

Stetson, H., *Man and the Stars* (New York: McGraw-Hill, 1930).

Stine, G.H., *Confrontation in Space* (Englewood Cliffs, NJ: Prentice-Hall, 1981).

Stinson, H., *Russia and America: Dangers and Prospects* (New York: Council on Foreign Relations, 1956).

Strassler, R., *The Landmark Thucydides: A Comprehensive Guide to the Peloponnesian War* (New York: Free Press, 1996).

Strausz-Hupé, R., *Geopolitics: The Struggle for Space and Power* (New York: Putnam and Sons, 1942).

Sun Tzu, *The Art of War*, trans S.B. Griffith (Cambridge: Cambridge University Press, 1972).

Thilly, F., *A History of Philosophy* (New York: Henry Holt, 1914).

Thompson, W., 'Democracy and Peace: Putting the Cart Before the Horse', *International Organization*, Vol. 50, No. 1 (January 1996), pp. 141–74.

Thucydides, *History of the Peloponnesian War*, trans S. Lattimore (Cambridge: Hackett, 1998).
Toynbee, A., *A Study of History* (London: Oxford University Press, 1956).
Tuchman, B., *The Guns of August* (New York: Macmillan, 1962).
Turner, F.J., *The Frontier in American History* (New York: Holt, Rinehart & Winston, 1962).
Twibel, T., 'Space Law: Legal Restraints on Commercialization and Development of Outer Space', *University of Missouri at Kansas City Law Review*, Vol. 65 (Spring 1997), pp. 589–97.
Vagts, A., *A History of Militarism: Romance and Realities of a Profession* (New York: W.W. Norton, 1937).
Van Creveld, M., *Command in War* (Cambridge: Cambridge University Press, 1985).
——, *The Art of War: War and Military Thought*, ed. J. Keegan (New York: Cassell, 2000).
Vaucher, M., 'Geographic Parameters for Military Doctrine in Space and the Defense of the Space-Based Enterprise', in U. Ra'anan and R. Pfaltzgraf (eds), *International Security Dimensions of Space* (Medfors, MA: Archon, 1984), pp. 32–46.
Veit, V., *The German People: Their History and Civilization from the Holy Roman Empire to the Third Reich* (New York: Alfred Knopf, 1946).
Von Bencke, M., *The Politics of Space: A History of US–Soviet Competition and Cooperation* (Boulder, CO: Westview, 1997).
Wadegoankar, D.,*The Orbit of Space Law* (London: Stevens & Sons, 1984).
Wagner, R.H., 'Peace, War, and the Balance of Power', *American Political Science Review*, Vol. 88, No. 3 (September 1994), pp. 593–607.
Walt, S., *The Origin of Alliances* (Ithaca, NY: Cornell University Press, 1993).
Waltz, K., *Theory of International Relations* (New York: McGraw-Hill, 1979).
Watkins, T., 'The Beginnings of Warfare', in J. Hackett (ed), *Warfare in the Ancient World* (New York: Facts on File, 1989), pp. 15–27.
Weede, E., 'Democracy and War Involvement', *Journal of Conflict Resolution*, Vol. 28, No. 4 (December 1984), pp. 649–664.
Wells, H.G., 'The Land Ironclads', *Selected Short Stories* ([1901] Harmondsworth: Penguin, 1958), pp. 85–112.
——, *Anticipations of the Reaction of Mechanical and Scientific Progress Upon Human Life and Thought* (New York: Harper, 1902).
Wendt, A., 'Anarchy Is What States Make of It: The Social Construction of Power Politics', *International Organization*, Vol. 46, No. 2 (Spring 1992), pp. 391–425.
White, I., *Decision-Making for Space: Law and Politics in Air, Sea, and Outer Space* (West LaFayette, IN: Purdue University Press, 1971).
Wiegert, H., 'US Strategic Bases and Collective Security', *Foreign Affairs* Vol. 25, No. 2 (1947), pp. 250–62.

——, *Principles of Political Geography* (New York: Appleton-Century-Crofts, 1957).
Williamson, R., 'International Cooperation and Competition in Space', in D. Papp and J. McIntyre (eds), *International Space Policy: Legal, Economic, and Strategic Options for the Twentieth Century and Beyond* (New York: Quorum Books, 1985), pp. 102–35.
Wilson, A. (ed.), *Interavia Spaceflight Directory* (Geneva: Interavia SA,1989),
Wilson, E.O., *Consilience: The Unity of Knowledge* (New York: Vintage/Random House, 1998).
Yadin, Y., *The Art of Warfare in Biblical Lands: In Light of Archaeological Study*, Vol. I (New York: A. Knopf, 1963).
Yost, J.G., *Spy-Tech* (New York: Facts On File, 1985).
Zeigler, D., 'Safe Havens: Military Strategy and Space Sanctuary', in M. DeBlois (ed.), *Beyond the Paths of Heaven: The Emergence of Space Power Thought* (Maxwell AFB, AL: Air University Press, 1999), pp. 185–245.
Zubrin, R., *Entering Space: Creating a Spacefaring Civilization* (New York: Jeremy P. Tarcher and Putnam, 1999).

Index

Printed in the USA/Agawam, MA
May 17, 2013